A Transdisciplinary Approach to Chinese and Japanese Language Teaching

A Transdisciplinary Approach to Chinese and Japanese Language Teaching illustrates how the transdisciplinary approach to second language acquisition (SLA) centers around collaboration to provide a learning-conducive environment with rich semiotic resources for second/foreign language learners.

The volume consists of 14 chapters from leading experts in SLA and Chinese and Japanese language educators from Canada, China, Japan, the United Kingdom, and the United States of America. As a first work of its kind, the contributions feature both theoretical interpretations of transdisciplinary concepts that can apply to Chinese/Japanese as a second language learning and case studies showcasing how college-level Chinese and Japanese language educators design and implement pedagogical projects in collaboration with partners across languages, disciplines, communities, and borders by adopting a transdisciplinary perspective to analyze students' learning outcomes.

This book will benefit researchers, administrators, educators, and teacher educators in higher education with an interest in world language education and interdisciplinary and project-based teaching.

Nobuko Chikamatsu is Associate Professor in the Department of Modern Languages and Co-director of the Japanese Language and Studies Program at DePaul University, USA. She teaches Japanese language, linguistics, and translation. Her research interests include second language acquisition, Japanese pedagogy, translation, and Japanese-American history and literature.

Li Jin is Associate Professor in the Department of Modern Languages and Director of the Chinese Studies Program and Global Asian Studies Program at DePaul University, USA. Her research interests include sociocultural theory and ecology of SLA, computer-assisted language teaching and learning, faculty perceptions of online language teaching, and Chinese pragmatic learning.

A Transdisciplinary Approach to Chinese and Japanese Language Teaching

Collaborative Pedagogy Across Languages, Disciplines, Communities, and Borders

Edited by Nobuko Chikamatsu and Li Jin

LONDON AND NEW YORK

First published 2023
by Routledge
4 Park Square, Milton Park, Abingdon, Oxon OX14 4RN

and by Routledge
605 Third Avenue, New York, NY 10158

Routledge is an imprint of the Taylor & Francis Group, an informa business

© 2023 selection and editorial matter, Nobuko Chikamatsu and Li Jin; individual chapters, the contributors

The right of Nobuko Chikamatsu and Li Jin to be identified as the authors of the editorial material, and of the authors for their individual chapters, has been asserted in accordance with sections 77 and 78 of the Copyright, Designs and Patents Act 1988.

All rights reserved. No part of this book may be reprinted or reproduced or utilised in any form or by any electronic, mechanical, or other means, now known or hereafter invented, including photocopying and recording, or in any information storage or retrieval system, without permission in writing from the publishers.

Trademark notice: Product or corporate names may be trademarks or registered trademarks, and are used only for identification and explanation without intent to infringe.

British Library Cataloguing-in-Publication Data
A catalogue record for this book is available from the British Library

Library of Congress Cataloging-in-Publication Data
Names: Chikamatsu, Nobuko, editor. | Jin, Li, 1978– editor.
Title: A transdisciplinary approach to Chinese and Japanese language teaching : collaborative pedagogy across languages, disciplines, communities, and borders / edited by Nobuko Chikamatsu and Li Jin.
Description: New York : Routledge, 2023. | Includes bibliographical references and index.
Identifiers: LCCN 2022045841 (print) | LCCN 2022045842 (ebook) | ISBN 9781032211503 (hardback) | ISBN 9781032211480 (paperback) | ISBN 9781003266976 (ebook)
Subjects: LCSH: Chinese language—Study and teaching. | Japanese language—Study and teaching. | Interdisciplinary approach in education. | Second language acquisition.
Classification: LCC PL1065 T73 2023 (print) | LCC PL1065 (ebook) | DDC 495.107—dc23/eng/20221108
LC record available at https://lccn.loc.gov/2022045841
LC ebook record available at https://lccn.loc.gov/2022045842

ISBN: 978-1-032-21150-3 (hbk)
ISBN: 978-1-032-21148-0 (pbk)
ISBN: 978-1-003-26697-6 (ebk)

DOI: 10.4324/9781003266976

Typeset in Times New Roman
by Apex CoVantage, LLC

Contents

List of figures viii
List of tables ix
About the contributors x
Acknowledgements xiii

1 **Introduction: collaborative Chinese and Japanese language teaching from a transdisciplinary perspective** 1
  LI JIN AND NOBUKO CHIKAMATSU

SECTION 1
Theoretical foundations and empirical evidence for a transdisciplinary approach to Chinese/Japanese language teaching 17

2 **Teaching and learning of East Asian languages in the era of "trans-"** 19
  JUNKO MORI

3 **Translanguaging and co-learning at the interface of language and culture** 38
  LI WEI

SECTION 2
Across disciplines: language and non-language faculty collaboration 47

4 **Translanguaging with food and ethics: translating languages, enhancing agencies, and expanding horizons** 49
  YUKI MIYAMOTO AND NOBUKO CHIKAMATSU

5 Teaching Chinese through classic literature: a cross-disciplinary collaboration 67
JINAI SUN AND STUART PATTERSON

6 Promoting translingual and transcultural literacies in a collaborative content-based Japanese classroom: audiovisual translation as pedagogy 81
SAORI HOSHI AND AYAKA YOSHIMIZU

7 Wellbeing and Chinese language study: a case of cross-disciplinary teaching 97
CHIEH LI, ANN CAI, AND DONGYING LIU

SECTION 3
Across communities: language and community partner collaboration 111

8 Negotiating C2 expectation and Third-Space personae in transdisciplinary L2 learning: collaboration with Chinese professionals in advanced Chinese language curricula 113
XIN ZHANG

9 Internships at Japanese orphanages: a case study of a first-year Japanese language student's growth 128
NOBUKO KOYAMA

SECTION 4
Across languages: Chinese-Japanese and multi-language collaboration 143

10 An experiment of cross-language and cross-disciplinary collaboration: integrating Xu Bing's text-based arts into Chinese and Japanese classrooms 145
NORIKO SUGIMORI AND LEIHUA WENG

11 Cross-language and cross-disciplinary collaborations in a Mandarin CLAC course 159
YAN LIU

SECTION 5
Across borders: international collaboration 177

12 **The United States-Japan online magazine project: international telecollaborations as translanguaging spaces** 179
YURI KUMAGAI AND MOMOYO SHIMAZU

13 **Transcending borders and limitations with digitally enhanced pedagogy: language Learning-focused COIL (LLC) for Japanese learners and prospective teachers** 196
KEIKO IKEDA AND NOBUKO CHIKAMATSU

14 **Coda** 212
NOBUKO CHIKAMATSU AND LI JIN

Index 219

Figures

2.1	The multifaceted nature of language learning and teaching	21
2.2	East Asian language enrollment in U.S. institutions of higher education	25
8.1	Collaboration timeline	119
10.1	Xu Bing's *Living Word*	148
10.2	Xu Bing's *Art for the People for the Met*	149
10.3	Greeting letter from CHIN102 students	152
10.4	Greeting letter from JAPN302 students	153
12.1	Project procedures (based on the U.S. college schedule)	184
12.2	Xinran's hand gesture	185
12.3	Slack interaction	186
12.4	Cover and sample page from *Corona and Education/ The Impact of COVID-19 on Higher Education*	189

Tables

4.1	Course outlines of the FLAC Japanese and ethics courses	53
4.2	The original Japanese poem and English translation of しんでくれた (Tanigawa, 2014)	56
4.3	Student A's response poem, いのちをあげる ("I give you my life")	58
4.4	Student B's final poem in Japanese 卵ちゃん "Little Egg"	60
5.1	Schedule of two coordinated courses	72
6.1	Course outline of "Japanese media and translation" (with assigned readings for Weeks 2–5)	85
7.1	Pre-trip weekly tasks	102
8.1	Themes and sample workplace scenarios	117
8.2	Topics covered in the Chinese resume workshop	121
8.3	Sample sections in a student resume: 1st draft and final draft	122
8.4	Sample interview questions and corresponding C2 expectations	123
9.1	Internship preparations	133
10.1	Project steps	151
11.1	Course outline of ENVIRON 201 and Mandarin CLAC courses	165
11.2	Specialist lectures: Themes and materials	167
11.3	Breakout room arrangement and students' final project topics	168
11.4	Student-led discussions: Themes, materials, and wrap-up activities	169
11.5	Students' perceived gains in the target language (Chinese)	170
11.6	Students' perceived gains in the course content	170
11.7	Students' perceived gains in global learning skills	171
12.1	Language profile of the group members	184
12.2	Titles of magazine and corresponding SDGs	188
13.1	DePaul University and Kansai University information	199

* The tables in Appendix I and Appendix II in Chapter 7 are not included in this list

About the contributors

Ann CAI, EdD, is Teaching Professor of Chinese in the World Language Center at Northeastern University (NEU), USA. She teaches Chinese language and leads the Summer China Dialogue Program. Her research interests include mindfulness in higher education, conversational artificial intelligence (AI) chatbots in foreign language learning, and incorporating Chinese rap into classroom practice.

Nobuko CHIKAMATSU is Associate Professor in the Department of Modern Languages and co-director of the Japanese Language and Studies Program at DePaul University, USA. She teaches Japanese language, linguistics, and translation. Her research interests include second language acquisition, Japanese pedagogy, translation, and Japanese-American history and literature.

Saori HOSHI is an assistant professor of teaching in Japanese applied linguistics in the Department of Asian Studies at University of British Columbia, Canada. She teaches Japanese language and content-based language courses. Her research interests include foreign language learning and acquisition, Japanese pedagogy and pragmatics, and critical content-based language teaching.

Keiko IKEDA is a professor in the Division of International Affairs and vice-director for the newly established organization at Kansai University, Institute for Innovative Global Education (IIGE). She received her PhD from the University of Hawai'i at Manoa, specializing in Japanese linguistics, foreign language education, and conversation analysis.

Li JIN is Associate Professor in the Department of Modern Languages and Director of the Chinese Studies Program and Global Asian Studies Program at DePaul University, USA. Her research interests include sociocultural theory and ecology of SLA, computer-assisted language teaching and learning, faculty perceptions of online language teaching, and Chinese pragmatic learning.

Nobuko KOYAMA is Associate Professor and Coordinator of the Japanese Language Program and Faculty Advisor for Japan Children's Home Internship Program (JCHIP) in the Department of East Asian Languages and Cultures at the University of California, Davis. Her research interests include overseas internship experiences, Academic Japanese (AJ), L2 writing, and Open Educational Resources (OER).

About the contributors xi

Yuri KUMAGAI is a senior lecturer in the Department of East Asian Languages and Cultures at Smith College, USA. She teaches Japanese language and culture courses. Her specializations are critical literacy and multiliteracies in world language education. Her research interests include critical discourse analysis and ideologies of language.

Chieh LI, EdD, NCSP, is an associate professor of school psychology at Northeastern University. Her research interests include advancing the understanding of culturally and linguistically diverse students and promoting their academic and psychological wellbeing in a culturally responsive manner, including incorporating bilingual guided meditation in the classrooms.

Dongying LIU, MA in teaching Chinese as a second language, is a research fellow at Kunming Academy of Social Sciences. She has been assisting and guest lecturing in the Summer China Dialogue Program of Northeastern University over 10 years. Her research interests include intercultural communication and Chinese history and culture.

Yan LIU is Assistant Professor of the Practice in the Department of Asian and Middle Eastern Studies and Assistant Director of the Chinese Program at Duke University, USA. She teaches Chinese language, sociolinguistics, and translation. Her research interests include second language acquisition, Chinese pedagogy, and interdisciplinary Chinese curriculum development.

Yuki MIYAMOTO is Professor of ethics in the Department of Religious Studies at DePaul University where she teaches nuclear and environmental ethics. In addition to articles, her monographs include *Beyond the Mushroom Cloud: Commemoration, Religion, and Responsibility After Hiroshima* (2011), *Naze genbaku ga aku dewa nainoka* (2020), and *A World Otherwise: Environmental Praxis in Minamata* (2021).

Junko MORI is Professor in the Department of Asian Languages and Cultures at the University of Wisconsin-Madison and a former president of the American Association of Japanese Teachers. As an applied linguist, she has investigated grammar in interaction, classroom discourse, intercultural/transnational workplace communication, and administrative issues concerning language programs.

Stuart PATTERSON (BA St John's College, PhD Emory University) is Associate Professor and Chair of the Shimer Great Books School at North Central College. Patterson teaches interdisciplinary seminars across the traditional liberal arts at both undergraduate and graduate levels. His most recent scholarship involves the role of gossip in Cao Xueqin's *Story of the Stone*.

Momoyo SHIMAZU is a professor in the faculty of Foreign Language Studies at Kansai University, Japan. She has been researching Japanese learners' discourses through examining their storytelling, creative language use, and communication styles. Recently she has also been working on an analysis of interviews and narratives of Japanese language teachers.

Noriko SUGIMORI is Associate Professor of Japanese at Kalamazoo College, USA. She is a sociolinguist with a PhD from Boston University. She teaches Japanese language and culture. Her research interests include historical sociolinguistics, language ideology, language policy, grapholinguistics, and oral history.

Jinai SUN is Associate Professor of Chinese at North Central College where she has taught since 2011. Dr. Sun also has served for 7 years as Program Director of the STARTALK Chinese immersion program at North Central. Her research focuses on curriculum and instructional design, particularly through the use of authentic materials toward student motivation in Chinese language classrooms in the United States.

Li WEI is Director and Dean of the UCL Institute of Education at University College London, where he holds a chair in applied linguistics. His research covers various aspects of language contact, bilingualism, and multilingualism. He is a fellow of the British Academy, Academia Europaea, Academy of Social Sciences (UK), and the Royal Society of Arts (UK).

Leihua WENG holds the position of Chinese Endowed Assistant Professor of Chinese language and literature at Kalamazoo College. She teaches Mandarin Chinese as well as courses on modern Chinese literature and culture. Her research covers a range of topics on the formation, transmission, and reception of tradition(s) in China.

Ayaka YOSHIMIZU is an assistant professor of teaching at the Department of Asian Studies at University of British Columbia. She teaches Japanese literature, films, and media and transpacific histories and cultures. Her educational projects focus on decolonial and anti-racist approaches to teaching and curriculum development and on embodied narrative as pedagogy.

Xin ZHANG is Assistant Professor of Chinese and intercultural communication at Duke Kunshan University where she coordinates the Chinese program and co-directs the Third Space Lab. Her research lies at the intersection of applied linguistics, language pedagogy, and intercultural communication with a focus on how multilinguals negotiate identities and socialize into globalized workplaces and educational contexts.

Acknowledgements

First and foremost, we would like to express our gratitude to the contributors in this volume for their commitment throughout the process. We are extremely grateful for the support provided by the Japan Foundation Sakura Grant and the DePaul University Research Council for the 2021 Teaching China and Japan Symposium, which provided the basis and was the initial stage of the entire project. We appreciate an additional grant from the Japan Foundation Sakura Grant, which assisted us to complete the current volume timely. We also would like to recognize the invaluable assistance of the Routledge editorial team, Iola Ashby and Andrea Hartill, and the Production team led by Marie Roberts. Lastly, we would like to express our deepest gratitude to our Chinese and Japanese language students for their passion of learning, which inspires us to continuously seek innovative teaching approaches.

1 Introduction

Collaborative Chinese and Japanese language teaching from a transdisciplinary perspective

Li Jin and Nobuko Chikamatsu

According to the Modern Language Association of America's most recent data on college-level non-English language enrollments (Looney & Lusin, 2018), more than 130,000 U.S. college students studied Japanese and Chinese in 2016; this makes Japanese the fifth most commonly learned language after Spanish, French, American Sign Language, and German and makes Chinese the seventh-ranked one after Italian. From 2006 to 2016, Chinese and Japanese courses experienced notable increases in enrollment in the United States—an extraordinary phenomenon considering the overall declining trend of U.S. college-level foreign language enrollments. Given the ascending global economic and geopolitical clout and rich histories and cultures in both China and Japan, many international education advocates have argued that an education in Chinese, especially Mandarin Chinese, and Japanese has become essential for students to be competitive and well-rounded global citizens (e.g., ACTFL, 2019; Goh, 2017).

In the 1980s, Chinese (Mandarin or Cantonese) and Japanese were designated as Category IV languages by the U.S. Defense Language Institute or Category V languages by the Foreign Service Institute, meaning they are among the most challenging languages for English native speakers to learn. Since then, this view has been widely cited by foreign language educators and researchers (Walton, 2016). The perceived challenges largely stem from linguistic features not found in Indo-European languages, such as the logographic orthography and tonal system (Crystal, 1997). In addition, cultural distance and identity-related issues can influence and sometimes impede language learning processes and outcomes. For instance, unique pragmalinguistic features in Chinese or Japanese could easily confuse learners of Chinese or Japanese who are not familiar with embedded gender roles or hierarchical relationships in a given conversation (e.g., Jin, 2015; Ohta, 2008). Many Chinese and Japanese language educators believe that the unique needs of their learners are not sufficiently addressed by concepts in traditional, usually Eurocentric, theoretical frameworks in second language acquisition (SLA)—namely, historically dominant cognitive linguistic approaches in language learning and teaching. In addition, given the changing student demographics in language classrooms, such as the surging number of Chinese international students in Japanese language classrooms at some—especially elite—public and private universities and the increasing heritage learners and non-English-speaking learners in Chinese language classrooms, the outdated categorization and misconceptions can mislead Chinese and Japanese language instructors.

This book aims to challenge certain outdated understandings about Chinese and Japanese language learning and introduce an innovative pedagogical approach by applying the Douglas Fir Group's (DFG, 2016) transdisciplinary framework of SLA to teaching college-level Chinese and Japanese language, particularly in North America. This approach centers around collaborative projects among language faculty, area studies specialists, local community organizations/members, and international partners with a synergized purpose to provide a learning-conducive environment with rich semiotic resources for second/foreign language learners. The chapters included in this volume feature both theoretical interpretations of transdisciplinary concepts in East Asian language teaching and case studies illustrating collaborative pedagogical practices adopted by college-level Chinese and Japanese language educators. In the following sections, we introduce the main tenets of the transdisciplinary perspective of SLA and explain why it is a useful framework guiding Chinese and Japanese as a second/foreign language pedagogy. We then review the origin, evolvement, and current trends of collaborative pedagogy in the field of foreign language education, with a particular focus on its adoption in Chinese and Japanese language teaching. We also discuss the need for a transdisciplinary perspective to understand evolving collaborative pedagogical practices in world language education in the subfields of Chinese and Japanese. Finally, we introduce each chapter included in the volume and elaborate how each of them contributes to our understanding of effective collaborative language pedagogy from a transdisciplinary perspective.

A transdisciplinary approach to Chinese and Japanese language teaching

After a century of research dominated by monolinguistic assumptions of language teaching and learning, many scholars have claimed that the field of SLA has entered a multilingual turn (Kramsch, 1997; May, 2013; Ortega, 2013). This turn signifies increasing criticism of viewing language as a standard and closed system and individuals learning an additional language as failed native speakers, and it focuses more attention on the complex and discursive nature of language use and language learning. The transdisciplinary framework for SLA, first synthesized by DFG in its 2016 seminal paper published in the *Modern Language Journal*, formally set the stage to reevaluate the multifaceted nature of language learning and teaching in the current diverse multilingual world (Byrd Clark, 2016; Duff & Byrnes, 2019). Expanding beyond conventional cognitive-linguistic views of SLA that focus on learners' cognitive development (i.e., what happens inside their heads) and hold monolingualism or native-speakerism (Holliday, 2006; Houghton & Hashimoto, 2018) as the norm, the transdisciplinary framework offers a "problem-oriented, rising above disciplines and particular strands within them" view of SLA with an aim to integrate many layers of existing knowledge about SLA and derive "coherent patterns and configurations of findings across domains"

(DFG, 2016, p. 20). As a result, it attempts to describe language learning as a complex, dynamic, and holistic meaning-making process in a multilingual world. From a transdisciplinary perspective, factors influencing SLA are organized into three levels:

> (a) micro-level features influencing individuals in interactional context, including their "semiotic resources"; (b) meso-level—mostly place-based—community institutions and the processes by which identities are formed in relation to them; and (c) macro-level ideological structures—various larger (and fundamentally abstract) value/belief systems.
>
> (Atkinson, 2019, p. 114)

What's important is that social activities at these three levels co-exist and constantly influence one other.

This new SLA framework sets two explicit goals—namely, to "expand the perspectives of researchers and teachers of [second language] L2 learners with regard to learners' diverse multilingual repertoires or meaning-making resources and identities" and to

> foster in learners a profound awareness not only of the cultural, historical, and institutional meanings that their language-mediated social actions have, but also . . . of the dynamic and evolving role their actions play in shaping their own and others' worlds.
>
> (Duff & Byrnes, 2019, p. 25)

An increasing number of researchers on language teacher education (e.g., Gao, 2019; Johnson, 2019) recognize the potential of the transdisciplinary approach to rectify the long-standing theory-practice divide that prevents language educators from gaining meaningful and practical insights from SLA research.

To bridge the initial DFG effort that lays out a transdisciplinary theoretical foundation to practical knowledge accessible to language educators, Joan Kelly Hall, one of the initial DFG members, published the book *Essentials of SLA for L2 Teachers: A Transdisciplinary Framework* in 2019. In this book, Hall explained what is language and what is second language learning from a transdisciplinary perspective; then she elaborated that the "learning environment should include purposeful activities that emphasize processes of experiencing, conceptualizing, analyzing and applying" and instructors should see that "teaching a second language is about creating increasingly complex meaning-making contexts in which students can use their cognitive and other capabilities to expand on the repertoires they already have" (Hall, 2019, p. 36). The book's content is organized around eight themes on L2 learning: (a) L2 learning knowledge is complex and dynamic; (b) L2 knowledge is a repertoire of diverse semiotic; (c) L2 learning is situated and attentional and socially gated; (d) L2 learning is mediated and embodied; (e) L2 learning is mediated by learners' social identities; (f) L2 learning is mediated by motivation, investment, and agency; (g) L2 learning is mediated by literacy and instructional practices; and (h) L2 learning is mediated by language ideologies. Despite considering L2 teachers to be her primary target audience, Hall provided no specific guidance for language educators to directly apply the concepts into their own teaching.

The pedagogical application of the transdisciplinary framework is particularly meaningful in non-European and non-Roman alphabetic languages, such as Chinese and Japanese, for a number of reasons. First, the traditional monolinguistic assumptions held by SLA researchers and language educators misconstrue the multilingual reality in which L2 learners have access to diverse semiotic repertoires that are different and even lacking for monolingual speakers. In addition, L2 learners' linguistic and sociocultural goals, status, roles, and functions in a target language environment are unique and different from those of native language (L1) speakers. As a result, traditional pedagogy that centers around monolingual standards can no longer meet L2 learners' needs. Although native-speakerism, which promotes a monolingual view of language proficiency, exists among nearly all language educators (Llurda & Calvet-Terré, 2022), it is particularly salient in Chinese and Japanese language teaching, which is dominated by teachers who are native speakers (Nomura & Mochizuki, 2018). The monolinguistic view of L2 learning also comes with an ideology that a target language is only represented by the national language. This belief is particularly common among Chinese and Japanese language educators, who tend to focus on their respective national standard languages: *Pǔtōnghuà*, which means "common language" based on northern Chinese dialects in China, and *Hyōjungo*, which also means "standard language," but is the formal Tokyo dialect in Japan. This approach to language teaching ignores the variations of languages spoken within each country or by its global diaspora, thereby depriving L2 learners of opportunities to learn about the richness and diversities of Chinese languages and Japanese languages. Having a more appropriate understanding of the complex multilingual nature of L2 learning would help Chinese and Japanese language educators develop more appropriate learning objectives and more carefully select and plan class materials and activities to meet students' needs. For instance, the ways and extent of using students' first language(s) (L1) in a Chinese and Japanese language classroom need to be reconceptualized to consider how translanguaging can be adopted (García & Kano, 2014).

Second, a transdisciplinary approach to second/foreign language teaching considers L2 knowledge as a repertoire of diverse semiotic resources and L2 learning a mediated and embodied process. From a transdisciplinary perspective, language learning should be supported with multimodal resources and meaningful social interactions to help learners develop meaning potentials. The traditional cognitive-linguistic approach to teaching Chinese and Japanese focuses more on vocabulary and grammar learning and less on the meaningful and contextual semiotic resources L2 learners need in diverse communicative activities. As previously mentioned, Chinese and Japanese are considered challenging for English-speaking learners, mostly due to the linguistic and cultural distance from their L1 English. Bringing in more multimodal semiotic resources such as images, audio, and video materials or tactical formats (e.g., diagrams, maps, anime, melody) that highlight diverse features of a linguistic form (e.g., tonal and prosodic variations in Chinese or pitch variations in Japanese) or nonverbal behaviors (e.g., facial expressions or hand gestures) in a specific context, as well as creating more opportunities for learners to use L2 language in various contexts, can greatly enrich the language learning experience and reduce learner anxiety. In the same vein, a transdisciplinary approach stresses the mediation of learners' literacy and instructional practices in language learning, which explains the challenges encountered by English-speaking learners when learning Chinese *hànzì* and Japanese *kanji*, the languages' distinct writing systems consisting of logographic characters. Thus, adopting this perspective can urge Chinese and Japanese language educators to pay close attention to learners' prior experience with learning an orthographic writing system and then adjust learning objectives and instructional approaches (e.g., to what extent and when to start learning *hànzì/kanji* and how to instruct character writing).

Third, a transdisciplinary approach highlights L2 learners' identities as a key factor that shapes their language learning experience across all the three levels of social activity (i.e., micro, meso, and macro). Neglecting the influence of L2 learners' identities on their learning would consequently limit the potential of their social, cognitive, and linguistic development. Study abroad research (e.g., Jin, 2015; Ohta, 2001) has documented that the pervasive ingroup mentality in China and Japan makes Chinese and Japanese language learners, especially those who are not Asian-looking, feel excluded and, in some cases, infantilized by local residents during foreign sojourns. The intentional or unintentional exclusion from being a full-fledged member of the community limits the quantity and quality of semiotic resources accessible to language learners. On the flip side, L2 learners' self-identities may also affect their motivation and investment in L2 language learning. For instance, American learners of Chinese language may refuse to act modestly when responding to a compliment from a senior interlocutor (Jin, 2012); American learners of Japanese may resist adopting feminine speech styles expected of female interlocutors in certain social contexts in Japan (Ohta, 2001). Having awareness of the interplay between learners' identities and language learning will help Chinese and Japanese language educators develop more reasonable teaching plans to support and motivate students and ultimately stimulate more agentive actions.

Finally, thanks to both increasing enrollments of Asian international students and continuously diversified domestic student demographics on North American tertiary-level campuses in recent years (Mori, Chapter 2 in this volume), today's language classrooms have become more complex with learners bringing with them a myriad of multilingual and multicultural repertoires. Determining how to tap into the rich semiotic resources that come with diverse students and motivate them to advance their language proficiency requires a holistic understanding of language learners and language learning. Adopting a transdisciplinary framework in Chinese and Japanese language teaching could potentially balance the disproportionate attention to cognitive development inherent in traditional language teaching approaches and encourage language educators to develop a holistic view of language learning and teaching that embraces the learner as a creative and productive communicator in today's flexible and dynamic Chinese/Japanese-speaking communities.

Although the transdisciplinary framework has not yet been widely adopted as an overarching pedagogical approach in foreign language education, Chinese and Japanese language educators have used some theoretical concepts (e.g., translanguaging, ecological language teaching, meaning potentials) to guide class design. In particular, there is a surging interest in adopting translanguaging in Chinese and Japanese language teaching where negotiation between a stronger and a weaker language facilitates language learning (e.g., Chikamatsu, 2022; García & Kano, 2014; Wang, 2019; Zheng, 2021). According to Leung and Valdés (2019), translanguaging is a "transmutable concept" (p. 358) that has been used variably by both researchers and practitioners. Basically, it allows us to reconceptualize language as "a multilingual, multisensory, and multimodal resource for sense- and meaning-making" (Li, 2018, p. 22). Emphasizing translanguaging as a form of empowerment of minoritized students, García and Kano (2014) defined translanguaging as "a process by which students and teachers engage in complex discourse practices that include all the language practices of all students in a class in order to develop new language practices and sustain old ones" (p. 261). Given that even advanced Chinese and Japanese language learners still need their first language to assist with text comprehension and communication, translanguaging has been largely adopted as a pedagogical practice in Chinese and Japanese language classrooms.

Collaborative teaching as a solution

Collaborative pedagogy is not new in the field of second/foreign language education. Language faculty members have been encouraged to work across disciplines and languages as well as with colleagues in the local and global communities. The first wave of collaborative pedagogy in foreign language is reflected in the development of Foreign Languages Across the Curriculum (FLAC), a term that later changed to Languages Across the Curriculum (LAC) and recently regrouped under Cultures and Languages Across the Curriculum (CLAC), which entails adding foreign language (FL) materials to a non-FL course for students who already possess certain proficiency in the said FL and requires collaboration among faculty in languages and other disciplines (Reisinger, 2018; Zilmer, 2018). As early as the 1970s, scholars and educators (e.g., Champagne, 1978) proposed multidisciplinary language courses to integrate foreign language studies into a university undergraduate curriculum so students can apply their language skills in other interest areas. In 1981, the National Assembly on Foreign Language and International Studies officially recommended integrating foreign language learning into general education (Sudermann & Cisar, 1992). The National Endowment for the Humanities also encouraged the practice of FLAC. Depending on institutional settings, students might receive a partial credit or no extra credit for completing the FLAC courses. Later on, to answer the call for internationalization, some American universities also started collaborative curricula between the department of foreign languages, college of business, and practical training (Kecht, 1999; Voght & Schaub, 1992). A wide variety of interdisciplinary models, ranging from one LAC course to weekly seminars and combined degrees, was launched, and this interdisciplinary approach to internationalization was considered successful (Bettencourt, 2011). As LAC programs require substantial institutional support for faculty development and coordination, many LAC programs had to reduce their curricular offerings or even ceased to exist due to reduced external funding in the 1990s (Klee, 2009).

In response to the Modern Language Association's (MLA) 2007 report on the "current language crisis that has occurred as a result of 9/11" (Geisler, 2007, p. 1) as well as the need to address the college-level non-English language enrollment issue, the call for developing more LAC courses has become urgent again. The MLA urges language departments to produce "educated speakers who have deep translingual and transcultural competence" (Geisler, 2007, p. 3) by creating new courses covering more subject areas, including interdisciplinary collaborative courses co-taught with faculty members from other departments. The American Council for Teachers of Foreign Languages (ACTFL), the official professional organization for K–16 foreign language educators in North America, also updated its world readiness standards for learning languages (National Standards Collaborative Board, 2015) to highlight the goals of guiding learners to develop competence to participate in multilingual communities at home and around the world. In line with the professional organizations' promotion, many second/foreign language researchers and educators (e.g., Allen et al., 1992; Met, 1991) are strong advocates for pedagogical cooperation across the curriculum and language. With a focus on intercultural citizenship as the ultimate goal of action-oriented world language education, Michael Byram and his colleagues (e.g., Byram & Wagner, 2018; Wagner et al., 2020) argued that language teaching needs to be linked to other disciplines so language classroom content can be cognitively and emotionally demanding and students can "engage with significant issues in their own and other countries, such as environmental problems or political and historical conflicts" (Byram & Wagner, 2018, p. 146). This approach also encourages language educators to collaborate across the language to develop "a vision of the complementarity of teaching skills and attitudes in intercultural competence even if the knowledge component may differ" (p. 147). Cross-disciplinary collaboration has increasingly been adopted in college-level Japanese language classrooms (e.g., Chikamatsu, 2012, 2019, 2022) and more recently in Chinese language classrooms (e.g., Reisinger et al., 2022).

Another type of collaborative pedagogy that has received increasing attention from world language educators is community engagement and service learning (e.g., Bettencourt, 2015; Overfield, 1997). This approach, believed to have a great impact on students' attitude toward civic engagement, diverse cultural communities, and language learning (Horst & Pearce, 2010; King de Ramírez, 2015), emphasizes integrating language learning in particular communicative settings beyond the classroom and requires careful project design through cooperation with selected community partners who can both provide support to students and help the language instructor gauge service-learning outcomes. To address the issue of limited access to non-Spanish-speaking local communities, Overfield (1997) suggested expanding the definition of community to both local and global communities of speakers of a target language. He and Qin (2017) reported on an innovative 8-week international internship program in China in which American students with intermediate proficiency in Mandarin Chinese (demonstrated through four semesters of language instruction as well as 8-week study abroad program in the previous year) were placed in Chinese-owned companies that provided service related to each individual student's major, future career plans, and/or research interests. Throughout the internship, each student was required to complete a variety of tasks and duties assigned by their onsite supervisors or mentors. In addition, on two afternoons per week, the students participated in community services and social activities, such as selling newspapers to benefit the Red Cross or visiting a school for children who were blind and on the autism spectrum. The authors highlighted the benefits of international internship experience in terms of language development and working cultural competence.

The advancement of computer technologies has made collaborative pedagogy more feasible and even ubiquitous nowadays. In the field of second/foreign language education, telecollaboration, which puts language learners in direct contact with native speakers of the target language via diverse internet technologies, has been practiced to promote bilingual—bicultural exchanges since the early 2000s (Thorne, 2006; Warschauer, 1995). Telecollaborative practice has been implemented in a variety of models and tasks, such as e-tandem and the *Cultura* model (Furstenberg et al., 2001). The most demanding tasks are collaborative tasks that require learners from both sides to work together on a joint project (e.g., Belz, 2007; O'Dowd & Ware, 2009). Although telecollaboration has been increasingly integrated into college-level Chinese and Japanese language teaching in the United States (e.g., Akiyama & Saito, 2016; Jin, 2018; Nishio & Nakatsugawa, 2020; Wang et al., 2013; Zhang, 2016), most existing projects tended to treat target language peers as linguistic and cultural consultants to American learners instead of partners working on a joint project (Luo & Yang, 2018).

In recent years, a new trend—cross-disciplinary telecollaborative initiatives—has emerged to "engage students in not only in 'pure' foreign language practice but also in collaborative projects based on different subject areas" (O'Dowd, 2018, p. 299). This trend is largely influenced by the collaborative online international learning network (COIL) created by the State University of New York system, which connects students at different geographical locations through online and hybrid courses to work on subject-specific collaborative projects (Robin, 2017; Schultheis Moore & Simon, 2015). The COIL initiatives have taken place in a wide variety of disciplines, such as business, history, music education, anthropology, and public health. Unlike traditional telecollaborative projects, COIL projects are institutional level virtual exchanges that require more structured faculty and student collaboration from both sides (i.e., well-designed team teaching and collaborative student learning) and encourage collaboration between language faculty and faculty in other disciplines (O'Dowd, 2018). COIL projects have been increasingly adopted in Chinese and Japanese language classrooms. For instance, in Nishio et al.'s (2020) project, each undergraduate learner of Japanese at an American university teamed up with two or three students in a Japanese university to conduct online discussions comparing American college life with Japanese college life. At the end of the project, students from both sides created an informational video in their respective target language to introduce one subtopic they discussed. In Huang's (2022) dissertation study, she reported on a COIL project engaging learners of Mandarin Chinese enrolled in two upper-level Chinese business courses in a rural university in the southeastern United States and graduate students who were training to become teachers of Chinese as a second language at a Chinese university. Students from both sides participated in weekly online discussions for 6 weeks, and the American students were required to create two cultural reports with the help of their Chinese counterparts. Students from both sides also conducted a debriefing and reflection meeting at the end of the project.

As previously discussed, although collaborative pedagogy has been widely practiced in the field of second/foreign language education, more growth is yet to be seen in Chinese and Japanese language-focused projects. In addition, challenges impeding language educators and learners from fully benefiting from these experiences still exist, and a deeper understanding of language learning affordances in these collaborative settings is still greatly needed (O'Dowd, 2018; Reisinger, 2018). We believe that well-thought-out collaboration between language faculty and diverse collaborators from local and global communities, as one type of pedagogical activity supporting micro-, meso-, and macro-level L2 learning, helps generate meaningful multimodal and complex real-life contexts in which language learners can learn and use Chinese or Japanese language (and English, in some cases) to access and interact with a wider range of "socially constituted repertoires of identification and affiliated resources" (Bauman, 2000, p. 1). To bring changes to the field of Chinese and Japanese as a second/foreign language teaching and learning, this book introduces collaborative pedagogical practices between language faculty and various partners across disciplines, communities, and borders, which are followed with pedagogical reflections from a transdisciplinary perspective by involved educators. The case studies shared in the book "showcase" detailed practical examples as to how to provide learners with not only "multiple encounters with particular linguistic forms (e.g., increased input frequencies), but also meaningful interactions that fundamentally help them expand their L2 linguistic sensitivities and thus their repertoires, semiotic resources, and registers" (Duff & Byrnes, 2019, p. 4).

Organization of the Chapters

This book consists of five sections: Section 1 focuses on theoretical interpretations of major transdisciplinary concepts, and Section 2, Section 3, Section 4, and Section 5 feature case studies describing collaborative courses or course projects in terms of the collaboration context, course design, implementation process, and pedagogical reflections and suggestions by Chinese and Japanese language educators and their collaborators. The Chinese and Japanese language classes reported in the case studies range from beginning to advanced classes, thereby providing examples for language educators at all levels.

Section 1 contains Chapter 2 and Chapter 3, which focus on theoretical foundations and empirical evidence for a transdisciplinary approach to Chinese and Japanese language teaching. In Chapter 2, "Teaching and learning of East Asian languages in the era of 'trans-,'" Junko Mori delineates the social, cultural, and historical contexts that shaped and are still shaping East Asian language programs in North America, with a focus on the meso- and macro-level layers of the ecological systems in which East Asian language teaching is situated. It includes notable discourses that have influenced program operations, assumptions, institutional policies, and structures before it points out future directions for East Asian language teaching in the United States. In Chapter 3, "Translanguaging and co-learning at the interface of language and culture," Li Wei advocates a foreign language teaching and learning approach from the lens of translanguaging, co-learning, and cultural translation. Using a college-level Chinese language class in the United Kingdom as an example, Li first explains the concepts of translanguaging, co-learning, and cultural translation, then illustrates how to use these concepts to interpret the language learning and teaching happening in the Chinese language classroom.

Section 2 features pedagogical projects on the theme of collaborative teaching between language and other disciplines. Chapter 4, "Translanguaging with food and ethics: translating languages, enhancing agencies, and expanding horizons," introduces collaborative teaching between one advanced Japanese language course in the United States and one Japanese food ethics course taught by a religious studies professor that were linked through a FLAC design model. Yuki Miyamoto and Nobuko Chikamatsu highlight translanguaging as a purposeful pedagogical practice to expand Japanese language learners' meaning potentials and construct their own semiotic repertoires across the languages. Chapter 5, "Teaching Chinese through classic literature: a cross-disciplinary collaboration," shares the collaboration between a Chinese language professor and a literature professor in one co-taught Chinese classic literature course and one advanced Chinese communication and composition course. In this chapter, Jinai Sun and Stewart Patterson explain how their collaboration afforded students access to rich Chinese semiotic resources and stimulated students' interest to identify with particular Chinese cultural values by reading and discussing Chinese classic novels. Chapter 6, "Promoting translingual and transcultural literacies in a collaborative content-based Japanese classroom: audiovisual translation as pedagogy," reports on an advanced Japanese language course adopting the critical content-based instruction design and co-taught by a Japanese linguist and an expert in media studies. Adopting translanguaging to engage Japanese native speakers, heritage speakers, and Japanese L2 learners, Saori Hoshi and Ayaka Yoshimizu had learners discuss sociolinguistic and sociocultural aspects of Japanese-English subtitle translation, particularly gender-identity construction through language use.

Chapter 7, "Wellbeing and Chinese language study: a case of cross-disciplinary teaching," features two collaborative projects developed by a Chinese language educator and colleagues from other disciplines with a shared interest in mental wellbeing: the Bilingual Meditation Program and the Bicultural Comparison Project. Through these two projects, which can be applied to Chinese language learners at all levels, Chieh Li, Ann Cai, and Dongying Liu emphasize the affective aspect of language learning and illustrate how to integrate language learning with understanding wellbeing as a multicultural and multidisciplinary concept.

Section 3 focuses on collaborative pedagogy between language educators and community partners. In Chapter 8, "Negotiating C2 expectation and Third-Space personae in transdisciplinary L2 learning: collaboration with Chinese professionals in advanced Chinese language curricula," Xin Zhang reports on her advanced Chinese language course at a United States-China joint-venture university. Drawing on the concept of the Third Space, Zhang purposefully integrates a career services specialist into course material development and class activities to enable the students to negotiate the expectations they receive as a learner and user of Chinese language as well as the personae they desire to project in a Chinese-speaking professional setting. Chapter 9, "Internships at Japanese orphanages: a case study of a first-year Japanese language student's growth," shares a first-year Japanese language learner's experience as an intern in the Japan Children's Home Internship Program in Japan. As the internship faculty advisor, Nobuko Koyama observes the gap between the learner's imagined community and the real communities he encountered during the internship, which triggered the learner's identity transformation and ultimately agency activation.

Section 4 is about cross-language pedagogical collaboration. Chapter 10, "An experiment of cross-language and cross-disciplinary collaboration: integrating Xu Bing's text-based arts into Chinese and Japanese classrooms," features the collaboration between a first-year Chinese language course and a third-year Japanese language course. Using Xu Bing's text-based artworks as a common subject and collaborative course projects, Noriko Sugimori and Leihua Weng draw attention to ownership of *hànzì/kanji* and ideologies in language education. In Chapter 11, "Cross-language and cross-disciplinary collaborations in a Mandarin CLAC course," Yan Liu introduces an advanced Chinese language tutorial course as an adjunct course to an environmental science and policy course, which was offered collaboratively with two other language tutorials (Spanish and French). Liu argues for the benefits of this unique cross-language and cross-disciplinary approach in providing multimodal resources for language teaching and learning.

Section 5 features international pedagogical collaboration. In Chapter 12, "The U.S.-Japan online magazine project: international telecollaborations as translanguaging spaces," Yuri Kumagai and Momoyo Shimazu share an international telecollaborative project connecting a third-year Japanese language course in the United States and two seminar courses in two different Japanese universities. By analyzing student collaboration on a multilingual online magazine, the authors stress translanguaging as a useful pedagogical practice to build relationships and negotiate meanings. Chapter 13, "Transcending borders and limitations with digitally enhanced pedagogy: Language Learning-focused COIL (LLC) for Japanese learners and prospective teachers," reports on the virtual collaboration between a Japanese translation course in a U.S. college and a teacher education course at a Japanese university for students wishing to pursue a career in teaching Japanese as a second/foreign language. Keiko Ikeda and Nobuko Chikamatsu analyze how the joint translation project enabled students from both sides to activate agency as intercultural communicators and collaborators.

The transdisciplinary approach to SLA is our answer to the call for "a multilingual turn" in applied linguistics to rectify the monolingual standards a second language learner is expected to meet. A transdisciplinary perspective of second/foreign language teaching and learning offers language educators and learners a more sensible and holistic view of what language learning entails in a multilingual and multicultural world that is interconnected economically and now virtually, despite the pandemic. On the other hand, as has been widely recognized in the field of second/foreign language education, collaborative teaching has become a very important pedagogical approach for engaging language learners in meaningful and fruitful language learning in the 21st century. We believe understanding language learning supported by collaborative teaching from a transdisciplinary perspective will give language educators an upper hand when facing diverse challenges such as stagnated student motivation or a declining student enrollment trend. This book provides both theoretical concepts to understand a transdisciplinary approach to Chinese and Japanese language teaching and learning and concrete pedagogical examples to illustrate how a language educator can design, implement, and reflect on collaborative projects with diverse local and global partners. Given the rarity of reports on collaborative teaching in Chinese and Japanese languages, we hope this book will stimulate more interest among fellow college-level Chinese and Japanese language educators to start thinking about or reaching out to potential partners to innovate their language teaching. We hope the transdisciplinary perspective adopted to analyze students' language learning in each case study in this book also offers insights to colleagues who teach languages other than Chinese and Japanese, as this approach has not yet been widely disseminated and is, thus, not well-known among language educators.

References

ACTFL. (2019). *ACTFL 2019 annual report*. www.actfl.org/sites/default/files/reports/annualreport2019/index.html

Akiyama, Y., & Saito, K. (2016). Development of comprehensibility and its linguistic correlates: A longitudinal study of video-mediated telecollaboration. *The Modern Language Journal*, *100*(3), 585–609.

Allen, W., Anderson, K., & Narváez, L. (1992). Foreign languages across the curriculum: The applied foreign language component. *Foreign Language Annals*, *25*(1), 11–19.

Atkinson, D. (2019). Second language acquisition beyond borders? The Douglas Fir Group searchers for transdisciplinary identity. *The Modern Language Journal*, *103*(S1), 113–121.

Bauman, R. (2000). Language, identity, performance. *Pragmatics*, *10*(1), 1–5.
Belz, J. A. (2007). The development of intercultural communicative competence in telecollaborative partnerships. In R. O'Dowd (Ed.), *Online intercultural exchange* (pp. 127–166). Multilingual Matters.
Bettencourt, M. (2011). Languages across the curriculum: A response to internationalization in foreign language education. *Multicultural Education*, *19*(1), 55–58.
Bettencourt, M. (2015). Supporting student learning outcomes through service learning. *Foreign Language Annals*, *48*(3), 473–490.
Byram, M., & Wagner, M. (2018). Making a difference: Language teaching for intercultural and international dialogue. *Foreign Language Annals*, *51*(1), 140–151.
Byrd Clark, J. S. (2016). Introduction to the special issue. *L2 Journal*, *8*(4), 3–19.
Champagne, R. A. (1978). Responding to the challenge of survival: Multidisciplinary language courses. *Foreign Language Annals*, *11*(1), 81–85.
Chikamatsu, N. (2012). Communication with community: Connecting an individual to the world through Japanese content-based instruction of Japanese-American history. *Japanese Language and Literature*, *46*(1), 171–199.
Chikamatsu, N. (2019). Collaborative teaching of a Japanese content-based course: 3.11 and nuclear power crisis. In C. A. Melin (Ed.), *Foreign language teaching and the environment: Theory, curricula, institutional structures* (pp. 148–162). Modern Language Association of America.
Chikamatsu, N. (2022). Translanguaging in language and area-studies curriculum: A Japanese FLAC course of Minamata and Fukushima in environmental humanities. In M. de la Fuente (Ed.), *Education for sustainable development in foreign language learning: Content-based instruction in college-level curricula* (pp. 215–232). Routledge.
Crystal, D. (1997). World languages. In D. Crystal (Ed.), *The Cambridge encyclopedia of language* (2nd ed., pp. 359–361). Cambridge University Press.
Douglas Fir Group. (2016). A transdisciplinary framework for SLA in a multilingual world. *The Modern Language Journal*, *100*(S1), 19–47.
Duff, P. A., & Byrnes, H. (2019). SLA across disciplinary borders: Introduction to the special issue. *The Modern Language Journal*, *103*(S1), 3–5.
Furstenberg, G., Levet, S., English, K., & Maillet, K. (2001). Giving a virtual voice to the silent language of culture: The Cultura project. *Language Learning & Technology*, *5*(1), 55–102.
Gao, X. (2019). The Douglas Fir Group framework as a resource map for language teacher education. *The Modern Language Journal*, *103*(S1), 161–166.
García, O., & Kano, N. (2014). Translanguaging as process and pedagogy: Developing the English writing of Japanese students in the US. In J. Conteh & G. Meier (Eds.), *The multilingual turn in languages education: Benefits for individuals and societies* (pp. 258–277). Multilingual Matters.
Geisler, M., Kramsch, C., McGinnis, S., Patrikis, P., Pratt, M. L., Ryding, K., & Saussy, H. (2007). Foreign languages and higher education: New structures for a changed world: MLA Ad hoc committee on Foreign languages. *Profession*, 234–245.
Goh, Y. (2017). *Teaching Chinese as an international language: A Singapore perspective*. Cambridge University Press.
Hall, J. K. (2019) *Essentials of SLA for L2 teachers: A transdisciplinary framework*. Taylor & Francis.
He, Y., & Qin, X. (2017). Students' perceptions of an internship experience in China: A pilot study. *Foreign Language Annals*, *50*(1), 57–70.

Holliday, A. (2006). Native-speakerism. *ELT Journal*, *60*(4), 385–387.

Horst, E. E., & Pearce, J. M. (2010). Foreign languages and sustainability: Addressing the connections, communities, and comparisons standards in higher education. *Foreign Language Annals*, *43*(3), 365–383.

Houghton, S. A., & Hashimoto, K. (2018). Foreword: Probing for a post-native-speakerist future. In S. A. Houghton & K. Hashimoto (Eds.), *Towards post-native-speakerism: Dynamics and shifts* (pp. v–xv). Springer.

Huang, Y. (2022). *Investigating student development of intercultural communication competence through collaborative online international learning* [Doctoral dissertation]. University of North Georgia.

Jin, L. (2012). When in China, do as the Chinese do? Learning compliment responding in a study abroad program. *Chinese as a Second Language Research*, *1*(2), 211–240.

Jin, L. (2015). Developing Chinese complimenting in a study abroad program. *Chinese Journal of Applied Linguistics*, *38*(3), 277–300.

Jin, L. (2018). Digital affordances on WeChat: Learning Chinese as a second language. *Computer Assisted Language Learning*, *31*(1–2), 27–52.

Johnson, K. E. (2019). The relevance of a transdisciplinary framework for SLA in language teacher education. *The Modern Language Journal*, *103*(S1), 167–174.

Kecht, M. R. (1999). Integrated learning and internationalized education through languages across the curriculum. *Association of Departments of Foreign Languages Bulletin*, *30*(3), 17–22.

King de Ramírez, C. (2015). Strategy and action: Assessing student-led culture workshops within the professions. *Foreign Language Annals*, *48*(1), 56–67.

Klee, C. A. (2009). Internationalization and foreign languages: The resurgence of interest in languages across the curriculum. *The Modern Language Journal*, *93*(4), 618–621.

Kramsch, C. (1997). The privilege of the nonnative speaker. *PMLA*, *112*, 359–369.

Leung, C., & Valdés, G. (2019). Translanguaging and the transdisciplinary framework for language teaching and learning in a multilingual world. *The Modern Language Journal*, *103*(2), 348–370.

Li, W. (2018). Translanguaging as a practical theory of language. *Applied Linguistics*, *39*, 9–30.

Llurda, E., & Calvet-Terré, J. (2022). Native-speakerism and non-native second language teachers: A research agenda. *Language Teaching*, 1–17. doi:10.1017/S0261444822000271

Looney, D., & Lusin, N. (2018). *Enrollments in language other than English in United States institutions of higher education, summer 2016 and fall 2016: Preliminary report*. The Modern Language Association of America. https://files.eric.ed.gov/fulltext/ED590075.pdf

Luo, H., & Yang, C. (2018). Twenty years of telecollaborative practice: Implications for teaching Chinese as a foreign language. *Computer Assisted Language Learning*, *31*(5/6), 546–571.

May, S. (Ed.). (2013). *The multilingual turn: Implications for SLA, TESOL and bilingual education*. Routledge.

Met, M. (1991). Learning language through content: Learning content through language. *Foreign Language Annals*, *24*(4), 281–195.

National Standards Collaborative Board. (2015). *World-readiness standards for learning languages* (4th ed). Author.

Nishio, T., Fujikake, C., & Osawa, M. (2020). Language learning motivation in collaborative online international learning: An activity theory analysis. *Journal of Virtual Exchange*, *3*(SI-IVEC2019), 27–47.

Nishio, T., & Nakatsugawa, M. (2020). Successful participation in intercultural exchange: Tensions in American-Japanese telecollaboration. *Language Learning & Technology*, *24*(1), 154–168.

Nomura, K., & Mochizuki, T. (2018). Native-speakerism perceived by "non-native-speaking" teachers of Japanese in Hong Kong. In S. Houghton & K. Hashimoto (Eds.), *Towards post-native-speakerism* (pp. 79–95). Springer.

O'Dowd, R. (2018). From telecollaboration to virtual exchange: State-of-the-art and the role of UNICollaboration in moving forward. *Journal of Virtual Exchange*, *1*, 1–23.

O'Dowd, R., & Ware, P. (2009). Critical issues in telecollaborative task design. *Computer Assisted Language Learning*, *22*(2), 173–188.

Ohta, A. S. (2001). *Second language acquisition processes in the classroom: Learning Japanese*. Lawrence Erlbaum Associates.

Ohta, A. S. (2008). Laughter and second language acquisition: A study of Japanese foreign language classes. In J. Mori & A. S. Ohta (Eds.), *Japanese applied linguistics: Discourse and social perspectives* (pp. 213–242). Continuum.

Ortega, L. (2013). SLA for the 21st century: Disciplinary progress, transdisciplinary relevance, and the bi/multilingual turn. *Language Learning*, *63*(Supplement 2019), 1–24.

Overfield, D. M. (1997). From the margins to the mainstream: Foreign language education and community-based learning. *Foreign Language Annals*, *30*(4), 485–491.

Reisinger, D. (2018). Measuring the impact of cultures and languages across the curriculum: New research directions. In D. Soneson & C. Zilmer (Eds.), *Developing responsible global citizenship through cultures and languages across the curriculum (CLAC): Selected papers from the 2016 CLAC conference* (pp. 17–40). University of Minnesota, Center for Advanced Research on Language Acquisition.

Reisinger, D., Quammen, S. V., Liu, Y., & Virguez, E. (2022). Sustainability across the curriculum: A multilingual and intercultural approach. In M. de la Fuente (Ed.), *Education for sustainable development in foreign language learning: Content-based instruction in college-level curricula* (pp. 197–214). Routledge.

Robin, J. (2017). Embedding collaborative online international learning (COIL) at higher education institutions: An evolutionary overview with exemplars. *Internationalization of Higher Education*, *2*, 27–44.

Schultheis Moore, A., & Simon, S. (2015). *Globally networked teaching in the humanities*. Routledge.

Sudermann, D. P., & Cisar, M. A. (1992). Foreign language across the curriculum: A critical appraisal. *The Modern Language Journal*, *76*(3), 295–308.

Thorne, S. L. (2006). Pedagogical and praxiological lessons from Internet-mediated intercultural foreign language education research. In J. Belz & S. L. Thorne (Eds.), *Internet-mediated intercultural foreign language education* (pp. 2–30). Heinle & Heinle.

Voght, G. M., & Schaub, R. (1992). Foreign languages and international business. *ERIC Digest* (ED347851).

Wagner, M., Cardetti, F., & Byram, M. (2020). *Teaching international citizenship across the curriculum: The role of language education*. ACTFL.

Walton, A. R. (2016). Expanding the vision of foreign language education: Enter the less commonly taught languages. In E. S. Silber (Ed.), *Critical issues in foreign language instruction* (3rd ed., pp. 160–185). Routledge.

Wang, D. (2019) Translanguaging in Chinese foreign language classrooms: Students and teachers' attitudes and practices. *International Journal of Bilingual Education and Bilingualism*, *22*(2), 138–149.

Wang, J., Zou, B., Wang, D., & Xing, M. (2013). Students' perceptions of a wiki platform and the impact of wiki engagement on intercultural communication. *System, 41,* 245–256.

Warschauer, M. (Ed.). (1995). *Virtual connections.* University of Hawai'i Second Language Teaching and Curriculum Center.

Zhang, S. (2016). Learning through a CMC-based tandem project with native speakers: A descriptive study of beginning CFL learners. *Journal of Technology and Chinese Language Teaching, 7*(2), 58–81.

Zheng, B. (2021). Translanguaging in a Chinese immersion classroom: An ecological examination of instructional discourses. *International Journal of Bilingual Education and Bilingualism, 24*(9), 1324–1339.

Zilmer, C. (2018). A CLAC framework. In D. Soneson & C. Zilmer (Eds.), *Developing responsible global citizenship through cultures and languages across the curriculum (CLAC): Selected papers from the 2016 CLAC conference* (pp. 9–16). University of Minnesota, Center for Advanced Research on Language Acquisition.

Section 1
Theoretical foundations and empirical evidence for a transdisciplinary approach to Chinese/Japanese language teaching

2 Teaching and learning of East Asian languages in the era of "trans-"

Junko Mori

Introduction

The last two decades have seen a surge in the use of the "trans-" prefix that acknowledges the fluidity and complexity of social practices and activities observed in late modernity. Terms such as *transnational, transcultural, translocal,* and *transpatial,* for instance, have been used in discussing the rapid circulation of people, ideas, goods, and practices, which suggests the interconnectedness of global society. In the field of applied linguistics, translingual practice (Canagarajah, 2013, 2018), translanguaging (García & Li, 2014; Li, 2018), and transmodality (Hawkins, 2018, 2021) have captured researchers' attention because of their ability to encapsulate the flexible and creative employment of resources from different (named) languages and semiotic systems ubiquitously found in both physical and digital worlds. Furthermore, the need for transdisciplinary approaches has been advocated in the investigation of the multifaceted nature of language use, acquisition, and learning taking place under the circumstances described by the aforementioned "trans-" terms (Douglas Fir Group, 2016).

These "trans-" terms, in essence, challenge the existence of borders, boundaries, categories, and associated ideologies and instead celebrate the possibilities of transcending these orthodox understandings. Yet, at the same time, these terms also recognize the very existence of the past and their continuous impact on our practices and activities today (cf. Hawkins & Mori, 2018). Indeed, Kramsch (2018) cautions applied linguists from blindly pursuing imaginations of "transpatial utopias," suggesting that sufficient attention must be given to a humanistic sense of history—the "dependency on infrastructural conditions and legacies of discourse and institutional power that precede and condition our existence" (Butler, 2016, p. 21). So what are the infrastructural conditions and legacies of discourse that continue to shape the current operation of East Asian language programs in U.S. higher education? The current chapter tackles this question with the hope that the examination of the key aspects of this particular contextual climate will help readers appreciate innovations and challenges associated with the instructional activities undertaken by the authors of later chapters.

In the following, I first offer a brief overview of the transdisciplinary framework presented by the Douglas Fir Group (2016) by focusing on the macro and meso layers of the ecological systems discussed in their framework. I subsequently review the history of East Asian language programs in U.S. higher education and identify notable discourses that have conditioned their operations. I then examine commonly observed institutional policies, practices, and structures in today's higher education and consider how they serve as enablers or obstacles for exploring and implementing innovations and collaborations inspired by the "trans-" turn. Finally, with the renewed understanding of constructs such as language, learners, teachers, and teaching and learning activities that have emerged from the critical reflection of the ecological layers, this chapter concludes by posing several fundamental questions that should continue to be explored as we imagine the future of language education in the United States.

A transdisciplinary framework: Ecological layers and their interrelatedness

As touched upon earlier, the Douglas Fir Group (2016), consisting of 15 scholars from diverse theoretical perspectives, proposed a transdisciplinary framework (hereafter, DFG framework) for understanding the complexities and dynamics of language learning and teaching taking place in the contemporary world. The scholars identified two goals to foster by proposing the framework:

> One goal is to expand the perspectives of researchers and teachers of L2 learners with regard to learners' diverse multilingual repertoires of meaning-making resources and identities so as to enable their participation in a wide range of social, cognitive, and emotional activities, networks, and forms of communication and learning in their multilingual lifeworlds. Another goal is to foster in learners a profound awareness not only of the cultural, historical, and institutional meanings that their language-mediated social actions have, but also, and just as importantly, of the dynamic and evolving role their actions play in shaping their own and others' worlds.
>
> (p. 25)

To capture the essence of their proposal, the group introduced a schematic figure of multilayered ecological systems inspired by Bronfenbrenner's (1979) model of human development (see Figure 2.1). The figure places "individuals engaging with others" at the center surrounded by the micro level of social activity, the meso level of sociocultural institutions and communities, and the macro level of ideological structures. Although solid lines and different colors visually separate these levels in the figure, the accompanying explanation underscored that "each exists only through constant interaction with the others, such that each gives shape to and is shaped by the next" (p. 25).

Limitations of the two-dimensional centric-circle figure, however, have been acknowledged by the contributing scholars. Duff (2019), a member of the Douglas Fir Group, for instance, stated that:

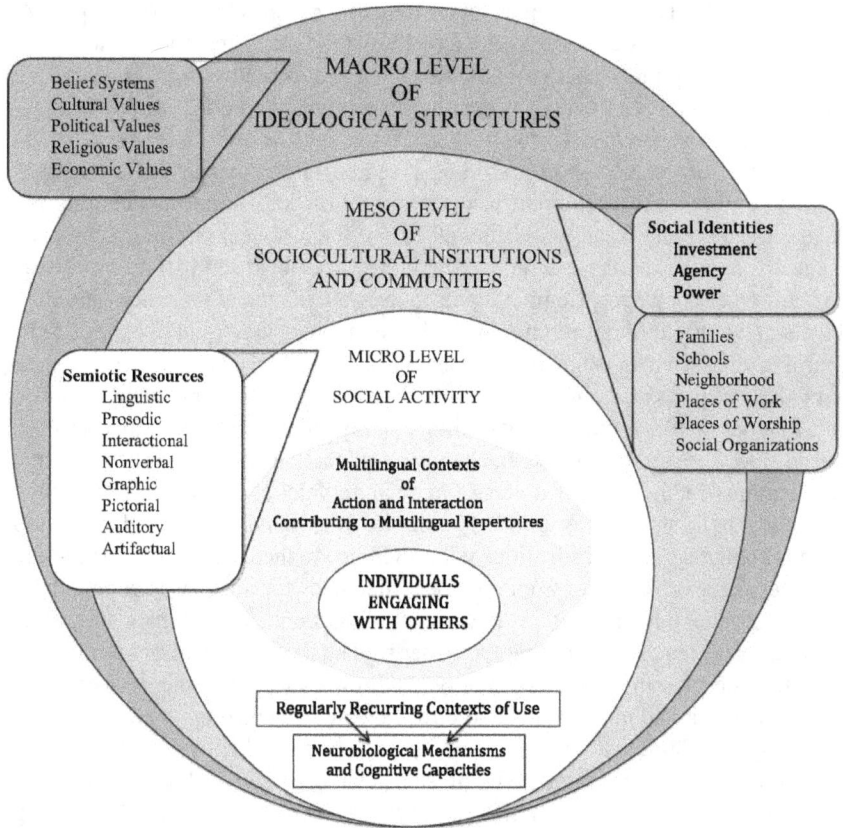

Figure 2.1 The multifaceted nature of language learning and teaching
Source: Douglas Fir Group (2016)

> The figure cannot easily capture multiple timescales—the relationship of the present to the past and future—or the manner in which these macro—meso—micro dynamics and particulars may change and differ concurrently or sequentially across contexts for a given learner.
>
> (pp. 9–10)

Atkinson (2019), another member, pointed out that "the continued lack of theoretical integration of the cognitive, the social, and the material is the single greatest barrier to transdisciplinarity in SLA studies" (p. 115). Yet another member, Johnson (2019), admitted that the DFG framework did not "address the relevance for language teachers, language teaching, or language teacher education" (p. 167) and warned that "institutional policies (i.e., mandated curriculum, high-stakes assessments) and dominant ideologies (i.e., the native speaker myth, English as economic capital) may make it impossible to enact instructional practices that reflect the theoretical principles of a transdisciplinary framework for SLA" (p. 173). The dissatisfaction expressed by these (and other) members reflects their respective disciplinary backgrounds, revealing the difficulty in making an ideal proposal that addresses every concern in this evolving and transforming field.

Despite the apparent need for further refinement, the DFG framework should be credited for its success in providing researchers and teachers of L2 learners with a common reference point in discussing a range of issues concerning language learning and teaching. Ushioda (2017), for instance, referred to this ecological framework when examining the impact of global English on motivation to learn other languages. Competing discourses circulating at the macro and meso levels inevitably influence individuals' decision to engage or not to engage in the learning of particular languages happening at the micro level. From instrumental values of particular languages in the global economy to humanistic values of understanding other cultures, possibilities of expanding cognitive capacities, and so on, these varied discourses on language education have generated different implications for learners of diverse linguistic, ethnic, and socioeconomic backgrounds. De Costa and Norton (2017), on the other hand, explored the development of language teacher identities with reference to the DFG framework. Macro and meso level discourses, from neoliberal demands for increased accountability for educational outcomes to top-down institutional policies and mandates, affect how language teachers who aspire to foster students' multilingual and multimodal repertoires design their classroom activities; how they present themselves to students, peers, and administrators; and how they are evaluated by institutions.

Navigating through obstacles posed by prevalent ideologies and conventional institutional structures undoubtedly presents challenges to teachers who embrace the goals put forth by the Douglas Fir Group. Nevertheless, as Gao (2019) suggested, the DFG framework prompts language teachers and teacher educators to reappraise the fundamentals of our profession—why we teach languages, what languages we teach, and how we teach languages—and establish a renewed understanding of their own professional positions. It also encourages teachers and teacher educators to recognize contextual conditions that contribute to the creation of inequity among language learners from diverse backgrounds. Accordingly, Gao called for the exercise of teacher agency, which he believes "will play a critical role in transforming our understanding and sustaining our pursuit of professional aspirations" (p. 165).

With this brief (and admittedly selective) overview of the DFG framework and debates that it triggered as a backdrop, the following sections turn to the critical reflection of macro and meso level contextual milieus that have shaped the teaching and learning of East Asian languages in U.S. institutions of higher education.

East Asian language programs in U.S. higher education

To begin this section with a rather blunt summation, the history of East Asian language programs in U.S. higher education can be characterized by the continuous process of othering and self-othering, which parallels the historical and geopolitical relationships between the United States and the East. Some of the labels and descriptors commonly used to describe East Asian languages in the United States exemplify this othering and self-othering practice. One example is less commonly taught languages (LCTLs). Despite the fact that enrollments in East Asian languages have dramatically increased over the last several decades (Japanese ranked fifth, Chinese ranked seventh, and Korean ranked eleventh according to the 2016 MLA enrollment survey results; Looney & Lusin, 2019), the practice of assigning the label LCTLs to all languages other than English, French, German, and Spanish continues to be observed in the profession.[1] Another label frequently used for East Asian languages is Category IV language. According to the Foreign Service Institute (FSI) (n.d.), Category IV languages—labeled as "super-hard languages" that are "exceptionally difficult for native English speakers"—require learners to spend three to four times more hours than Category I languages, which are "more similar to English," in order to reach "professional working proficiency." This categorization has been widely circulated as a justification for various programmatic decisions, but its origin and validity have not received sufficient attention. The FSI states that their categorization reflects "70 years of experience in teaching languages to U.S. diplomats," but it is important to remember that those who have been selected to serve as U.S. diplomats represent a small fraction of college and university graduates. Furthermore, given that more than 20% of people in the United States speak a language other than English at home today (U.S. Census Bureau, n.d.), the FSI categories, which are based on the assumption that leaners are (monolingual) native speakers of English, must be taken with a degree of skepticism. In light of the transdisciplinary framework, the idea that East Asian languages are different, difficult, and demanding for students in U.S. higher education can therefore be considered a product of the past, and this influential ideology that has been maintained for decades warrants critical examination.

From "neglected" languages to languages of national security interest

The development of this ideology can be traced to the history of U.S. higher education, whose foundations were established by White colonists, following British and European models. In the early 19th century, heavy emphasis was placed on the classics, and prospective students were expected to have an understanding of Greek and Latin along with basic mathematics (Snyder, 1993). Under these circumstances, the Modern Language Association (MLA) was founded in 1883 with the aim to promote the teaching of modern languages and literatures. At the time of its inception, the MLA focused on English, French, and German, which were deemed essential for sustaining the interaction with the West for the advancement of various academic and professional fields. Parker (1953), who chronicled the MLA's activities in 1883–1953, referred to the subsequent developments concerning the teaching of Spanish, Italian, and Slavic languages, but there was no mention of Asian languages in his article.

According to Tsu (1970) and Miura (1990), however, Chinese and Japanese were taught in U.S. higher education as early as the 1870s–1880s.[2] The website of the Department of East Asian Languages and Cultures (https://ealc.berkeley.edu/about/about-ealc) at the University of California, Berkeley, indeed indicates that the department's history dates back to 1872. By the 1930s, several other large universities started to offer Chinese and Japanese, but the number of institutions offering East Asian languages was still significantly smaller than that of institutions offering the major languages of the West.

What actually propelled the teaching of East Asian languages more widely in the United States was the series of wars starting in the 1940s. By drawing a comparison with the earlier development of the European national language departments, Shirane (2003, p. 72) stated:

> Large East Asian language departments in major universities were originally created for strategic purposes to defend the United States; the last three major wars, World War II, the Korean War, and the Vietnam War, were fought against or involved East Asian countries.

During World War II, the U.S. military developed intensive area and language study curriculum to equip officers and enlisted men with the knowledge and facility necessary to fight wars in the other's territory (Hyneman, 1945). These programs, typically housed at large universities, impacted the subsequent development of East Asian language programs.

During the Cold War, the federal funding for language and area studies programs in higher education continued to be motivated by national security considerations. The launch of Sputnik prompted the creation of Title VI of the National Defense Education Act (NDEA) of 1958 "to insure trained manpower of sufficient quality and quantity to meet the national defense needs of the United States" (U.S. Department of Education, n.d.). Around the time of these developments, the MLA started to direct its attention to the conditions of these "neglected" languages (Harmon et al., 1964). Furthermore, the Chinese Language Teachers Association and the Association of Teachers of Japanese were founded in the early 1960s—more than three decades after the establishment of their European language counterparts—to promote the study of East Asian languages, cultures, and pedagogies.

Rapid enrollment growth and teacher shortage

Starting in the 1980s, changes in the socioeconomic dynamics of the Pacific Rim became notable, and East Asia began to be seen as competitors (and collaborators) in business, science, technology, and beyond. As shown in Figure 2.2, which was created based on the historical enrollment data released by the MLA, the first rapid enrollment growth of Japanese language corresponds to the rise of Japan's economic power in the 1980s. The sharpest growth of enrollment in Chinese language, on the other hand, was observed in the 2000s, corresponding to the period of the rapid growth of China's economy.

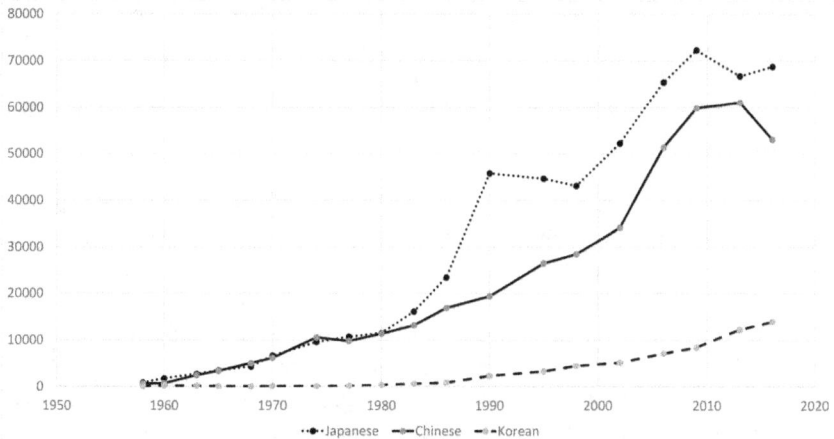

Figure 2.2 East Asian language enrollment in U.S. institutions of higher education
Source: MLA (n.d.)

During these periods, the instrumental value of these languages began to be discussed in regard to capitalist economy in addition to national security. In the 2000s—early 2010s, the media painted the image of Chinese language as a prized new commodity, which was enhanced by the fact that Chinese had not previously been taught as commonly as major European languages in these Anglophone countries (Duff et al., 2015). As a result, Anglophones not of Chinese ancestry who possess proficiency in Chinese, an exceptionally difficult language, have been considered rare, and this understanding has also contributed to the discursive construction of linguistic capital and competitive edge associated with the advanced proficiency in the language. Similar discourse widely circulated in the media during the peak of the Japanese economy in the late 1980s–early 1990s.

What draws our attention is how U.S. institutions of higher education responded to these periods of rapid enrollment growth and the resulting teacher shortages. The void of qualified instructors of these less commonly taught languages that are considered to be exceptionally difficult for English speakers has largely been filled by those who were born and raised in East Asia and relocated to the United States. This movement of language teachers from the East to the United States has also been supported by various initiatives on the part of East Asian countries that promoted their national language in the global market and sustained by a large number of individuals who have found the United States to be a destination where their aspirations can be satisfied.

Among the initiatives, the most notable are the roles played by the Office of Chinese Language Council International (i.e., *Hanban*) and the Confucius Institutes in the rapid expansion of Chinese language education seen in the early 21st century (Pan, 2013; Starr, 2009; Zhu & Li, 2014). According to Wang and Ruan

(2016), from 2004–2014, they prepared approximately 200,000 Chinese language teachers for more than 100 countries, and the United States housed the largest number of the Confucius Institutes and Confucius Classes during the period. On a lesser scale, federal and private foundations in Japan, South Korea, and Taiwan have also provided both financial and human resources to promote the teaching and learning of their national languages abroad. These initiatives have arguably contributed to the reaffirmation of the link among the language, the nation, and the people or the native-speakerism that still permeates in the profession. According to Shirane's (2003, p. 68) account, the most pressing pedagogical issues at the turn of the century were "how to train nonnative speakers to teach East Asian languages" and "how to construct East Asian language programs so that they can employ nonnative speakers alongside native speakers while maintaining a high standard." Two decades later, this condition remains mostly unchanged (Mori, 2020; Mori et al., 2020). According to the Japan Foundation (2020), as of 2018, 77.4% of Japanese language teachers in North America were native speakers of Japanese. The profiles of the contributors to this current volume also appear to reflect this imbalance, which is particularly notable in higher education.

Cultural diplomacy of the East, the generation of digital natives, and increased student diversity

The socioeconomic growth of East Asian countries endangered various initiatives of cultural diplomacy originating in East Asian countries, including the previously discussed initiatives of sending language teachers and teaching materials overseas. Other initiatives that have been undertaken as part of the geopolitical strategies to enhance their images include national branding efforts, as epitomized by phrases such as "Cool Japan" and the "Korean wave," and the promotion of inbound tourism, as exemplified by their successful bids to host Olympic games (Ang et al., 2015). This era also corresponds to the birth of the digital native generation who have been exposed to East Asian popular culture from early in life. For the current and future generations of students, who have had abundant opportunities to explore popular cultural materials originating from East Asia, certain aspects of East Asian languages and cultures may no longer appear "foreign" or "distant" but rather something for which they have a strong affinity. In fact, the reason why enrollment in Japanese saw another sharp rise in the 2000s (see Figure 2.2) despite Japan's post-bubble economic slump can be attributed to the global circulation of Japanese popular culture. The recent rise of Korean enrollment can also be linked to the surge of interest in K-pop, K-drama, etc.

Meanwhile, the surge of international students from Asia has altered the demographic profiles of students in U.S. higher education. According to the statistics published by the Institute of International Education (IIE), students from Asian countries accounted for more than a half of all international students in 2018/2019.[3] Furthermore, the enrollment of Asian Americans and Pacific Islanders (AAPI) in higher education also increased by 36% between 2000–2018 (Postsecondary National Policy Institute, 2021). On some campuses, Asian and Asian

American students, who are still the minority on White-dominant campuses, may find themselves to be a majority in the East Asian language classroom. First-generation college students who are descendants of refugees from Asia raised in multilingual households and privileged international students from Asia who have learned English as a second language may be learning together with students who may fit the image of monolingual English speakers. This reality complicates the basis for the FSI categorization of languages. For some, the participation in a study abroad program in East Asia may not mean the first immersion experience in a different, distant culture but rather a rediscovery of their ancestry or a reunion with compatriots who happened to take different transnational pathways to arrive at the destination. Given such super-diversity (Vertovec, 2007) observed in the classroom, the continuous characterization of East Asian languages as "different," "difficult," and "demanding" Category IV languages, without the critical evaluation of their implications, may harm efforts to acknowledge and embrace "trans-" realities and possibilities presented in the classroom.

The broad-brush sketch presented in this section does not do justice to the complex and varied histories of different programs situated in different types of institutions. However, the intent was to encourage the readers to be aware of how colonial and racial foundations of U.S. higher education and legacies of discourse on East Asian languages and cultures still influence today's teaching and learning. At the same time, it is equally important to appreciate how "trans-" realities that manifest inside and outside the classroom offer different possibilities and necessities and call for the transformation of the infrastructural conditions and discourse that we have inherited from the past.

Institutional policies, practices, and structures concerning language education

During the last two to three decades, the landscape of higher education has undergone remarkable changes, which can be characterized by the corporatization of higher education driven by neoliberal ideals (Giroux, 2002; Saunders, 2010). These changes have increased the precarity of language education in U.S. higher education. As previously discussed, the same period has also seen increased diversity in student populations. The changing demographics of the U.S. population have not yet been fully reflected in the statistics of those enrolled in higher education, but colleges and universities have recently intensified their efforts to recruit and support underrepresented populations of students. Under the circumstances, the mission and structure of language programs in higher education require reevaluation.

"Foreign" language requirement

One of the ongoing controversies surrounding language education concerns its place and role in general education requirements. According to the MLA survey conducted in 2009–2010 (Lusin, 2012), the percentage of 4-year U.S. colleges and universities that enforce requirements for languages other than English for the baccalaureate declined almost 17% between 1994–1995 (67.5%) and 2009–2010 (50.7%). According to Lord (2020), a similar downward trend was observed in the results of a smaller but more recent survey conducted in fall 2017, which confirmed that the decline was still in progress. This decline may be attributed to various factors including the emergence of new fields of study that take precedence, the ever-increasing power of English as a global lingua franca, and the increased availability of digital language learning resources and machine translation.

The increased diversity in the student population has also added further complications. The 2009–2010 MLA survey report (Lusin, 2012) conveyed that, although the fulfillment of a requirement is typically discussed based on the length of study and specified by the number of semesters of language courses, institutions also offer various alternative pathways including results of a proficiency or placement exam (e.g., Advanced Placement [AP] exam; International Baccalaureate [IB] exam), participation in study abroad, or recognition of students' native language other than English. However, it is questionable whether the current mechanism concerning language requirements equitably serves different populations of students given the fundamental difference in the nature of language learning and development that ranges from majority English speakers to those who speak minoritized languages and dialects (cf. Leung & Valdés, 2019). These complexities give rise to the following fundamental, interrelated questions: What are the purpose and goal of language requirements? What should be required for whom? How should the fulfillment of the requirements, or more importantly, the fulfillment of the purpose and goal of the requirements, be assessed? The lack of clear, convincing, and coherent answers to these questions has often become a target of criticism from non-specialists.

For instance, Neuman (2017), a professor of media technology, pointed out the discrepancy between the stated rationale for the language requirement—the development of students' cultural and linguistic sensitivities as well as critical thinking skills—and the emphasis on language proficiency seen in the actual requirement descriptions and assessment methods. Based on his own survey study, Neuman argued that three or four semesters of language instruction do not make a major difference in students' linguistic capacities. He shared his view that "the current tradition of language-proficiency requirements has it backward. It requires the study of foreign language vocabulary and grammar under a potentially false pretense that exposure of a few semesters leads to cultural and linguistic sensitivity and critical thinking skills." This shortfall has also been recognized by insiders, as exemplified by Reagan and Osborn's (2019, p. 83) following admission:

> Given the normative monolingualism of U.S. society, the overwhelming failure of foreign language education programs at all levels to produce meaningful fluency in all but a tiny percentage of students, and the suspicions of individuals who are bilingual (and especially those who are bilingual in many of the "critical languages") in our society, it seems to us that we have a "truth in advertising" problem in making the case for the importance of foreign language education in the United States.

With this continued perception of language proficiency as a fundamental outcome of language education, the apprehension concerning anticipated workload or the sense of unfulfilled promises could be even higher for East Asian languages that have been portrayed as exceptionally difficult for native English speakers.

In the meantime, recent literature on language education has advocated for the incorporation of activities to enhance critical literacy skills and to introduce social justice concerns and activism early on in the curriculum (Glynn et al., 2014; Kumagai et al., 2016; Osborn, 2006). However, doing so in the courses that bear the name of a specific language and a specific sequenced number of semesters or years may also be viewed as false advertisement by some students who have already developed their own view regarding what language learning is about (Kubota et al., 2003). Indeed, the fact that the satisfaction of language requirements is tied to the number of semesters of language courses taken, or alternatively to the results of widely used standardized assessment tools that identify their proficiency levels, contributes to the formation of the belief that the primary purpose of language courses is the development of linguistic knowledge and capacities.

The integration of proficiency development and the fostering of critical awareness of and engagement in sociocultural issues continues to be explored by a growing number of informed language educators, including the authors featured in the current volume. However, it appears that this intention has not yet been clearly articulated and widely communicated beyond the profession in a way to alter the public discourse on language requirements and fundamental infrastructural conditions under which instructional activities take place.

Academic unit structures

In addition to general education requirements, language courses may also be considered part of the essential requirements for different academic majors and minors. East Asian languages may be taught (a) within a foreign language department or program; (b) as part of an East Asian languages and literatures program; and/or (c) as part of an East Asian languages and civilizations/cultures program, which encompasses various disciplines including history, religion, and literature (Shirane, 2003).

As noted by Shirane (2003), in some ways, East Asian language specialists may have had advantages over European language specialists for exploring interdisciplinary or transdisciplinary approaches. Whereas European language programs established by the national language and literature model tend to have housed faculty positions created based on canonical genres or major periods, East Asian languages that came on the scene later did not—or could not—duplicate such a traditional European model. The relatively low enrollments at the time of program inception did not justify the comparable investment on the part of colleges and universities. As a result, the limited financial and human resources necessitated a small number of faculty who specialize in East Asia to cover a wide range of subject matters and/or to collaborate with other specialists on East Asia across the campus for the development of interdisciplinary regional or international studies major and minor programs. This necessity of serving as generalists has effectively facilitated the kind of transdisciplinary approaches explored in this volume.

On the other hand, the limited allocation of resources also meant that differently named language programs have been put into competition. This situation has often created unfortunate consequences of division and tension, which can also be influenced by socioeconomic and geopolitical conditions of East Asia and the relationship between the respective nations and the United States. One example is that many colleges and universities still do not offer Korean, despite its well-acknowledged significance, due to the decision to prioritize other languages that have already gained an established status.

Another critical organizational issue identified as a major obstacle for making innovative curricular changes is the bifurcation of those who contribute to language education in higher education. Geisler et al. (2007, p. 236) described the condition as follows:

> Foreign language instructors often work entirely outside departmental power structures and have little or no say in the educational mission of their department, even in areas where they have particular expertise. . . . This two-track model endows one set of language professionals not only with autonomy in designing their curricula but also with the power to set the goals that the other set of professionals must pursue. In this model, humanists do research while language specialists provide technical support and basic training.

Ten years later, Lomicka and Lord (2018) reported that 45.1% of 134 faculty and administrators who responded to their survey indicated that they had not attempted to make any curricular modifications while generally agreeing with the statements made by Geisler et al. (2007). Only 39.1% of them indicated that they had attempted to bridge that divide.

The division and the power differential described in these documents tend to be exacerbated in the case of East Asian languages where tenured or tenure-track positions in literatures and cultures tend to be held by Americans who learned East Asian languages as a second language while non-tenure-track language instructor positions tend to be held by first-language speakers of East Asian languages (Mori et al., 2020; Shirane, 2003). The continued bifurcation of academic positions combined with the differences in disciplinary, ethnic, and linguistic backgrounds seen in East Asian programs may serve to reinforce the perceived association between language and race (Kubota, 2020; Rosa & Flores, 2020) and the division between humanities courses taught in English by first language speakers of English and language courses considered to focus on the development of linguistic skills through the exposure to native speakers of Asian languages.

Summary

To borrow Kramsch's (2019, p. 53) expression, much of the last few decades' advocacy efforts for foreign language education can be characterized as "jumping onto the globalization bandwagon and capturing the attention of politicians and school administrators regarding the need to prepare youngsters for the 'global realities' of tomorrow." This tendency to highlight its contribution to the neoliberal globalization project reflects the precarity of language programs in educational institutions and the insecurity felt by language teachers. However, the world affairs of the last few years, including COVID-19, Black Lives Matter, anti-Asian racism, the 2021 U.S. Capitol attack, and the Russo-Ukrainian War, have drastically altered the macro level context and increased the uncertainty of the future. These series of events have also made the systemic inequality as well as the ideological divisions painfully visible and have clearly exposed the vulnerability of human societies. In this climate, the humanistic goals underscored by the DFG framework have become more relevant than ever. To reiterate, the second goal of the framework is

> To foster in learners a profound awareness not only of the cultural, historical, and institutional meanings that their language-mediated social actions have, but also, and just as importantly, of the dynamic and evolving role their actions play in shaping their own and others' worlds.
>
> (Douglas Fir Group, 2016, p. 25)

Such an awareness is indeed what needs to be first ensured among language teachers. With such awareness, language teachers are encouraged to undertake critical reevaluation of institutional policies, practices, and structures that affect their work and to consider how their own actions (or inactions) may contribute to the shaping of the future world.

Imagining the future of language education

As discussed in the previous sections, various aspects of the current operations of East Asian language programs in U.S. higher education have been shaped by infrastructural conditions and surrounding discourses that we inherited from the past. Meanwhile, institutions of higher education now accommodate diverse populations of students who embody various aspects of "trans-" realities, and the world for which we aim to prepare these students also continues to evolve at a rapid pace. Although an immediate overhaul of existing conditions may not be possible, it is essential to continue engaging in critical reflection of the macro and meso layers of the ecological systems that impact the teaching and learning of East Asian languages and to question how our own actions as language teachers may contribute to the reaffirmation of pervasive ideologies that shape the conditions of language education. As a way of concluding this chapter, I would like to pose several fundamental questions that should continue to be explored as we envision the future of language education that will align with the goals set by the DFG framework.

What kinds of languages should be taught and how?

The practice of naming programs with names of particular languages continues to emphasize "the idea that languages are distinctive and separate entities" and gives "the impression that learning an additional language means focusing on that language alone" (Leung & Valdés, 2019, p. 353). Although it may be difficult (or may not be necessary) to discontinue this program-naming practice altogether, it is conceivable for us to include critical reflection of the selected name of the program as part of the language courses. For instance, the teaching of the standardized variation of the named languages, *Putonghua* or *Hyōjungo*, should be augmented with teachers' and learners' exploration of what it means to aspire to become a speaker of the idealized standard variation. This process entails explicit acknowledgement of linguistic diversities within a given society as well as the historical discursive process of the language standardization and minoritization of other variations. Creative utilization of translingual and transmodal practices that blend elements of a particular named language with various other semiotic resources should also be objects of inquiry. For the teaching of East Asian languages, in particular, both historically and currently observed translingual phenomena among Chinese, Japanese, Korean, English, and beyond could enrich learners' understanding of sociohistorical and geopolitical dynamics of the region (cf. Sato, 2022).

How can we reach out to diverse learners, accommodate their different needs and aspirations, and create a space where they can learn from each other?

Whereas traditional language classrooms in U.S. higher education tend to have been tailored for (monolingual) first-language speakers of English, the demographic shift observed in recent years demands the acknowledgment of diverse linguistic, ethnic, and socioeconomic backgrounds, motivations, and aspirations that learners bring to the classroom. East Asian language programs today may serve as a community where multilingual students, who might have been characterized as English as a second language or English language learners, can be empowered due to their extensive prior experience of language learning and border crossing. On the other hand, for monolingual speakers of English, the programs can offer opportunities to be exposed not only to the one particular named language and culture that they selected but also to the varied experiences of minoritized language speakers and how they relate to the language and culture of their common choice. Together they can explore how being a speaker of a particular East Asian language with their respective linguistic and cultural roots may generate different expectations and treatments from first language speakers of the language (Kumagai & Sato, 2009; Mori & Takeuchi, 2016) and consider how the difference came about and whether it can be changed in the future.

What would be the role of classroom-based teaching and learning?

The rearticulation of the role of classroom-based teaching and learning in higher education is of critical importance. What are the distinct features of the language learning experience in institutions of higher education that set them apart from other ubiquitous language learning programs, tutorial websites, apps, and other tools available elsewhere? As summed up by Johnson (2019, p. 173), if we were to adopt the vision presented by the DFG framework, language teachers and learners will "need to learn to work together to continuously interrogate the language and culture in order to uncover the meaning potentials of the semiotic resources that language users use to carry out different social actions in different contexts of use." To this end, the traditional tendency to focus on determining "correct" answers needs to be replaced with the exploration of a range of expressions and structures available to perform the same speech act in a given context and the realization that each choice can convey different social meanings and that the process of meaning creation intricately relates to the speakers' varying identities.

What are the essential qualifications and training requirements for future language educators?

The traditional emphasis on the development of proficiency in the standardized variation of a named language tends to have foregrounded the ability to provide idealized models of the standard variation as desired qualifications for language teachers. Many of the job announcements that circulate today still include expressions such as "native" or "near-native" to describe the required qualifications for language teaching positions (Mori, 2020). Despite the diversification of student populations, the diversification of teachers lags behind in East Asian language programs and continues to reinforce the perception that the goal of language education is to become native-like or to be able to interact with native speakers. Considering what is discussed in the previous paragraphs, what needs to be emphasized for those who engage in language teaching in higher education is not the mere native or near-native fluency/competence in the language. Rather, we should strive to instill in current and future language teachers the ability to integrate a wide range of activities and tools available outside of the classroom into the formal instruction for the acceleration of learners' proficiency development as well as the ability to facilitate learners' development of profound awareness of cultural, historical, and institutional meanings of their language-mediated social actions.

The authors of the following chapters indeed showcase their attempts to push this agenda forward in their own classrooms. The accumulation of these innovations at the micro level is essential for changing the meso and macro level structures over time. At the same time, we should be reminded that it is equally important to continue questioning the status quo of infrastructural conditions and critically examining how some of our own professional conduct (e.g., in promoting language learning or making hiring decisions) may inadvertently contribute to the reinforcement of the conditions and ideologies behind them.

Notes

1 See, for instance, https://carla.umn.edu/lctl/definition.html and https://lilac.msu.edu/lctl/ (accessed on March 20, 2022).

2 Prior to this, East Asian language education was offered primarily for heritage learners or descendants of migrants from East Asia.
3 According to IIE (n.d.), the decline in international students' enrollment was 1.8% in 2019–2020 and 15% in 2020–2021. However, 2021–2022 saw an increase by 3.8%. At this author's home institution, international student enrollment has returned to pre-COVID levels, and the number of international applications for 2022–2023 has increased more than 30%.

References

Ang, I., Isar, Y. R., & Mar, P. (Eds.). (2015). Special issue: Cultural diplomacy: Beyond the national interest? *International Journal of Cultural Policy*, *21*(4), 365–508.

Atkinson, D. (2019). Second language acquisition beyond borders? The Douglas Fir Group searches for transdisciplinary identity. *Modern Language Journal*, *103*(Supplement 2019), 113–121.

Bronfenbrenner, U. (1979). *The ecology of human development: Experiments by nature and design*. Harvard University Press.

Butler, J. (2016). Rethinking vulnerability and resistance. In J. Butler, Z. Gambetti, & L. Sabsay (Eds.), *Vulnerability in resistance* (pp. 12–27). Duke University Press.

Canagarajah, S. (2013). *Translingual practice: Global Englishes and cosmopolitan relations*. Routledge.

Canagarajah, S. (2018). Translingual practice as spatial repertoires: Expanding the paradigm beyond structuralist orientations. *Applied Linguistics*, *39*(1), 31–54.

De Costa, P. I., & Norton, B. (2017). Introduction: Identity, transdisciplinarity, and the good language teacher. *Modern Language Journal*, *101*(Supplement 2017), 3–14.

Douglas Fir Group. (2016). A transdisciplinary framework for SLA in a multilingual world. *Modern Language Journal*, *100*(Supplement 2016), 19–47.

Duff, P. A. (2019). Social dimensions and processes in second language acquisition: Multilingual socialization in transnational contexts. *Modern Language Journal*, *103*(Supplement 2019), 6–22.

Duff, P. A., Anderson, T., Doherty, L., & Wang, R. (2015). Representations of Chinese language learning in contemporary English-language news media: Hope, hype, and fear. *Global Chinese*, *1*(1), 139–168.

Foreign Service Institute. (n.d.). *Foreign language training*. www.state.gov/foreign-language-training/

Gao, X. (2019). The Douglas Fir Group framework as a resource map for language teacher education. *Modern Language Journal*, *103*(Supplement 2019), 161–166.

García, O., & Li, W. (2014). *Translanguaging: Language, bilingualism and education*. Palgrave Macmillan.

Geisler, M., Kramsch, C., McGinnis, S., Patrikis, P., Pratt, M. L., Ryding, K., & Saussy, H. (2007). Foreign languages and higher education: New structures for a changed world: MLA Ad Hoc committee on Foreign languages. *Profession*, 234–245.

Giroux, H. (2002). Neoliberalism, corporate culture, and the promise of higher education: The university as a democratic public sphere. *Harvard Educational Review*, *72*(4), 425–464.

Glynn, C., Wesely, P. M., & Wassell, B. A. (2014). *Words and actions: Teaching languages through the lens of social justice*. ACTFL.

Harmon, J., Simms, J., & Tierney, H. (1964). Manpower in the neglected languages, fall 1962. *PMLA*, *79*(4), 91–106.

Hawkins, M. R. (2018). Transmodalities and transnational encounters: Fostering critical cosmopolitan relations. *Applied Linguistics, 39*(1), 55–77.

Hawkins, M. R. (Ed.). (2021). *Transmodal communications: Transporting semiotics and relations*. Multilingual Matters.

Hawkins, M. R., & Mori, J. (2018). Considering "trans-" perspectives in language theories and practices. *Applied Linguistics, 39*(1), 1–8.

Hyneman, C. S. (1945). The wartime area and language courses. *Bulletin of the American Association of University Professors, 31*(3), 434–447.

Institute of International Education. (n.d.). *International students enrollment trends*. Open Doors Data. https://opendoorsdata.org/data/international-students/enrollment-trends/

Japan Foundation. (2020). *Survey report on Japanese-language education abroad 2018*. www.jpf.go.jp/j/project/japanese/survey/result/dl/survey2018/all.pdf

Johnson, K. (2019). The relevance of a transdisciplinary framework for SLA in language teacher education. *Modern Language Journal, 103*(Supplement 2019), 167–174.

Kramsch, C. (2018). Trans-spatial utopia. *Applied Linguistics, 39*(1), 108–115.

Kramsch, C. (2019). Between globalization and decolonization: Foreign languages in the cross-fire. In D. Macedo & M. Degraff (Eds.), *Decolonizing foreign language education: The misteaching of English and other colonial languages* (pp. 50–72). Routledge.

Kubota, R. (2020). Confronting epistemological racism, decolonizing scholarly knowledge: Race and gender in applied linguistics. *Applied Linguistics, 41*(5), 712–732.

Kubota, R., Austin, T., & Saito-Abbott, Y. (2003). Diversity and inclusion of sociopolitical issues in foreign language classrooms: An exploratory survey. *Foreign Language Annals, 36*(1), 12–24.

Kumagai, Y., López-Sánchez, A., & Wu, S. (Eds.). (2016). *Multiliteracies in world language education*. Routledge.

Kumagai, Y., & Sato, S. (2009). "Ignorance" as a rhetorical strategy: How Japanese language learners living in Japan maneuver their subject positions to shift power dynamics. *Critical Studies in Education, 50*(3), 309–321.

Leung, C., & Valdés, G. (2019). Translanguaging and the transdisciplinary framework for language teaching and learning in a multilingual world. *Modern Language Journal, 103*(2), 348–370.

Li, W. (2018). Translanguaging as a practical theory of language. *Applied Linguistics, 39*, 9–30.

Lomicka, L., & Lord, G. (2018). Ten years after the MLJ report: What has changed in foreign language departments? *ADFL Bulletin, 44*(2), 116–120.

Looney, D., & Lusin, N. (2019). *Enrollments in languages other than English in United States institutions of higher education, summer 2016 and fall 2016: Final report*. Modern Language Association. www.mla.org/content/download/110154/2406932/2016-Enrollments-Final-Report.pdf

Lord, G. (2020). Is the sky falling (again)? Observations on the language requirement in United States higher education. *ADFL Bulletin, 46*(1), 114–122.

Lusin, N. (2012). *The MLA survey of postsecondary entrance and degree requirements for languages other than English, 2009–2010*. Modern Language Association. www.mla.org/content/download/3316/81618/requirements_survey_200910.pdf

Miura, A. (1990). *America shakai niokeru nihongokyooiku no tenkai* [Development of Japanese language education in American Society]. *Nihongo Kyooiku* [Japanese-Language Education], *70*, 21–33.

Modern Language Association. (n.d.). *Enrollments in languages other than English in United States institutions of higher education*. www.mla.org/Resources/Research/

Surveys-Reports-and-Other-Documents/Teaching-Enrollments-and-Programs/Enrollments-in-Languages-Other-Than-English-in-United-States-Institutions-of-Higher-Education

Mori, J. (2020). Reaffirming professional qualifications for Japanese-language educators: Towards the cultivation of the next generation. In S. Suzuki, S. Dorsey, & D. Iskos (Eds.), *Proceedings of the 28th Central Association of Teachers of Japanese (CATJ 28) Japanese language education in diversifying communities* (pp. 15–33). www.macalester.edu/asian/wp-content/uploads/sites/23/2020/11/CATJ28-Proceedings-2020-8.pdf

Mori, J., Hasegawa, A., Park, J., & Suzuki, K. (2020). On goals of language education and teacher diversity: Beliefs and experiences of Japanese-language educators in North America. *Japanese Language and Literature, 54*(2), 267–304.

Mori, J., & Takeuchi, J. D. (2016). Campus diversity and global education: A case study of a Japanese program. *Foreign Language Annals, 49*(1), 146–161.

Neuman, W. R. (2017). *Setting aside bureaucratic requirements*. Inside Higher Ed. www.insidehighered.com/views/2017/05/18/undergraduate-foreign-language-requirements-arent-particularly-effective-essay

Osborn, T. A. (2006). *Teaching world languages for social justice: A sourcebook of principles and practices*. Routledge.

Pan, S. (2013). Confucius Institute project: China's cultural diplomacy and soft power projection. *Asian Education and Development Studies, 2*(1), 22–33.

Parker, W. R. (1953). The MLA, 1883–1953. *PMLA, 68*(4), 3–39.

Postsecondary National Policy Institute. (2021). *Asian American and Pacific Islander students in higher education*. https://pnpi.org/asian-americans-and-pacific-islanders/

Reagan, T., & Osborn, T. A. (2019). Time for a paradigm shift in U.S. foreign language education? Revising rationales, evidence, and outcomes. In D. Macedo & M. Degraff (Eds.), *Decolonizing foreign language education: The misteaching of English and other colonial languages* (pp. 73–110). Routledge.

Rosa, J., & Flores, N. (2020). Reimagining race and language. In H. S. Alim, A. Reyes, & P. V. Kroskrity (Eds.), *The Oxford handbook of language and race* (pp. 90–107). Oxford University Press.

Sato, E. (2022). *Translanguaging in translation: Invisible contributions that shape our language and society*. Multilingual Matters.

Saunders, D. B. (2010). Neoliberal ideology and public higher education in the United States. *Journal for Critical Education Policy Studies, 8*(1), 41–77.

Shirane, H. (2003). Attraction and isolation: The past and future of East Asian languages and cultures. *Profession, 2003*, 66–75.

Snyder, T. D. (1993). Higher education. In T. D. Snyder (Ed.), *120 years of American education: A statistical analysis* (pp. 63–94). National Center for Education Statistics.

Starr, D. (2009). Chinese language education in Europe: The confucius institutes. *European Journal of Education, 44*(1), 65–82.

Tsu, J. B. (1970). The teaching of Chinese in colleges and schools of the United States. *Modern Language Journal, 54*(8), 562–579.

U.S. Census Bureau. (n.d.). *Why we ask questions about . . . language spoken at home*. www.census.gov/acs/www/about/why-we-ask-each-question/language/

U.S. Department of Education. (n.d.). *The history of Title VI and Fulbright-Hays: An impressive international timeline*. www2.ed.gov/about/offices/list/ope/iegps/history.html

Ushioda, E. (2017). The impact of global English on motivation to learn other languages: Toward an ideal multilingual self. *Modern Language Journal, 101*(3), 469–482.

Vertovec, S. (2007). Super-diversity and its implications. *Ethnic and Racial Studies, 30*(6), 1024–1054.

Wang, W., & Ruan, J. (2016). Historical overview of Chinese language education for speakers of other languages in China and the United States. In J. Ruan, J. Zhang, & C. B. Leung (Eds.), *Chinese language education in the United States* (pp. 1–28). Springer.

Zhu, H., & Li, W. (2014). Geopolitics and the changing hierarchies of the Chinese language: Implications for policy and practice of Chinese language teaching in Britain. *Modern Language Journal, 98*(1), 326–339.

3 Translanguaging and co-learning at the interface of language and culture

Li Wei

A classroom example

Picture the scene: It is an evening class for beginner Mandarin Chinese, run by a university's language center in central London. The teacher speaks Mandarin as a first language (L1) and is from China, where she taught Chinese as a foreign language. She has been in the United Kingdom for 2.5 years, but this is the first time she has taught at this London university. The class has approximately 20 students from very diverse linguistic and cultural backgrounds. Some are European and some Asian. All of the students are bilingual or multilingual with English as one of their languages; their other languages include English, German, Dutch, Italian, Russian, Korean, Japanese, and Cantonese. It is the sixth lesson, and the teacher is explaining the different uses of the expression 对不起 (*duì bùqǐ*). She is teaching in English. She says to the class that 对不起 means "sorry" in English and offers a range of examples: "对不起, can you pass me that book?"; "对不起, can I pass?"; and "对不起, I need to get out for a second." She is mixing Chinese and English in her examples because the students would not yet have sufficient vocabulary to understand or produce those utterances wholly in Chinese. Some people might call this mixed use translanguaging, but that is not what I am interested in here. One of the European students comments loudly, "That sounds incredibly apologetic." The teacher pauses and says, "Yes, it means 'sorry.'" The student questions, "But why? I don't say 'Sorry, can I borrow your pen?' I say 'excuse me.'" The teacher responds, "Yes, it means 'excuse me.'" Another European student asks, "What does it actually mean then?" The teacher looks quite puzzled. The first student then asks, "Is it an apology or is it just like a polite thing, like 'excuse me'?" The teacher turns to the Cantonese-speaking student, a British-born Chinese individual, and asks, "What do you say in Cantonese?" The student says, "對唔住" (*deoi3 m4 zyu6*), which is a literal translation of 对不起. The first European student asks, "Is it the same thing?" The Cantonese-speaking student says, "more or less." The European student becomes somewhat frustrated and asks, "But what does it actually mean?!" The teacher seems unable to offer a direct answer. The Cantonese-speaking student then says to the teacher, "Is it like 唔该 (*m4 goi1*)? Or should it be like 唔该 (*m4 goi1*)?" The teacher does not know the Cantonese expression but seems to sense what it means, so she offers

DOI: 10.4324/9781003266976-4

another expression, 劳驾 (láo jià), which is indeed the Mandarin equivalent to the Cantonese 唔该 and a good translation equivalent to "excuse me" in English. The second European student then says, "Okay, so that one—*lao* something—is it 'excuse me' and *duì bùqǐ* is 'sorry'—is that right?" The teacher then says, "Yes, sorry, yes." The first European student then says, "谢谢老师 (Thank you, teacher). We should all stop apologizing so much."

After the lesson, I asked the teacher how she felt about this session. The teacher said that English language teaching textbooks in China often translate both "excuse me" and "sorry" as "对不起." However, when Chinese teaching textbooks mention "对不起," they often simply translate it as "sorry." She admitted that she did not know the literal meaning of 对不起 (literal meaning: "not having the capacity to face or confront"), which is why she did not know how to respond to the European students' queries during that session. However, she was glad that she had learned something and seemed very positive about the experience. She also said that she learned another expression from the Cantonese-speaking student after class: 唔好意思 (*m4 hou2 ji3 si1*), which could be used in some similar situations. In addition, when the teacher asked the Japanese student of the class whether 对不起 sounded too apologetic to her, the Japanese student reportedly said that it did not. The teacher commented to me: "They say 'sorry' a lot in Japanese. Europeans don't [say] sorry as much."

Linguistically, these pragmatic expressions are very hard to translate literally. Teaching them is not easy. Apart from the crucial role context plays in the usage of such expressions, there are significant intercultural differences in people's perceptions of and experiences with the tone of such expressions. What may be perceived as overly apologetic in one culture may be quite routine in another. But what I am particularly interested in here and what I what to explore in this chapter are the concepts of translanguaging, co-learning, and language learning as cultural translation, which the preceding story illustrates very well.

Translanguaging

The classroom interaction as shown in the preceding story is a good example of the flexible use of different languages, especially on behalf of the teacher who showed considerable willingness and skills in bringing the students' prior languages into learning, all of which are good translanguaging practices. But translanguaging is more than flexible and dynamic use of different named languages. The idea of translanguaging originated from the Welsh revitalization context. Cen Williams (1994) and Colin Baker (2001) were responsible for introducing the concept to the wider bilingual education research community. They emphasized that translanguaging was not conceived as an object or a linguistic structural phenomenon to describe and analyze but rather as a practice and a process: a practice that involves the dynamic and functionally integrated use of different languages and language varieties through different modalities, and a process of knowledge construction that goes beyond (i.e., transcending) different knowledge systems.

In taking the concept to bilingual education worldwide in the 21st century, Ofelia García defined translanguaging as "multiple discursive practices in which bilinguals engage in order to makes sense of their bilingual worlds" (2009, p. 45).

As a pedagogical philosophy, translanguaging aims to empower the learner and maximize their potential for learning. It also empowers the instructor and transforms the way we teach and support our students in the process of knowledge construction—a point I will return to in the next section about co-learning. As pointed out in Li (2022) and Li and García (2022), translanguaging is not additive or about allowing different languages to be used in the classroom. Translanguaging is fundamentally reconstitutive—of the language status, of language ideologies, and of authorities and power relations in learning—through transgressive practices that disturb the existing hierarchies. It urges us to think about questions, such as:

- If education is about knowledge construction, does the language in which knowledge is constructed matter?
- Does the cultural context in which the knowledge system is constructed matter?
- What impact do pedagogical practices and classroom interaction have on knowledge construction?
- What is the role of prior knowledge?

Translanguaging therefore seeks to find a different language to talk about learning and education and to find a different narrative(s) about the learners and their cultural experiences including experiences with language learning and use.

Co-learning

I first wrote about co-learning in Li (2013) in the context of heritage language education in complementary schools in the United Kingdom, inspired by Edward Brantmeier's (n.d.) work. The concept of co-learning did not come from education but rather from other disciplines ranging from artificial intelligence and computer simulation to global security systems and business information management. In essence, co-learning is a process in which several agents simultaneously try to adapt to one another's behavior so as to produce desirable global outcomes shared by the contributing agents. In the classroom context, co-learning changes the role sets of teachers and learners from what Brantmeier (2020, p. 97) called "dispensers and receptacles of knowledge" to "joint sojourners" on the quest for knowledge, understanding, and wisdom. In particular, the teacher-versus-learner dichotomy would be broken, and the teacher would become a learning facilitator, a scaffolder, and a critical reflection enhancer while the learner becomes an empowered explorer, a meaning maker, and a responsible knowledge constructor. A facilitator "guides the process of student learning" and "does not get in the way of learning by imposing information." A scaffolder "assesses the learner's knowledge and builds scaffolding to extend that knowledge to a broader and deeper understanding." A critical reflection enhancer asks the learner to "reflect on what is being learned and the process of learning (meta-reflection about process)" (Brantmeier, n.d.). At the same time, an empowered explorer is "an independent or collective explorer of knowledge," while a meaning maker and responsible knowledge constructor is "one who engages in meaningful knowledge construction that promotes relevancy to her/his own life" (Brantmeier, n.d.). In co-learning, mutual adaptation of behavior is the key. In order to achieve desirable learning outcomes, all co-participants need to constantly monitor and adapt their actions and learn from each other.

Co-learning in the classroom does not simply involve the teacher developing strategies to allow equitable participation for all; co-learning requires much unlearning of cultural conditioning because, as Brantmeier (n.d.) pointed out, "it challenges the traditional authoritative, dominant and subordinate role sets in schooling environments and the unequal power relationships in wider spheres of our world." It empowers the learner, and "builds a more genuine community of practice" (Brantmeier, n.d.). It moves the teacher and the learner toward a more "dynamic and participatory engagement" (Brantmeier, n.d.) in knowledge construction. According to Brantmeier (2020), the characteristics of a co-learning relationship include:

- all knowledge is valued;
- reciprocal value of knowledge sharers;
- care for each other as people and co-learners;
- trust;
- learning from one another.

The characteristics of a co-learning classroom environment include:

- shared power among co-learners;
- social and individualized learning;
- collective and individual meaning making and identity exploration;
- community of practice with situated learning;
- real-world engagement and action.

Translanguaging and co-learning share a great deal of common values. In particular, both translanguaging and co-learning emphasize that all knowledge, acquired through all languages and in all cultural contexts, should be valued. In the classroom, this is shown through the reciprocal value of knowledge sharers who care for each other as people and co-learners. Their mutual trust is essential in order to learn from one another. In what he describes as the pedagogy of vulnerability, Brantmeier (2020) urged instructors to open themselves and contextualize that self in societal constructs and systems. For him, co-learning entails admitting one does not know everything and is human. It also entails taking risks: risks of self-disclosure, of change, of not knowing, and of failing. Whereas translanguaging focuses on valuing all languages and promotes the learning of each other's languages and perspectives of the world, co-learning advocates valuing the knowledge, values, and insights of all involved. Both advocate creating opportunities of different ways of learning and talking about learning, and both point to the need to unlearn cultural conditioning as well as dismantle asymmetrical power relationships.

Today it is commonplace for language classes to include learners with very different linguistic, cultural, and educational backgrounds, as those in the preceding example exemplify, with some having very complex migration and language-learning experiences. They bring with them "funds of knowledge"—"the historically accumulated and culturally developed bodies of knowledge and skills essential for households and individual functioning and well-being" (Moll et al., 1992, p. 133; see also Moll & Gonzalez, 1994). Such funds of knowledge contain rich cultural and cognitive resources that can be used in the classroom in order to provide culturally responsive, meaningful, and effective teaching. Teachers, as well as learners, have much to gain from using these funds of knowledge in the classroom—not only to make the classrooms more inclusive but also to engage in real-world meaning making and identity exploration, which are crucial yet often neglected aspects of learning.

Language learning as cultural translation

One important aspect of the funds of knowledge diverse learners bring to the classroom and the learning process is the cultural context in which a prior language or language variety has been learned. Language and culture are intertwined. One cannot divorce one from the other in teaching and learning languages. In Zhu et al. (2020), we proposed the idea of language teaching and learning as a process of cultural translation. For us, culture is a value system that evolves in a specific community that encourages specific kinds of sense-making and meaning-making practices with specific semiotic resources. Cultural variations and differences are therefore rooted in the ecologies of the communities where the availability of the sense-making and meaning-making resources may vary. Thus, their symbolic values are different and give rise to different traditions and practices. Language learning is about learning a different way of meaning-making and sense-making, even when the same semiotic resources, including named languages, are involved. It presents potential challenges to the existing value systems. Translation and adaptation are then needed. Language practices vary from community to community because of the different ecologies, and they gain different symbolic values across communities. Members of a specific community are socialized into specific language practices (Kramsch & Steffensen, 2008) and develop symbolic competence (Kramsch, 2006; Kramsch & Whiteside, 2008), of which awareness of the symbolic values of specific languages and language practices as well as the ecology of the value system of the community is a crucial part. Learning a language entails learning to recognize and interpret the symbolic value of language practices traditionally associated with a different community.

By translation, we mean "a way of thinking about how languages, people, and cultures are transformed as they move between different places" (Young, 2020,

p. 29). Therefore, it is not just an interlingual process but may also be intermedial, intersystemic, and intercultural. Cultural translation is then about bringing values and practices that have evolved in a specific community to another community so that members of both communities can interact with each other to achieve a certain level of understanding. The process of translation entails adaptation, appropriation, and transformation, which in turn entails changes, gains, and losses much in the same spirit of translanguaging and co-learning. The purpose of translation is often to meet specific local and individual needs. Thus, translation needs to fit the local conditions where environmental affordances may determine what may be translated and how.

From a cultural translation perspective, affinity between the teacher's experience and background and those of the students is an important issue in the language classroom. But in the case of not having much in common, such as in a foreign language classroom where the teacher's background is drastically different from that of the students', the principles of co-learning and mutual respect are crucial. Everybody has the knowledge and experience with the value systems and symbolic practices of their own community, and they are familiar with the sense-making and meaning-making resources that are available and can be exploited in different contexts. However, making connections and comparisons between and reshaping the prior and new ecological systems is a process of translation rather than complete abandonment of one cultural practice and complete acceptance of and integration into another. Let us now revisit the example of the Chinese class from the lens of translanguaging, co-learning, and cultural translation.

Example

As previously indicated, the class is very diverse in linguistic and cultural terms, and each co-learner brings with them their own knowledge, experiences, and perspectives. As a relative newcomer to the United Kingdom who grew up in China and learned Chinese there, the teacher has knowledge of the language and the cultural practice of linguistic politeness that is conditioned by her own upbringing. She wants to teach the Chinese expression 对不起 (*duì bùqi*) as a politeness marker, but she translates it as "sorry" rather than "excuse me" because in English language teaching textbooks in China both of these English expressions are sometimes translated as 对不起 (*duì bùqi*). To the European students in the class, however, "sorry" is too apologetic, and the examples the teacher uses to illustrate the contexts in which 对不起 (*duì bùqi*) can be used do not seem to warrant apologies. They want an equivalent to "excuse me" instead. What we have here is a classic example of the intertwining of language and culture and the complex process of cultural translation.

However, the way the teacher handles the situation is precisely what Brantmeier (2020) advocated in his pedagogy of vulnerability. She admits the limit to her own knowledge, both linguistic and cultural, and is prepared to unlearn and co-learn from the students. She actively involves other students, particularly the Cantonese-speaking student whom she thinks might have the relevant cultural knowledge. When she learns something new from the students, she immediately corrects herself. She even asks more questions of the East Asian students after class about their perceptions of the politeness and relevant linguistic expressions. As a result, her cultural knowledge increases, which she can put to use in future classes. That being said, her comment to me about the differences between the Japanese and the Europeans still shows a certain level of cultural stereotype. The learning journey continues.

As the same time, the students learn from each other. They develop better knowledge of the subtleties and complexities of linguistic politeness markers in Chinese and enhance their cultural awareness. Two students commented much later in the term that they learned that Cantonese and Mandarin were very different and asked why they were regarded as dialects of Chinese rather than different languages. The East Asian students in the class said that one of the benefits of attending this Mandarin class was the realization of the differences in politeness routines among different nations of East Asia as well as in European cultures. These are value systems, and the learners are able to learn and adapt to them because of the co-learning opportunities the class created for them.

The co-learning opportunities are created through fluid and flexible translanguaging practices across different named languages and knowledge systems. The co-learners use whatever resources they have to make meaning and make sense of each other. It is a good example of translanguaging at work. It is also a process of translating cultures to achieve better understanding. In particular, notions of politeness are negotiated between co-learners of different cultural backgrounds, moving from an apparent lack of understanding of each other's intent to a better appreciation of each other's thinking.

Conclusion

The landscape of language teaching and learning has fundamentally changed. Increased diversity in learning conditions, learner backgrounds, and motivations requires new thinking and new approaches to the way we teach and learn languages. Learners, as well as teachers, bring with them rich and diverse experiences with different languages and cultures. These funds of knowledge are important resources for learning without which language classes will be boring. Thus, the practical and philosophical question is how to make the best use of such funds of knowledge not only for knowledge transmission but also for enriching the learning experience.

This chapter advocates translanguaging and co-learning approaches to language teaching and learning where all languages are valued and all knowledge that may have been acquired through different languages and in different cultural conditions are valued. This requires co-learners' willingness to adapt and unlearn, trust and respect each other, and support each other on the same journey of exploration.

Particularly relevant to co-learning and mutual adaptation is the idea of language learning as cultural translation, which entails adapting to new value systems and raising cultural sensitivities toward diversity and difference. Learning a new language is about learning a way of making meaning and making sense as well as achieving an understanding of the world around us with people from different linguistic and cultural backgrounds by transcending and even transgressing the boundaries that have been created by named languages and cultural traditions.

There are, of course, practical challenges in adopting a translanguaging and co-learning pedagogy, especially in a foreign language classroom, such as the challenge of time; the challenge of the diversity of learners' backgrounds, motivations, capacities, and needs; and the challenge from the traditional assumption that an exclusive target-language focus is more effective than flexible plurilingual pedagogies. None of these challenges are insurmountable if we remind ourselves that the goal of learning a new language, whatever it may be, is not to replace the language(s) and culture(s) one already has but to become bilingual and multilingual as well as intercultural.

Acknowledgments

The example scene presented herein came from observations of language classes conducted during the 2018–2019 session at the Language Centre at a University of London college in Bloomsbury. All participants gave consent to the observations and informal chats and to anonymous fieldnotes being used for research purposes.

Note

1 This website is no longer accessible. We have contacted the author, but he does not have a copy of the original posting. Instead, he recommended Brantmeier (2020). However, some of the words were taken directly from the previous PDF, and I want to ensure that the source is properly acknowledged. This reference is therefore listed here.

References

Baker, C. (2001). *Foundations of bilingual education and bilingualism* (3rd ed.). Multilingual Matters.
Brantmeier, E. J. (n.d.). *Empowerment pedagogy: Co-learning and teaching.* [previously published at www.indiana.edu/~leeehman/Brantmeier.pdf[1]]
Brantmeier, E. J. (2020). Pedagogy of vulnerability: Definitions, assumptions, and applications. In J. Lin, R. L. Oxford, & E. J. Brantmeier (Eds.). (2013). *Re-envisioning higher education: Embodied pathways to wisdom and social transformation* (pp. 95–106). Information Age Publishing.
García, O. (2009). *Bilingual education in the 21st century: A global perspective.* Wiley-Blackwell.
Kramsch, C. (2006). From communicative competence to symbolic competence. *The Modern Language Journal, 90,* 249–252.
Kramsch, C., & Steffensen, S. V. (2008). Ecological perspectives on second language acquisition and socialization. *Encyclopedia of Language and Education, 8,* 17–28.
Kramsch, C., & Whiteside, A. (2008). Language ecology in multilingual settings: Towards a theory of symbolic competence. *Applied Linguistics, 29,* 645–671.

Li, W. (2013). Who's teaching whom? Co-learning in multilingual classrooms. In S. May (Ed.), *The multilingual turn: Implications for SLA, TESOL, and bilingual education* (pp. 177–200). Routledge.

Li, W. (2022). Translanguaging as a political stance: Implications for English language education. *ELT Journal, 76*(2), 172–182.

Li, W., & García, O. (2022). Not a first language but one repertoire: Translanguaging as a decolonizing project. *RELC Journal, 53*(2), 313–324. https://doi.org/10.1177/00336882221092841

Moll, L. C., Amanti, C., Neff, D., & Gonzalez, N. (1992). Funds of knowledge for teaching: Using a qualitative approach to connect homes and classrooms. *Theory Into Practice, 31*(2), 132–141.

Moll, L. C., & Gonzalez, N. (1994). Lessons from research with language-minority children. *Journal of Reading Behavior, 26*(4), 439–456.

Williams, C. (1994). *Arfarniad o Ddulliau Dysgu ac Addysgu yng Nghyddestun Addysg Uwchradd Ddwyieithog* [An evaluation of teaching and learning methods in the context of bilingual secondary education] [Unpublished doctoral thesis]. University of Wales.

Young, R. J. (2020). *Postcolonialism: A very short introduction.* Oxford University Press.

Zhu, H., Li, W., & Jankowicz-Pytel, D. (2020). Whose karate? Language and cultural learning in a multilingual karate club in London. *Applied Linguistics, 41*(1), 52–83.

Section 2
Across disciplines
Language and non-language faculty collaboration

4 Translanguaging with food and ethics

Translating languages, enhancing agencies, and expanding horizons

Yuki Miyamoto and Nobuko Chikamatsu

Introduction

With a focus on the nature of food—culturally particular, yet universally concerned—this chapter highlights two courses on food offered collaboratively in the fields of Japanese language and area studies at DePaul University, a midwestern urban university in the United States. Adopting DePaul's Foreign Languages Across the Curriculum (FLAC) model, these two courses were designed to communicate the same themes whereby the learner of the second language (L2) acquires knowledge through content learning in the first/stronger language (L1) (Hall & Caldwell, 2001; Klee, 2009). The FLAC structure combines a full-credit course in English, entitled "Religion and ethics in Japanese foodscapes" (REL/L1), taught by an ethicist, and a half-credit language course, "Food and ethics in Japan" (JPN/L2), that caters to advanced learners of Japanese. These two courses, focusing on the issue of food, are organized into these themes: food and occupational discrimination in Japan; food and nationalism; and food, health, and illness. Alongside these topics, the L1 course imparts historical and philosophical knowledge of Japan, and the L2 course offers the opportunity to examine and discuss the topics drawing upon primary sources.

Employing more than one language during analysis can enhance a learner's awareness of the differences of each culture's food discourse, which not only reveals a given culture's customary diet but also indicates how people relate to each other and their environment (Melin, 2019; Okazaki, 2009). Thus, the FLAC courses expand the learners' intellectual horizons by recognizing the functions of the language and the food, both of which produce cultural knowledge and awareness that are crucial components of one's identity and source of social status. The exploration of identity through the above themes allows learners to experience the meaning potentials of a semiotic repertoire (Hall, 2019) in which context-sensitive "conventionalized meanings . . . develop from their uses" (p. 48) across two languages. Consequently, learners are given greater access to multimodal and multisensory semiotic resources thereby evoking a greater sense of agency to shape their own L2 learning on the basis of thorough content knowledge and L1-mediated analysis.

To demonstrate how reciprocal content learning can effectively facilitate critical thinking and self-expression in two languages, we introduced this FLAC structure into the previously mentioned courses, centering upon translanguaging, which is a process involving two or more languages used interchangeably or simultaneously for the comprehension and communication of a subject matter (García & Li, 2014; Kumagai & Kono, 2018). We then highlight the synthesizing effects of L1 and L2 in three class activities: a film screening, poetry translation, and poetry composition. The chapter concludes with reflections on the FLAC program as well as its challenges, together with students' feedback, to underscore the potential of the FLAC framework.

Translanguaging in a Japanese FLAC course

The FLAC pedagogy is widely practiced in the field of second language learning or second language acquisition (SLA). Pointing out SLA's transdisciplinary philosophy, the Douglas Fir Group (2016) emphasized the importance of sociocultural and sociocognitive dimensions in L2 learning as multilingual individuals' command of language in today's plurilingual world is being reassessed by researchers and educators. In particular, the FLAC model, which allows students to move between L1 and L2 contexts, heightens their sociocultural consciousness and thereby deepens their L2 comprehension (Kaufman, 2004; Reisinger et al., 2022). With increasing cross-border traffic and virtual communication, a bilingual individual has more occasions to manage two (or more) languages interchangeably and simultaneously according to the context; in particular, the person draws upon one integrated repertoire rather than two sets of separate language worlds (Leung & Valdes, 2019). This process is called translanguaging (García & Kano, 2014; García & Li, 2014), and FLAC, by encouraging learners to explore two language worlds on a particular subject matter, provides a meaningful environment in which to integrate them.

The FLAC model allows learners to acquire knowledge and discuss the issues in their stronger language (e.g., L1) while it facilitates learning in their weaker language (e.g., L2). In other words, this process allows learners to access "different linguistic features or various modes of what are described as autonomous languages, in order to maximize communicative potential" (García, 2009). In the translanguaging framework, L2 learning is not merely a bilingual exercise to develop the capacity for which both L1 and L2 are coactivated but to initiate "the fluid mixing of semiotic codes irrespective of named languages." (Ortega, 2019, p. 26). It is also important to note that the translanguaging pedagogy promotes a non-hierarchical relationship between L1 and L2, which alleviates the linguistic insecurity detected among L2 learners bounded by monolingualism or native-speakerism. Consequently, learners become more confident in their own capability of using the learned language, which assists in building their repertoire of diverse semiotic resources while making their own choices and in fortifying their sense of agency by initiating actions and negotiating with others in a wider range of contexts accessible via multilingual language uses (Hall, 2019).

FLAC in environmental ethics

In the mid 2010s, FLAC courses were implemented within multiple language programs in the authors' university. Despite the rising numbers of Japanese advanced learners, which have enhanced the demand for content-based instruction (CBI) courses over the last decade (Chikamatsu, 2019; Sato et al., 2015), the required number of students per classroom (due to universities' financial constraints) has made it difficult for learners of less commonly taught languages to maintain full credit advanced CBI courses (Ananth & Lyons, 2020). To respond to the concerns of instructors and learners, FLAC is served as a solution, allowing language programs to maintain advanced level classes with smaller enrollments.

Japanese FLAC courses have been offered since 2015 in the Modern Languages Department (MOL) paired with a course in the Religious Studies Department (REL) by the two faculty members—a linguist (MOL) and an ethicist (REL)—who teach and administrate the university's Japanese Studies program. The first FLAC courses, themed on industrial diseases, focused on Minamata Disease and the Fukushima Nuclear Disaster (Chikamatsu, 2022; Miyamoto, 2021). After offering these FLAC courses, the authors created a new course on food, which was first offered during the pandemic. The preparation for the FLAC course requires the two faculty members' close communication over years to decide on the course theme, compose a proposal, and select course materials. In particular, a Japanese course needs to be developed around the topic corresponding to the ethics course while also taking into consideration the accessibility of the resources and materials in the Japanese language. Once the course is approved and launched, each faculty member regularly attends the other's course. Furthermore, in order to enhance students' learning experiences, the instructors plan at least one campus event during the course (e.g., a film screening with a director). When the course is over, the instructors reflect on the course and discuss successful points as well as those that need to be altered.

L1 course: religion and ethics in Japanese foodscapes (REL)

The core content course for the FLAC topic "Religion and ethics in Japanese foodscapes" meets twice a week for 90-minute sessions for 10 weeks to explore our relationship to food, which can be quite personal and intimate as well as communal and social. Reflecting on the versatile roles that food plays in a given culture, the course investigates food as a powerful analytical tool for understanding ourselves and our place in society. Given food's ubiquity in Japanese popular culture, from literature to TV shows, food holds a unique position for equipping students not only with a grasp of Japanese society but also with applicable skills to view food as one of the contributors that determines our view of ourselves, others, and the world. Because the course defines ethics as a provider of theoretical frameworks as well as an indicator of the intersections and transactions between the self and the other (Wyschogrod, 1990)—including non-human subjects (Bennett, 2009)—investigating the social constructs that dictate the norms of our society is an ethical task. To this end, the course is designed to analyze how food construes one's identity—both personal and collective—by bringing people together and, conversely, how food divides people by placing them in hierarchical strata in a given society. The assigned readings train students to discuss the underlying key concepts of cultural authenticity, nationalism, and discrimination.

L2 course: food and ethics in Japan (JPN)

The Japanese FLAC course, entitled "食と倫理: Food and ethics in Japan," is a half-credit, 10-week language course that meets once a week for 90 minutes. The goals of the course are to (a) examine historical, environmental, sociocultural, and gender issues related to food production and consumption; (b) develop critical thinking skills for the linguistic and literary analysis of Japanese textual and visual materials; and (c) present one's understanding of and relationship with food through the creative use of one's own languages (English and/or Japanese). The course is designed for students who are learning advanced level (fourth year or higher) Japanese and are concurrently enrolled in the L1 course. Three advanced Japanese students enrolled in the course in spring 2021, which was offered virtually via Zoom due to the pandemic.

Table 4.1 outlines the two courses. Japanese textual and visual materials used in class included children's picture books, manga, anime, poetry, essays, novels, documentaries, and feature films. A worksheet was assigned weekly along with readings and/or visual materials based on classroom discussions conducted in both Japanese and English. A term project, assigned during the second half of the course, focused on poetry translation and writing. Collaborative online international learning (COIL) was also implemented, and students at a Japanese university participated in it. One American and two Japanese students formed a group and met every other week to discuss course-related topics in Japanese, such as food rituals, discrimination in the meat industry, the identification of food, and cooperation with the government regarding food contamination inspections. This international component will not be further discussed, however, as it is beyond the scope of this chapter.

Discussion of translanguaging pedagogy in FLAC

We present three learning practices reflecting the translanguaging pedagogy. Each practice exemplifies how theories and practices were intertwined. Learning Activity 1 focused on the expansion of meaning potentials via a documentary film screening. Activity 2 centered around poetry translation to build one's voice. Finally, Activity 3 highlighted poetry writing to enact one's identity and agency as language learner and user.

Activity 1: film screening and discussion of expanding meaning potentials

In spring 2021, we hosted a Zoom event and invited a special guest: documentarian Aya Hanabusa, director of *Tale of a Butcher Shop* (ある精肉店の話), a documentary released in 2013. The film introduced a small butcher shop in Osaka run by

Table 4.1 Course outlines of the FLAC Japanese and ethics courses

Class	JPN395 Topics and materials	REL244 Topics and materials (selected readings)
Week 1	Course introduction History of Japanese cuisine	Religion and food Menon (2018)
Week 2	Food and heroism Picture books: 桃太郎 *Peach Boy* (Matsui, 1965); アンパンマン *Anpan* ["Sweet Bun"] *Man* (Yanase, 1975); おでんくん *Oden* ["Fish Cake"] *Boy* (Franky, 2001)	Acculturation of tea Benn (2015); Rath (2013)
Week 3	Food and discrimination: meat industry Documentary film: ある精肉店のはなし *Tale of a Butcher Shop* (Hanabusa, 2013)	Cultural praxis; The praxis of meat-eating Krämer (2008)
Film screening of *Tale of a Butcher Shop* with Director Aya Hanabusa (via Zoom)		
Week 4	Food and discrimination: outcasts Essay: 被差別の食卓 "Meals at Outcast Households" (Uehara, 2005) Poem: しんでくれた "You Die for Me" (Tanigawa, 2014)	Politics of meat Jaffe (2005)
Week 5	Food and discrimination: purity Feature film: あん *Sweet Bean* (Kawase, 2015)	Religious significance of rice Ohnuki-Tierney (1995)
Week 6	Food and nationalism: Washoku *Intangible Cultural Heritage* (MAFF, 2013); *Certificate for Japanese Cooking* (MAFF, 2016)	Food and nationalism Cwiertka (2018)
Week 7	Food and nationalism: identity Essay: ウマし "Yummy!" (Ito, 2018)	Food fight Cwiertka (2006); Arch (2018)
Week 8	Food and discrimination: disease Novel: あん *Sweet Bean Paste* (Sukegawa, 2013)	Food and discrimination Kajiwara and Catt (2004); Sukegawa (2017)
Week 9	Food and contamination: Fukushima Manga: 美味しんぼ (Kariya, 2013; 2014)	Food, disaster, and gender discourse Kimura (2016); Ochiai (2013)
Week 10	Term project presentation	Final project presentation

the Kitade family who raised cows, slaughtered them, and sold the meat directly to consumers. It depicts the butchers' philosophy about life and death, which was demonstrated by their grateful and respectful treatment of the animals and their meat. The film captured their everyday life just before the closure of their slaughter business, which had lasted more than 100 years, due to the declining local population and growing competition with grocery store chains. Notably, despite the family's pride and their customers' appreciation, handling and processing animal meat was considered a job relegated to the outcasts, the *burakumin*, in Japan.

To prepare for the film screening event, the L1 class was assigned readings that discussed food, identity, and social status, such as Menon's "Ruminations on beef" and Krämer's "Not befitting our divine country." The former introduced the idea that the consumption of certain foods is closely connected to one's (religious) identity and social status, and the accessibility to and consumption of beef were weaponized to sharply divide Hindus and Muslims in India. After examining the case of contemporary India, students read Krämer's article, which examined the ways in which food production similarly demarcated the self and the other in Japan. Such a division not only maintained the social hierarchy, but also justified discriminatory attitudes toward a certain population that had historically dealt with animal skin, meat, and bones. The L2 students' preparation involved reading part of a middle school history textbook to learn about the assigned occupations in medieval to early modern Japanese society such as butchery or leatherworking. A worksheet was designed to aid the students' understanding of the content and linguistic expressions used in the film.

Overall, the students were impressed by the Kitade family's respect for their cattle presented in the film. The discussion in L1 revolved around the following thought: Although, or perhaps precisely because, the Kitade family had to end a cow's life to sell its meat, they did not waste any parts of the slaughtered animal. The film reminds viewers of the nature of human beings whose lives can be sustained only by consuming others' lives. If that is the human condition, we must at least be grateful for the lives given for us. However, in an era of mass production/consumption, the production of food and its market are completely separated. Consequently, most of the production sites that are automated, depending upon the exploited laborers, remain invisible to consumers.

This view was also shared in the L2 students' discussion after the screening, as seen in the following comments provided by Student A [translated from Japanese]: "In America, we generally feel that we eat 'meat,' not 'life.' We view beef as something we consume. Since we do not want to think that we are indebted to other lives, meat is 'meat' but not 'life.'"

The L2 class discussion revolved particularly around language use. For instance, Student A commented as follows: "I realized *itadakimasu* means we are given the lives of animals and plants, which humbles me," and "I was surprised to learn that the Kitades used *waru*, or 'to divide,' instead of *korosu*, 'to kill/slaughter' [for slaughtering], which gave me [the] impression they [had] profound respect for the lives of their cattle." いただきます, *itadakimasu*, a phrase customarily uttered before a meal in Japan, was introduced in an early stage of L2 Japanese learning as formulaic speech. It may have been recognized as a humble form of the verb *morau* ("to receive") or *itadaku* ("to receive humbly") when the dynamic usage of giving-receiving verbs was introduced later in the course. However, Student A identified the phrase to represent humans' as humble receivers of the respected lives of animals and plants (instead of the cook who prepared the food, which is a common interpretation of the expression). In short, Student A conceptualized the non-hierarchal relationship between humans and

Translanguaging with food and ethics 55

nature through the discussions in L1 and L2 courses. As previously stated, Student A further analyzed the expressions for the act of slaughtering from different perspectives and identified that 割る (*waru*, "to divide") was used by the Kitades instead of 屠畜 [*tochiku*, "to slaughter (cattle)"] or 殺す (*korosu*, "to kill"). The concept of "slaughtering" was transformed in the student's integrated semiotic system, regardless of the language, because of the respectful interaction the Kitade family displayed in the film. This was the moment Student A expanded their meaning potentials in the peculiar yet shared context for the personalized meaning-making process carried out recursively in L1 and L2. The fluid use of two languages (i.e., translanguaging) made it possible for the students to redefine the concepts of "eating," "slaughtering," "meat," "life," and "death" as well as reshape meaning potentials.

The topic was followed by Week 4's reading of the foreword for 被差別の食卓 (*hisabetsu no shokutaku*, "Meals at outcast households") (Uehara, 2005), a nonfiction book about food culture that was based on the author's upbringing in the *buraku* district.

Activity 2: translating poetry to find one's voice

In Week 4, right after the film screening and discussions, L2 students read しんでくれた, (*shinde kureta*, "You die for me") composed by renowned Japanese poet Tanigawa Shuntaro (2014). The poem expresses a young boy's feelings of appreciation and guilt toward cows and other animals whose lives were taken to feed humans. The poem is written in *hiragana*, a syllabic script and the first of three Japanese scripts learned by children. The poem was published in a picture book with phrases placed on two open pages of lively, colorful illustrations. Students first shared their interpretations to identify the intended audience, linguistic and rhetorical features, and the poet's message and then translated it into English. The first draft was presented and critiqued in class during Week 4; it was revised during the following week. All students in the class and both instructors exchanged comments and edits for each translation, both in class and on Google Docs when each shared their translation.

Table 4.2 shows the original Japanese poem and the English translation created by Student A. Student A evaluated the poem's linguistic features and commented that it was "primarily written in casual form with very short stanzas [and] with . . . simplistic grammar" and was written "only in hiragana," suggesting that the poem was most likely aimed toward younger readers. It was presented "with the underlying themes of life, death, and respect"; "the author [was] trying to communicate . . . the hierarchy of life [and] the appreciation and respect for the lives of the animals that sustain us as human beings." Based on this interpretation, the poem was translated into English (L1) "to preserve the intents of the author" and to "maintain the feelings of respect as well as the concepts of life and death." Particular linguistic features, such as "childish language (mommy, daddy, etc.) and fairly simple sentence structures," were

Table 4.2 The original Japanese poem and English translation of しんでくれた (Tanigawa, 2014)

The original poem しんでくれた	Student A's translation "You die for me"
うし	Cow,
しんでくれた　ぼくのために	Who gave your life for me—
そいではんばーぐになった	Reduced to but a hamburg steak.
ありがとう　うし	Thank you, Cow.
ほんとはね	But in reality,
ぶたもしんでくれてる	Pig too gave their life,
にわとりも　それから	Chicken as well—
いわしやさんまやさけやあさりや	And so did Sardine, Mackerel, Salmon, and Clam.
いっぱいしんでくれてる	Many have given their life.
ぼくはしんでやれない	But I can't give my life,
だれもぼくをたべないから	For no one would eat me.
それに　もししんだら	Besides, if I were to give my life,
おかあさんがなく	Mommy would cry,
おとうさんがなく	Daddy would cry,
おばあちゃんも　いもうとも	Granny and little sis, too.
だからぼくはいきる	That's why I'll keep my life.
うしのぶん　ぶたのぶん	Cow's share, Pig's share—
しんでくれたいきもののぶん	The share for all those that gave their life.
ぜんぶ	All of it

© Koseisha Shuppan, 2014

employed while "some liberties were taken with translation due to [the lack of] straight forward [*sic*] equivalents in English." For instance, "Cow" and "Pig" were singular and capitalized, instead of being plural and lowercase, in order to underscore the individuality of each animal that is worthy of not only respect—the theme discussed in the session after the screening—but also equality and equity in the non-hierarchical nature, which is the student's own interpretation of lives beyond the author's message.

LaScotte and Tarone (2019) claimed that learning and using language involve a "set of personalized 'voices' constituting complexes of linguistic and nonlinguistic features, each of which communicates a particular person's emotion, personality, and social stance" (p. 97). Student A's translation did not merely pass along the message of the original work in another language, but it also expressed an individual's interpretation and linguistic sensibility enriched via the discursive discussions in the two courses. Furthermore, by keeping readership, message, and semiotic resources in mind, Student A seemed to discover a clearer picture about their viewpoint and voice. Thus, the students' translation task exemplified a few things: the ability to create their own patterns with meanings and uses to expand meaning potentials and the use of their own expressions to find their own voice via the fluid usage of all semiotic resources.

Activity 3: creating poetry to express identity

During Week 5, a term project was assigned. Students composed a poem in Japanese to reflect their understanding of both courses' materials while using their individual voices to express the course theme—namely, their relationship with food and identity intertwined with food.

Responding to the poem

In addition to asking students to compose a poem, the L2 instructor wanted students to write, in Japanese, a poem in response to Tanigawa's (2014) poem. They were encouraged to first decide on a theme, emotion, tone, or intended audience and then write using rhetorical and linguistic devices (e.g., inversion, omission, script choice, alignment, font, rhyme, stanza, symbolism, ambiguity, polysemy). Students shared their first drafts during class in Week 5 and revised their work through Week 7.

Student A wrote a poem from the cow's perspective entitled 「いのちをあげる」, or "I give you my life," as a direct response to 「しんでくれた」 (See Table 4.3). The student employed a similar rhetorical style as Tanigawa (2014)—a monologue of short, simple sentences written completely in hiragana—and wrote, not as the boy but as the cow. In the first draft, the student tried to express the cow's sense of resentment for being exploited, as in ハンバーグになるほどに、どう思うの ("How do you feel as my life is changed merely to a hamburger steak?"). In class, the butcher family's respect toward their cow in the film was recalled. Therefore, in the second draft, Student A changed the tone behind "exemplifying the selfless actions demonstrated by the animals for the sake of the other side—the boy"; the emotional distance was diminished by changing key words such as しょうねん ("boy") and

Table 4.3 Student A's response poem, いのちをあげる ("I give you my life")

Draft 1	Draft 2[1]
しょうねん	きみ
いのちをあげる あなたのために	いのちをあげる
ハンバーグになるほどに	たとえハンバーグになっても
どうおもうの	きみのために
みんな がいのちをあげたいよ	ぼくたちのいのちをあげる
ぶたもいのちをあげたい	ぶたもいのちをあげる
にわとりも それから	にわとりも それから
いわしやさんまやさけやあさりや	いわしやさんまやさけやあさりも
みんないのちをあげたい	みんないのちをあげる
あなたはしんでやれない	きみはしんでくれない
だれもあなたをたべられないから	だれもきみをたべられないから
それに もししんだら	それに もししんだら
おかあさんがなく	きみのおかあさんがなく
おとうさんがなく	おとうさんがなく
おばあさんも いもうとさんも	おばあさんも いもうとも
だからあなたはいきないと	だからきみはいきないと
ぼくのいのち ぶたのいのち	ぼくのいのち ぶたのいのち
みんなのいのちも	みんなのいのちも
ぜんぶ	ぜんぶ

あなた ["you" (formal)] to きみ ["you" (casual)] and みんな ("everyone") to ぼくたち ("we all"). The intimacy suggested by the new words reflects the author's realization that taking food is not merely an act of consumption but is also an act of receiving others' lives. The lives of cows and pigs will continue to live in ourselves and nurture us. Eating inevitably involves taking others' lives, whether animals or plants, and precisely because that is the human condition, humans should not take it for granted but should take seriously the message from the cow in the poem: "to live." Eating is, thus, building an intimate relationship between the one who eats and the other who is eaten. As Student A describes, the changes were made to "give the sense that maybe the boy and the animals have been with each other for a long duration of time, and, as such, they are much closer." Moreover, the poem, in which the cow voluntarily gives up its life for the life of a boy, upends the commonly viewed hierarchy in which humans are above all the food chain. However, the poem suggests that the humans are rather at the bottom of the hierarchy as humans owe their lives to all others who gave up their lives. Acknowledging the poem calls into question the human superiority over other beings, Student A also made comments that humans do not own nature. Through this assignment, students were able to understand the nuances that those Japanese words carry and utilize them in their translation; at the same time, they also reconsidered their relationship with food, leading to a reshaping of their identity and worldview, as underscored by the L1 students who unpacked the socially constructed categories and worldview.

Creating a final poem

Identity was further explored when nationalism (or the lack thereof) and food were discussed in Week 6 and Week 7. For example, the L2 students were each asked to choose a food that represents themselves after reading Ito Hiromi's (2018) essay ウマし：カリフォルニアの無形文化遺産, in which the author identifies with a California roll because they both are transnational and borderless. The final project included the composition of a poem on their own identity and their relationship with food. Although the previous exercises involved reconsidering human relationships with food, thereby questioning the social constructs, this exercise prepared students to think about their fluid identity. As our lives are an accumulation of many lives offered to us, our identity is not static and perhaps not even a singular. By consuming a cow, using the previous practice, a cow becomes a part of a human. By the cow consuming grains, grains become a part of the cow. By nurturing grains, the soil becomes a part of the grains. Similar to the notion of selfhood in Buddhism, in which the self is a reflection of all influences around the individual, rather than something given, this assignment directs students' attention to a new perspective of self and identity—specifically the way they are constructed and perceived. Encountering the notion of the self that is envisioned differently serves as a window for understanding a culture and its language that they are learning. Students were required to translate this understanding into a longer poem in Japanese that considers one's selfhood and identity through food.

Drafts were shared in Week 8 and, after revisions (both in class and in Google Docs), students presented their final versions in Week 10 along with content and linguistic analysis. The following poem in Table 4.4, entitled 卵ちゃん ("Little

Table 4.4 Student B's final poem in Japanese 卵ちゃん "Little Egg"

卵ちゃん	*Little Egg (translated by Student B)*
こもる太陽、生卵	A concealed sun, raw egg:
殻にこもる、殻が守る	Hidden away, protected in your shell
ツルツルとまあるい顔をする	With a smoooooth and round face.
何色にも、命を生かす	Any color you take, you create life.
あのう、きずつけないでください	"Uhmm, please be careful with me!"
ってその卵ちゃん	So said the little
が私に言う	Egg to me
スーパーの通路で	In the aisle of the grocery
卵箱の点検中	In the middle of my inspecting the carton.
ハッとして、落としてしまう	I gasp, and drop the little one!
日光のように輝く	Glinting like sunlight,
スーパーの床を塗る黄身	The yolk paints the supermarket floor
私の顔を映す	And my face is reflected
蛍光灯の下で卵白が	In the tiny egg white beneath the fluorescent lights.
すぐスーパーを逃げ出す私	I run out of the store at once!
映った顔がピシャっと	My face, reflected, clings
ペッタリと善心・全身にくっつく	Splat! right onto my heart.
卵ちゃんの故郷さえ知らず	Knowing not even that little egg's hometown,
母の鶏に謝れない	How can I apologize to the mother chicken?
突然のカラスの鳴き声が聞こえる	Audible in the distance, the sudden cry of a crow!
帰り道、セミが耳に響いて	Homebound, as cicadas ring in my ears,
風に草の香りがする	And on the wind, the scent of grass.
日がジリジリと光り	The sun beats down
顔が卵のように焼ける	And fries my face like an egg.

Egg"), was written by Student B, who identified with an egg, *tamago*, in the earlier discussion.

This final project effectively expressed students' identity and their relationship with food, which is manifested in the following comment:

> For this poem, I took a lot of influence from the activity from Worksheet 7 where we compared ourselves to food. It helped me realize that a theme of this course, as well as [the L1] course, is the use of food for the creation of identity and the importance of identifying with the food one consumes in order to have consideration for the environment of its production. So, I wanted to write a poem in which the connections between humans, nature, food, and death are all present.

However, synthetizing these exercises was not easy. In the first, much shorter draft, Student B's poem sounded incomplete because it was one-dimensional, written only from *watashi*'s perspective. In the second draft, after receiving feedback from classmates and the instructors, Student B added the second half of the poem (underlined) "to elucidate the human/nature binary" and immersed *watashi* in nature to "use comparisons of light/sunlight vs. fluorescence," which demonstrated the ability to integrate more than one perspective into a poem and suggested the expansion of semiotic, ethical, and intellectual horizons. Student B also inventively employed linguistic devises. For example, the egg's line, あのう、きずつけないでください, "Uhmm, please be careful with me," is the only one written solely in hiragana, conveying a childlike tone.

Furthermore, four free-standing lines include actions by or toward *watashi*, "I," while five four-line stanzas describe the world around the egg and *watashi*. The paradox is that Student B self-identified as the egg while incorporating *watashi* as a human counterpart in this poem. In the very last stanza, Student B ended the poem with the following resolution:

> Outside, the sound of a crow and cicadas (symbols of life and death) reminds me that life and death exist in a natural balance and I cannot escape nature, and therefore must embrace and protect it as if it were a part of myself.

Hall (2019) discussed the significant role of learners' identities that mediate access to the development of their repertoires of semiotic resources and negotiate their self-expressions. Identity is fluid and reflective of our life experiences; therefore, providing opportunities to evoke multifaceted identities in complex and contradictory ways is crucial for enriching one's sense of self. Through a series of intellectual challenges, including the film screening, poetry reading, and translation of themes surrounding the act of eating, the L2 students were guided in two languages to expand their semiotic resources. The expanded and enriched resources also helped the students find their own voices and identities when writing an original poem. Student B self-identified via symbolism in the final poem assignment of the course. We believe the thread of the translanguaging practices provided students with the optimization of language conditions to enact their sense of agency to express oneself as a language learner and user in their own path of learning and communication.

Conclusion

In this chapter we highlighted the merits of the FLAC model when integrated with the translanguaging pedagogy, which were manifested in optimizing the accessibility of diverse semiotic resources, including L1 English and L2 Japanese, to discuss food, ethics, and individual and collective identities. L2 Japanese learning is often viewed as a challenge due to basic linguistic features such as the overwhelming number of kanji characters and unique linguistic features that are largely different from English conventions. However, if one language is viewed as the tool for human engagement in meaning making, adding resources in another language will expand the semiotic resources and provide more accessibility for meaning making. The FLAC platform serves fittingly to this end. The current FLAC courses showcase from a transdisciplinary—in particular, translanguaging—perspective with the strong effect of enacting learners' voices, self-agencies, and identities by maximizing the accessibility of their semiotic resources. The Douglas Fir Group (2016) recognized that the transdisciplinary approach to human meaning making is both multimodal and situated, and it involves much more than linguistic resources as there is no perfect correspondence between language and meaning. In their ultimate task with meaning making, where their semiotic resources, thought patterns, and identities are reflected, learners become more cognizant of their responsibility. Thus, Larsen-Freeman (2019) highlighted the importance of "ethical consideration beyond the classroom" (p. 72), and three central characteristics must be considered when it comes to agency in the language classroom: "the learner's ability to self-regulate, the socially mediated nature of sociocultural context, and awareness of one's responsibility for one's own act" (p. 73). Such ethical consideration was synthesized effectively in the reported FLAC courses.

Delivering successful FLAC courses requires meticulous planning and close pedagogical collaboration between the content specialist and the language educator. First, the curriculum must be carefully planned with (a) intellectually challenging themes both familiar and essential to our lives and (b) multimodal tasks designed to guide learners from understanding content to actively engaging in meaning-making activities with their enhanced sense of agency. Second, it is important to consider the obstacles: the L2 course, worth half a course credit, usually meets less frequently than the content course, which can make it quite challenging to select a shared theme that fits both courses and schedules as well as find appropriate materials, especially for the L2 course. Thus, the instructors need to be in constant communication to keep up with each other's class and understand each other's pedagogy.

In sum, the FLAC curriculum helped L2 Japanese students develop confidence in their linguistic and cultural competence in Japanese and prepared them to execute their agency in L2 learning by taking on more challenging tasks. In the fall quarter of 2021, when the campus reopened, the three L2 students who had enrolled in the previous year's FLAC courses enrolled in the Japanese language seminar. During the term, the L1 course instructor's newly published book, entitled 『なぜ原爆が悪ではないのか：アメリカの核意識』 (*Why the atomic bomb isn't wrong: Nuclear discourse in the US*) (Miyamoto, 2020), was translated. Reading a book written for a Japanese audience seemed unfeasible for students in a college Japanese course, yet they led lively discussions in every session, shared their own interpretations and voices candidly, and translated the first chapter successfully. These achievements were made possible by the FLAC program that had prepared them for the challenging tasks while helping them further expand their horizons.

Note

1 Student A's English translation of いのちをあげる "I give you my life"

I'll give my life for you—
Even if I must become a hamburg steak.
For your sake.

We'll give our lives for you.
Pig will do the same,
Chicken as well—
Sardine, Mackerel, Salmon, and Clam, too.
Everyone will give their lives.

But you couldn't give your life for us,
For no one could eat you.
Besides, if you were to give your life,
Your mother would cry,
Your father would cry,
Your grandma and little sister, too.

That's why you must live.

My share, Pig's share—
Everyone's share of life.
All of it.

References

Ananth, P., & Lyons, L. T. (2020). *Incorporating foreign language content in a humanities course*. Routledge.
Arch, J. K. (2018). *Bringing whales ashore: Oceans and the environment of early modern Japan*. University of Washington Press.

Benn, J. A. (2015). Tea as a religious and cultural commodity in traditional China. In *Tea in China: A religious and cultural history* (pp. 1–20). University of Hawai'i Press.

Bennett, J. (2009). *Vibrant matter: A political ecology of things*. Duke University Press.

Chikamatsu, N. (2019). Collaborative teaching of a Japanese content-based course: 3.11 and nuclear power crisis. In C. A. Melin (Ed.), *Foreign language teaching and the environment: Theory, curricula, institutional structures* (pp. 146–160). The Modern Language Association of America.

Chikamatsu, N. (2022). Translanguaging in language and area-studies curriculum: A Japanese FLAC course of Minamata and Fukushima in environmental humanities. In M. de la Fuente (Ed.), *Education for sustainable development in foreign language learning* (pp. 215–232). Routledge.

Cwiertka, K. J. (2006). *Modern Japanese cuisine: Food, power and national identity*. Reaktion Books.

Cwiertka, K. J. (2018). Serving the nation: The myth of washoku. In K. J. Cwiertka & E. Machotka (Eds.), *Consuming life in post-bubble Japan: A transdisciplinary perspective* (pp. 89–106). Amsterdam University Press.

Douglas Fir Group. (2016). A transdisciplinary framework for SLA in a multilingual world. *The Modern Language Journal, 100*(Supplemental 2016), 19–47.

Franky, L. (2001). おでんくん [Fish-cake boy]. Shogakukan.

García, O. (2009). Education, multilingualism, and translanguaging in the 21st century. In A. Mohanty, A. M. Panda, R. Phillipson, & T. Skutnabb-Kangas (Eds.), *Multilingual education for social justice: Globalizing the local* (pp. 128–145). Orient BlackSwan.

García, O., & Kano, N. (2014). Translanguaging as process and pedagogy: Developing the English writing of Japanese students in the US. In J. Conteh & G. Meier (Eds.), *The multilingual turn in language education: Opportunities and challenges* (pp. 258–277). Multilingual Matters.

García, O., & Li, W. (2014). *Translanguaging: Language, bilingualism, and education*. Palgrave Pivot.

Hall, J. K. (2019). *Essentials of SLA for L2 teachers: A transdisciplinary framework*. Routledge.

Hall, J. K., & Caldwell, A. M. (2001). A FLAC model for increasing enrollment in foreign language classes. *The French Review, 74*, 1125–1137.

Hanabusa, A. (Director). (2013). ある精肉店のはなし [Tale of a butcher shop] [Film]. Yashiho Films.

Ito, H. (2018). カリフォルニアの無形文化遺産 [Intangible cultural heritage in California] (T. Aoyama & M. Kishi-Debski, Trans.). In H. Ito, ウマレ！[Delicious!]. Chuokoronshinsha. https://exchanges.uiowa.edu/issues/borders/four-essays-on-food-from-ito-hiromis-delicious/

Jaffe, R. M. (2005). The debate over meat eating in Japanese Buddhism. In W. M. Bodiford, (Ed.), *Going forth: Visions of Buddhisst vinaya* (pp. 255–275). University of Hawa'i Press.

Kajiwara, K., & Catt, A. (2004). Buddhism and Hansen's disease. *The Eastern Buddhist, 36*(1/2), 40–45.

Kariya, T. (2013). 美味しんぼ 110巻 [Oishinbo, Vol. 110]. Shogakukan.

Kariya, T. (2014). 美味しんぼ 111巻 [Oishinbo, Vol. 111]. Shogakukan.

Kaufman, D. (2004). Constructivist issues in language learning and teaching. *Annual Review of Applied Linguistics, 24*, 303–319.

Kawase, N. (Director). (2015). *Sweet bean*. Comme des Cinémas.
Kimura, A. H. (2016). *Radiation brain moms and citizen scientists: The gender politics of food contamination after Fukushima*. Duke University Press.
Klee, C. A. (2009). The resurgence of interest in languages across the curriculum. *The Modern Language Journal, 93*, 618–621.
Krämer, H. M. (2008). "Not befitting our divine country": Eating meat in Japanese discourse of self and other from the seventeenth century to the present. *Food and Foodways, 16*, 33–62.
Kumagai, Y., & Kono, K. (2018). Collaborative curricular initiatives: Linking language and literature courses for critical and cultural literacies. *Japanese Language and Literature, 52*, 247–276.
Larsen-Freeman, D. (2019). On language learner agency: A complex dynamic systems theory perspective. *The Modern Language Journal, 103*, 61–79.
LaScotte, D., & Tarone, E. (2019). Heteroglossia and constructed dialogue in SLA. *The Modern Language Journal, 103*, 95–112.
Leung, C., & Valdes, G. (2019). Translanguaging and the transdisciplinary framework for language teaching and learning in a multilingual world. *The Modern Language Journal, 103*, 348–370.
Matsui, T. (1965). ももたろう [Peach boy]. Fukuinkan.
Melin, C. A. (2019). *Foreign language teaching and the environment: Theory, curricula, institutional structures*. The Modern Language Association of America.
Menon, K. D. (2018). Ruminations on beef. *Shuddhashar, 10*. https://shuddhashar.com/kalyani-devaki-menon-ruminations-on-beef-2/
Ministry of Agriculture, Forestry and Fisheries (MAFF). (2013). 和食 [Washoku]. www.maff.go.jp/j/keikaku/syokubunka/ich/pdf/leaflet_jjpg.pdf
Ministry of Agriculture, Forestry and Fisheries (MAFF). (2016). 海外における日本料理の調理技能認定制度 [Guidelines for certification of cooking skills for Japanese cuisine in foreign countries]. www.maff.go.jp/j/shokusan/syokubun/tyori.html
Miyamoto, Y. (2020). なぜ原爆が悪ではないのか：アメリカの核意識 [Why the atomic bomb isn't wrong: Nuclear discourse in the US]. Iwanami shoten.
Miyamoto, Y. (2021). *A world otherwise: Environmental praxis in Minamata*. Lexington Books.
Ochiai, E. (2013). The manga "Oishinbo" controversy: Radiation and nose bleeding in the wake of 3.11. *The Asia-Pacific Journal/Japan Focus, 11*(25), 4.
Ohnuki-Tierney, E. (1995). Structure, event and historical metaphor: Rice and identities in Japanese history. *The Journal of the Royal Anthropological Institute, 1*(2), 227–253.
Okazaki, T. (2009). 言語生態学と言語教育：人間の存在を支えるものとしての言語 [Language ecology and language education]. Bonjinsha.
Ortega, L. (2019). SLA and the study of equitable multilingualism. *The Modern Language Journal, 103*, 23–28.
Rath, E. (2013). Reevaluating Rikyū: Kaiseki and the origins of Japanese cuisine. *The Journal of Japanese Studies, 39*(1), 67–96.
Reisinger, D. R., Quammen, S. V., Liu, Y., & Virguez, E. (2022). Sustainability across the curriculum: A multilingual and intercultural approach. In M. de la Fuente (Ed.), *Education for sustainable development in foreign language learning* (pp. 197–214). Routledge.
Sato, S., Takami, T., Kamiyoshi, U., & Kumagai, Y. (2015). 未来を創ることばの教育をめざして内容重視の批判的言語教育 [Language education for social future: Critical content-based instruction]. Coco Publishing.

Sukegawa, D. (2013). あん [Sweet bean paste]. Poplar sha.
Sukegawa, D. (2017). *Sweet bean paste* (A. Watts, Trans.). Oneworld Publication.
Tanigawa, S. (2014). しんでくれた [You die for me]. Kosei Shuppan.
Uehara, Y. (2005). 被差別の食卓 [Meals at outcast households]. Shinchosha.
Wyschogrod, E. (1990). *Saints and postmodernism: Revisioning moral philosophy*. The University of Chicago Press.
Yanase, T. (1975). それいけ！アンパンマン [Go! Sweet-bun man]. Froebel-kan.

5 Teaching Chinese through classic literature

A cross-disciplinary collaboration

Jinai Sun and Stuart Patterson

Introduction

Mandarin Chinese is the most widely spoken first language in the world (Goh, 2017). Given its thousands of years of history, the Chinese language reflects the many rich cultures and diverse people who speak it. Today, with China's growing importance in the global market, the need for interculturally competent speakers of Chinese is more pressing than ever. Whereas a 2019 report from the American Council on the Teaching of Foreign Languages placed Chinese second only to Spanish as the most in-demand language on the side of employers, a 2019 Modern Language Association report ranked it seventh among the most commonly learned non-English languages in U.S. higher educational settings in 2016, after Spanish, French, American Sign Language, German, Japanese, and Italian (ACTFL, 2019; Looney & Lusin, 2019). However, the report also pointed out the worrisome trend that nearly all most commonly taught languages, including Mandarin Chinese, experienced decreasing enrollment at the advanced level in 2013–2016. To tackle this issue, we should revisit Geisler et al.'s (2007) report, which offered recommendations for structural changes for foreign language departments facing such enrollment issues. One suggestion calls for less division and hierarchy between language teaching and literature teaching (Geisler et al., 2007).

This chapter reports on a cross-disciplinary project that features pedagogical collaboration between an advanced level Mandarin Chinese course and a Chinese literature course offered in the spring semester of 2021 at North Central College, a regional liberal arts college in Illinois. The literature course, entitled "Two Chinese novels," was cotaught by both authors, largely in English, through a program featuring the great books of world literature. The language course "Communication and composition" was taught by a language specialist (one of our coauthors) in Chinese for upper level L2 Chinese students. We first review the pedagogical frameworks and institutional contexts that guided the planning and implementation of both courses. We then briefly describe the genesis and development of our collaborative relationship. We also share key themes and activities adopted between the two courses to stimulate investment and agency of students enrolled in both courses. The chapter concludes with an analysis of students' learning

DOI: 10.4324/9781003266976-7

outcomes and pedagogical reflections on our ongoing collaboration to link the study of literature and language toward their mutual enrichment.

Theoretical, pedagogical, and institutional framework

FLAC model for collaboration

The design of our two courses was inspired by content-based instruction (CBI)—specifically, Foreign Languages Across the Curriculum (FLAC), which is a variation of the CBI language teaching approach that allows students to use a target language to study a theme or topic appropriate to another academic field (Stryker & Leaver, 1997). Unlike other CBI models, the FLAC model requires collaboration between a language instructor and a content expert. Later called Languages Across the Curriculum (LAC) (Klee & Barnes-Karol, 2006), it is viewed as both a concept and a pedagogical approach that links language education with all academic disciplines (Bettencourt, 2011; Brinton et al., 1989; Klee, 2009; Kumagai & Kono, 2018; Lin, 2016). FLAC programs can take many forms, depending on how language learning is integrated with content learning. Our collaboration, guided by the concepts and collaborative models in FLAC programs, features designing lesson content with themes shared between two full credit courses offered during a given semester (Bettencourt, 2011; Stryker & Leaver, 1997).

As our college has not yet instituted a formalized FLAC program, the courses were offered independently of one another with students receiving full credit for each. Our collaboration was, thus, institutionally egalitarian insofar as each course's pedagogical methods and objects remained well within the disciplinary framework of our respective programs: language and literature. In this way, at least initially, the literature course took the form described in the recently published book *Incorporating Foreign Language Content in Humanities Courses* (Ananth & Lyons, 2020), with the similar intent to develop "a strategy for increasing foreign language enrollments by reaching a target audience of students who may have little or no previous experience with foreign language learning" (p. 20).

Language learning from a transdisciplinary perspective

The field of second language acquisition (SLA) has been evolving along with new understandings of language learners and the purposes of second language (L2) learning. The transdisciplinary approach to SLA is a concerted and multidisciplinary effort taken by leading SLA researchers (Douglas Fir Group [DFG], 2016) to address the multifaceted and dynamic processes of L2 learning in diverse social contexts over learners' lifespans. As a foundational understanding, language learning in the transdisciplinary framework is shaped by three mutually dependent levels of social activity: the micro, meso, and macro levels. At the micro level, L2 learners use their internal cognitive and emotional mechanisms in engagement with others in various multilingual contexts to develop their multilingual repertoires. At the meso level, the semiotic resources accessible to a learner in a specific social context are shaped by "particular sociocultural institutions and particular sociocultural communities" (p. 24) in which the learner is situated; these in turn affect the possibilities and nature of learners' social identities and ultimately their access to particular types of social experiences. At the macro level, the ways that learners interact with their social contexts shape and are shaped by society-wide ideologies, common social beliefs, and values about language use and language learning.

Among the themes derived from these three levels of social activity (Douglas Fir Group, 2016; Hall, 2019), we focus on those at the micro level and meso level of language learning specifically pertinent to the collaborative project: L2 learning involves learning of a repertoire of diverse semiotic resources including both linguistic and nonverbal, visual, graphic, and auditory resources; L2 learning is situated in local iterative contexts and is attentionally and socially gated; L2 learning is embodied and mediated by semiotic resources accessible to learners; and L2 learning is mediated by learners' social identities, which could motivate or demotivate learners to take agency in L2 development.

In order to enhance learners' access to such multilingual and multimodal semiotic resources, we employed translanguaging practice in our collaborative teaching. Translanguaging has caused a shift away from traditional monolingual practices in the language classroom, necessarily making use of a "fluidity between language system(s)" to develop learners' language competencies (García & Li, 2014, p. 36). It is described as a process in which two or more languages

> are used in a dynamic and functionally integrated manner to organize and mediate mental processes in understanding, speaking, literacy, and, not least, learning... [it] concerns effective communication, function rather than form, cognitive activity, as well as language production.
> (Lewis et al., 2012, p. 641)

Although translanguaging has typically been practiced to support language-minoritized students, it has also been adopted for foreign language instruction (Chikamatsu, 2022; Zheng, 2021). In Zheng's (2021) study, a Chinese instructor adopted translanguaging in a fourth-grade and fifth-grade grade Chinese immersion classroom to help English-dominant students co-construct and negotiate meaning with their peers. This study found that translanguaging facilitated a dynamic and creative learning environment in which students accessed a variety of resources, in both English and Chinese, to learn target linguistic forms. Therefore, we adopted translanguaging as an important pedagogical practice in the literature course reported in this chapter to help increase students' access to translingual and transcultural semiotic resources when reading Chinese literature.

Planning cross-disciplinary collaboration

Chinese classical literature serves as the centerpiece of our collaboration, which began on a research trip we took to China with five North Central students in the summer of 2019. Our project was to research the contemporary reception of the classic novel *Hongloumeng*《红楼梦》 (*Dream of the red chamber*) by Cao Xueqin, written in the mid-18th century but not published until 1792 (Cao et al., 1792/1973–1986). *Dream of the red chamber* (hereafter, *Dream*) is the most recently composed and published of China's canon of "four great novels" that "embody the deepest spirit of the grand civilization of old China" (Plaks, 2007, p. 109). This monumental work, which runs just over 2,300 pages in English, tells the story of a divinely-wrought stone that sojourns on Earth in the form of Jia Bao-yu, the young scion of a noble house in the early Qing dynasty, and his tragic love for his beautiful but dour cousin, Lin Dai-yu. Celebrated by the Chinese almost since its publication as a veritable encyclopedia of late imperial Chinese culture, our research sought to understand the contemporary reception of Cao's masterpiece as a reflection of Chinese culture today.

As this research project wound down in the second half of 2020, we began designing our course "Two Chinese novels." We decided to read another of the four canonical novels, *Xiyouji* (*Journey to the West*) alongside *Dream* as a comparative project (Wu, 1592/2006). First published in 1592 and attributed to Wu Cheng-en, *Journey to the West* (hereafter, *Journey*) narrates a fantastical pilgrimage, led by the irrepressible "Monkey King" Sun Wu Kong, to introduce Buddhist scriptures from India into China. Although they present quite distinct literary styles, *Dream* and *Journey* are comparable for their deep reflections on the mutual influences among the so-called three teachings of China (i.e., Taoism, Confucianism, and Buddhism) and how all three traditions guide the sometimes agonizing progress of each novel's hero toward enlightenment.

Beyond pursuing our literary interest in both novels, we sought to build a pedagogical bridge that would enable us to adopt methods and objects of study from each other. The literature specialist had only begun reading classical Chinese fiction in 2015 when he had assigned *Dream* to a class of students who had demanded to read works outside the so-called Western tradition. In 2017 he started collaborating with the language specialist on the previously described research project. His specific objective in this collaboration was to teach *Dream* again but with a better-informed sense of its full literary and cultural dimensions. The language specialist entered the collaboration seeking strategies for introducing classical fiction into her L2 Chinese courses; her goal was to introduce students at the undergraduate level to culturally rich and authentic materials that deeply inform Chinese life.

Designing the FLAC courses

One of our ulterior aims in offering the "Two Chinese novels" course as a general elective to all students was to test strategies for teaching classical Chinese fiction effectively to American students. Due to the fact that the course attracted students who already had, on average, intermediate proficiency in Chinese, we found ourselves instead strategizing methods for delving as deeply as possible into the text of a classical Chinese novel. Although the language specialist had already coordinated certain elements in the Chinese language course with our literature course (as we relate later in this chapter), she was able to work intensively on certain points of language study with two students taking both courses. Both courses were offered for full credit (four semester hours) over the 15 weeks of a semester. The calendar had been shortened by a week from its standard 16-week length to ease pressures on students during the ongoing COVID-19 pandemic; for the same reason, both courses were taught online in synchronous meetings over the Zoom platform. The "Two Chinese novels" course met once a week (in the evening) for a 2-hour discussion of each weekly reading portion. The language course met three times a week for 65 minutes each meeting.

"Two Chinese novels" course

As previously noted, in the "Two Chinese novels" course, students read both *Dream* and *Journey*, albeit in a somewhat abridged form in English; our reading of *Dream* occupied the first 8 weeks of the course, and we then read *Journey* over the remaining 7 weeks. In addition to the novels themselves, we presented students with a collection of secondary materials in English on each novel including chapter-by-chapter synopses of the entirety of the work, a range of recent scholarly commentary on select topics, and web-based resources such as YouTube lectures (in English) and televisual and/or cinematic adaptations. Students were not required to use any of these materials, although we occasionally urged students to look into one or another secondary source based on their questions or expressed interests that emerged during a class discussion.

The most salient goal of the course was for students to develop their skills in reading and analyzing Chinese long-form fictions. They did so in two ways: through weekly conversations on successive portions of each novel and in written reflections. In our weekly conversations, students were required to pose at least one question about each weekly reading portion and to come to that week's class session ready to respond to each other's questions through conversation. We acted as facilitators of these conversations, typically by helping students elaborate their own views, whether by reformulating a question or suggesting ways to elaborate on a point of interpretation initiated by a student. Students' written work took two forms: twice-weekly discussion board postings and two interpretive essays. Students' first discussion post each week offered reflections on the class discussion of the previous day; in the second, later in the week, they proposed questions on the portion to be discussed in the next class session. Essays were roughly 1500 words in length, with one on *Dream* due in the middle of the term and one on *Journey* due at the end of the term; both essays required students to research a specific topic in relation to each novel, whether literary, historical, or otherwise.

"Communication and composition" course

In the Chinese language "Communication and composition" course, the first 7 weeks of the semester were devoted to the study of classical literature (i.e., works

Table 5.1 Schedule of two coordinated courses

Week	"Communication and composition"	"Two Chinese novels"
1	人类文明的开始：神话故事和传说 (The beginning of human civilization: myths and legends)	Dream of the red chamber
2	《庄子》寓言故事给我们的启发 (Inspiration from the Parables of Zhuangzi)	
3–4	中国古典文学的最高峰《红楼梦》(Dream of the red chamber, the summit of Chinese classical literature)	
5	为什么要教小孩子背古诗？(Why teach children to memorize ancient poems?)	
6–7	西游记之三打白骨精 (Journey to the West: "Three bouts with the White Bone Spirit")	
8–15	Modern Chinese literature	Journey to the West

composed prior to the final dissolution of the Qing dynasty in 1919). In the second half of the course, students studied modern Chinese literature composed after this historical watershed (Feng, 1996). Thus, our two courses were loosely coordinated through the first 7 weeks of the semester and within an even narrower period within that timeframe as the 7 weeks devoted to classical literature also covered five topics (see Table 5.1).

Each of the five topics indicated in Table 5.1 were covered through a variety of weekly exercises including vocabulary and grammar exercises, short composition and translation exercises, recorded speaking exercises, five-paragraph essays in Chinese, reading comprehension exercises (including Chinese children's adaptations of both *Dream* and *Journey*), and aural comprehension exercises (including excerpts from television and film adaptations of *Dream* and *Journey*). Students were also encouraged to meet weekly with the teaching assistant to practice speaking on each week's topic. At the end of the 7 weeks on classical literature, students completed a mid-term project in which all students worked together as a team to write, design, and develop a roleplay video titled "Journey to North Central College." Students loosely imitated the storyline in *Journey* and created their own version of the novel to reflect their life experience in the college while applying the values and worldviews studied in class.

The salient goals toward which these exercises were designed were for students to (a) develop their spoken and written proficiency, (b) broaden their knowledge of Chinese literary culture through comparative and evaluative analyses of prominent classical and modern narratives, and (c) apply the enhanced proficiency and new knowledge about Chinese literature and culture to communication in both Chinese and English.

Examples of collaborative literature and language teaching

Given that the most intense focus of our collaboration was on *Dream*, we now present specific examples of collaborative pedagogy in both courses dealing with that novel.

Qíng 情 as pivotal term

Although we can only hint here at the richness of our weekly translanguaging Socratic dialogues, we can illustrate the myriad semiotic boundaries we traversed in the literature course alone by reference to the single term *qíng* 情 (Li, 2018). One feature of *Dream* that has captivated Chinese readers since its publication is the author Cao's masterful deployment of what Wai-yee Li and Yuri Pines have identified as Chinese "keywords" or "pivotal terms of political, ethical, literary and philosophical discourse" (Li, 2020, p. ix) that focus what Raymond Williams (1985, p. 23) describes as "conflicts of value and belief" through these terms' shifting and contested usages over historical time. Having featured in or near the center of Chinese debates about human nature since at least the first century of the common era, *qíng* 情 has been variously translated into English as "feelings," "love," "romantic sentiments," "passions," and/or "desire" (Huang, 1998; Levy, 1999; Yu, 1997). In short, readers of *Dream*, whether in Chinese or (if only more so) any language into which it has been translated, must come to terms with the ineluctable ambiguity of such pivotal terms.

However, to suggest anything like the full significance of the term *qíng* 情 within the translanguaging space of our two courses, we must recall that *Dream* is, at its core, a love story. That is, given the (abbreviated) range of previously listed meanings, it only makes sense that we find the concept *qíng* 情 (among related terms) at the center of *Dream*'s symbolic universe. Yet this leads us directly to elaborate on a further feature of Cao Xueqin's text, which is its profound playfulness with the Chinese language itself. Here we call attention to the nickname of one of the more vividly drawn but enigmatic figures in the novel, Qín Kěqīng 秦可卿, whose name forms a near-homophonic pun for the phrase *qíng kěqīng* 情可倾, which can be faithfully translated as "loveable." Furthermore, this character's chief role in the narrative is to orchestrate, by way of the very dream that gives the novel its title, the hero Jia Bao-yu's first sexual encounter as a young boy along with a portentous lesson in the difference between love and lust.

We corroborate Anthony Yu's (1997) judgment that the novel is indeed "highly traditional" among classical Chinese literary works in its masterful use of such punning and figurative linguistic means, but that it excels all others in exploiting these features of its "linguistic medium—the peculiarities of the Chinese language in both its phonetic and ideographic elements" (p. 4) to explore the very nature of language and meaning in literary contexts. Thus, in the literature course we could, through our dialogues on *Dream*, see how aspects of the central concept *qíng* 情 took on a kind of enacted significance in the *qíng kěqīng* 情可倾 figure of Qín Kěqīng 秦可卿. This was just one of dozens of instances of concept/name puns that lent a layer of significance to the English text we read through our awareness of the layers already within the Chinese original. To enrich students' learning of *Dream*, we also arranged a dialogue on the first five chapters between our class and five Chinese undergraduate students in Shanghai through an "online intercultural exchange" (O'Dowd & Lewis, 2016, p. ix *passim*). Although the hour we spent online together was not extensive enough to generate a truly collaborative relationship with our Chinese counterparts (students and professor) toward literary insights, we nonetheless were able to trade appreciable views on, for example, who we liked or disliked among the characters.

Dream *for linguistic and cultural references from the past to the present*

In the week and a half she spent studying *Dream* with her Chinese language students, Sun began with the model five-paragraph essay describing *Dream* as "the summit of classical literature (中国古典文学的最高峰)." For the students taking only the Chinese language course, this essay served primarily as a model for their subsequent exercises in composing a five-paragraph essay (in Chinese) on literature. They also learned from it the very basic outline of the love story between Jia Bao-yu and his cousin Lin Dai-yu as well as how and why *Dream* occupies such an exalted place in Chinese culture and history generally. Sun supplemented the information in this essay with a description of how Cao embedded within *Dream*'s narrative an exceedingly elaborate, allusive pastiche of a thousand years of Chinese literature from songs and poems to folktales and plays (Schonebaum & Lu, 2012).

The Chinese language students' next main encounter with *Dream* was while watching the first episode of a 2010 television adaptation of the entire novel (in Chinese with English subtitles). This hour-long television episode highlighted one scene, the first encounter between Dai-yu and Bao-yu, in which both have an immediate sense of already knowing each other. The language specialist supplemented this enigmatic scene with some background on the novel's opening passages. In these passages, we learn that the pair had already met on another plane of existence as a stone (Bao-yu) who waters and brings to life a flower (Dai-yu) who must repay this debt through her tears in the "dust-stained human realm" into which they both descend together to expiate their "love karma" (Cao et al., 1792/1973–1986, p. 130).

To enrich students' exposure to diverse Chinese linguistic forms, Sun also discussed basic expressive and formal features of *shi* 诗, or classical Chinese poetry, through analyses of the commonly taught poem by Li Bai "Quiet night thoughts" 静夜思, and then invited students to try their hand at composing their own.

Pedagogical reflections

The joint design of the "Two Chinese novels" course and the "Communication and composition" course enabled both instructors to provide diverse semiotic resources, including both linguistic and visual ones, to help students, especially the two students enrolled in both courses (June and Jose), develop deep understandings of key linguistic and cultural concepts such as *qíng* 情, 爱情, 命运 by reading *Dream* and *Journey*. For as fascinating a text as *Dream* is, our ulterior aim in "Two Chinese novels" was to let it serve as the pretext, however elaborate, for our own Socratic, dialogical explorations of the truth and value of such ideas as *qíng* 情 in our own experience. Although we describe the "Two Chinese novels" course as a literature course, we conceived it more so as an opportunity for our students to encounter themselves and each other by way of—or, we might even say, within—an encounter with Chinese culture. In this way, we relied centrally on the use of translanguaging as a pedagogical practice insofar as cases such as *qíng* 情 inevitably sharpen students' attention to the choices made in transmitting complex ideas from one named language to another (Chikamatsu, 2022; Kumagai & Kono, 2018).

The translanguaging space that resulted served, as Li described, to "break down the ideologically-laden dichotomies between the macro and the micro, the societal and individual, and the social and psychological through interactions" (2018, p. 23) in which we deployed our collective semiotic resources toward addressing the "self-chosen questions" through which we bridged the novel and our own experiences and opinions in our weekly Socratic dialogues (Van Rossem, 2006, p. 48). This same space for translanguaging further bridged both courses as both June and Jose found opportunities to rehearse a new semiotic repertoire they had developed in the literature course toward newly creative linguistic practices in the language course. Ultimately, we aimed to offer students a rewarding opportunity to practice crossing linguistic boundaries—between named languages and within a single language—and a sense of the semiotic rewards of increased insight not just into the novel but also into both a foreign culture and, ultimately, one's own culture and self.

Taking advantage of the affective power of literature in language acquisition and retention corresponds to the transdisciplinary view of L2 learning as a mediated and socially gated process. Daniel Shanahan (1997) eloquently attested to this power in an account of his own first reading of *Dream*, just a few paragraphs into which (in the English translation) transported him to memories of "almost hallucinogenic intensity" (p. 167) back to a visit to China many years earlier. By his own account, the language of *Dream* (again, even in English translation) somehow encoded "elements of Chinese culture . . . with powerful emotional underpinnings" (Shanahan, 2008, p. 17) that had escaped being effaced by even two centuries of dramatic historical change, which demonstrated to him "the profound ability" that "the affective element of language has . . . to engage us, to motivate us" (Shanahan, 1997, p. 167). In addition, the online exchange with Chinese undergraduate students, however short it was, confirmed that the students and their Chinese counterparts could meaningfully share views on the novel. A few students also took agency to become pen pals with their new Chinese friends after the online exchange session. This outcome indicates that the positive intercultural communication experiences helped students emotionally engage in further learning the language and culture (Hall, 2019).

In the instructor's presentation of Dai-yu's emotionally laden arrival at the Jia family compound, she intended specifically to engage the "emotional capacities" through which the Chinese language students selected and attended to "particular meaning-making semiotic resources and their patterns of use" as they interpreted this episode by mapping both functional similarities and dissimilarities between Chinese and American concepts of fate and romantic love (Hall, 2019, p. 7). Specifically, she first pre-taught targeted vocabulary terms such as *àiqíng* 爱情 or, roughly, "romantic love," and *mìngyùn* 命运, or "fate," and offered a brief description (in English) of Buddhist notions of karma and the transmigration of souls—concepts *Dream* clearly draws upon throughout its story (Yu, 1989). She then invited students to compare the story of Bao-yu and Dai-yu to the idea of love at first sight and their own ideas or experiences of what makes for such immediate chemistry with someone else. Given the students' ages and situations, these concepts could not fail to stir latent affective energy among her students as she bid them—as we had done—to consider their own experiences with love in light of the powerful example of Cao's monumental literary masterpiece.

As noted, two students, June and Jose (pseudonyms), took both "Two Chinese novels" and "Communication and composition." June was a heritage student adopted from China in infancy and raised speaking English. For his part, Jose had already graduated from North Central the year before but returned to audit both courses in the spring of 2021 (completing all coursework). The outcomes they both demonstrated and reported show how, in combination, our courses helped students grasp complex Chinese linguistic and cultural concepts while developing their motivation to learn Chinese language further.

In June's responses to an evaluative questionnaire at the end of the "Two Chinese novels" course, she expressed that she was "motivated . . . a lot to learn more Chinese" and "to want to continue my research . . . and expand my knowledge [of] Chinese historical novels [to] understand Chinese culture, government, politics, religion and many other aspects" of Chinese life. She also indicated that "it was really helpful to learn about the stories in English too," which made her "feel confident I can tell others about these books." Furthermore, in response to an evaluative questionnaire on her experience in the "Communication and composition" course, she commented that

> this term I . . . felt more connected with the Chinese language because we could see the styles of influential Chinese writers. It really provided a unique perspective that translated into how I can perceive Chinese ideals within their society.

In June's case, we should stress that, in personal communications with the instructor, she more than once described her motivation for learning Chinese as being strong enough to train to teach it at the elementary level. Her motivation to learn and teach Chinese further revealed her sense of herself as Chinese despite having been raised almost entirely in the United States by her adoptive White parents. Through her studies, June also indicated her interest in understanding China in order to understand how her life had been changed by being adopted rather than having grown up as a woman in China. More than once June expressed special interest in the study of Chinese women's conditions, including in her research paper in the "Two Chinese novels" course on *Dream*. Thus, for June, much of her study of Chinese language and culture stems from a personal interest in uniting disparate aspects of herself. June also demonstrated her commitment to her Chinese identity during our courses by making a televised statement questioning a local store owner's decision to post a notice denouncing the "demonic Chinese influence in our country."

Given June's larger motivations in studying Chinese, we would argue that her remarks regarding new insights into Chinese culture can be read as assertions of her ability to better understand the "imagined community" of her Chinese heritage. June's participation in this kind of imaginative project suggests her "investment" in developing new forms of "cultural capital" through knowledge of Chinese literature and the historical vantage it provides on the vast tableau of Chinese civilization (Norton, 2013, p. 8; see also Anderson, 1991; Bourdieu, 1977; Hall, 2019). The translanguaging practice adopted in both courses also afforded rich semiotic resources that stimulated June's "agency" in her new confidence in her ability to present that imagined community to others as both a learner of as well as a representative of both Chinese language and culture to eventually realize her aim to become a teacher of Chinese (Hall, 2019).

Like June, Jose also concretely demonstrated a deep understanding of cultural concepts, enhanced linguistic competence, and—more importantly—an increased motivation for Chinese learning that he tied to his participation in our linked courses. In the speech contest he entered, Jose composed and recited by memory an original five-paragraph essay on *Journey* in which he argued how the small group of pilgrims depicted in *Journey* can be read as representing distinct but related aspects of universal human qualities and drives. As he put it in his written responses to our questions about the "Two Chinese novels" course, his message was that "anyone from any culture can learn about themselves through this story." Jose also developed this theme in his final paper in "Two Chinese novels," in which he explored the many ways that Chinese Americans have identified themselves in literary and other expressive forms with Sun Wukong's pointedly hybrid identity as a monkey who, by the end of the story, has become a bodhisattva. He explained in a follow-up correspondence with the instructor that some of his interest in Sun Wukong was the character's appeal as a kind of hybrid hero who spoke to Jose's identity as a Mexican American.

For the creative expression in the speech contest, Jose recited an original poem he had written in response to a homework assignment in "Communication and composition." From the first draft of his own poem, Jose sought to emulate Daiyu by borrowing and adapting words and phrases from her poem. Yet his larger aim was to explore a new sense of "an excellent metaphor" we had discussed in class "relating the garden from [*Dream*] and the garden of Eden." Jose observed,

> The Chinese can place themselves as a natural part of their world, and the garden serves as a way to replicate the world around them on a condensed scale. In contrast, the garden of Eden is forbidden. A human being in the garden would taint it, and it would lose its value. Humans are naturally separated from that world.

Jose's first attempt at writing poetry in Chinese, in this light, was not simply a linguistic exercise; rather, it represented an extended effort to enlarge his communicative repertoire through a highly motivated development of new semiotic resources in Chinese in order to pursue a sympathetic identification with a worldview that he had first encountered in an English translation of *Dream* (Hall, 2019).

Conclusion

Although we have yet to offer another Chinese literature course, we have been motivated to new practices in our respective teaching that build on insights we took from the collaboration we have described herein, not least of all from our students themselves. The literature instructor, for example, has taken Jose's lead in thinking about hybrid identities through the example of Sun Wukong by assigning both *Journey* and a series of modern and contemporary works by Chinese American writers in his general introductory course on world literature. For her part, the language instructor continues to develop resources that can meld the emphasis on communicative competence with meaningful, student-centered encounters with Chinese culture that are available through open-ended dialogues on literature, film, art, philosophy, and similarly humanistic materials.

This collaborative pedagogical project offers great insights for Chinese language educators interested in integrating classic Chinese fictions in the language classroom. First, it is important to balance the cognitive challenges of communicative competence with the emotional investment that can come of open-ended dialogues. Classical literature can clearly supply content—namely, stories freighted with moral, affective, and even spiritual values that will readily and reliably engage students. However, the instructor needs to make sure such classical materials can be delivered in a variety of formats suited to different ages and levels of language proficiency. For instance, an open translanguaging space in which students could use both languages, deployed strategically, could help language students become familiar with new vocabulary and clarify difficult new concepts in L2 through the kind of combined affective and cognitive investment required in an open but supported discussion of the rich contexts such new materials invoke. Second, as they design learning outcomes, instructors should keep in mind that language, intercultural communication skills, and content learning are equally important. When students are cognitively challenged and emotionally involved, they are more likely to be motivated to use and learn the target language. Last but not least, language instructors should be open to adopting and adapting literary and other "high" cultural materials for lessons, which both elicit and reward student input toward lessons about subjects that clearly matter beyond the classroom. It is more important to tailor the task to be age appropriate to engage students than to teach them the comprehensive masterwork.

References

ACTFL. (2019). *ACTFL 2019 annual report*. www.actfl.org/sites/default/files/reports/annualreport2019/index.html

Ananth, P., & Lyons, L. T. (Eds.). (2020). *Incorporating foreign language content in humanities courses*. Routledge.

Anderson, B. R. O. (1991). *Imagined communities: Reflections on the origin and spread of nationalism*. Verso.

Bettencourt, M. (2011). Languages across the curriculum: A response to internationalization in foreign language education. *Multicultural Education, 19*(1), 55–58.

Bourdieu, P. (1977). The economics of linguistic exchanges. *Social Science in Formation, 16*(6), 645–668.

Brinton, D. M., Snow, M. A., & Wesche, M. B. (1989). *Content-based second language instruction*. Heinle & Heinle Publishers.

Cao, X., Hawkes, D., Gao, E., & Minford, J. (1973–1986). *The story of the stone: A Chinese novel in five volumes*. Penguin. (Original work published 1792).

Chikamatsu, N. (2022). Translanguaging in language and area-studies curriculum: A Japanese FLAC course of Minamata and Fukushima in environmental humanities. In M. J. de la Fuente (Ed.), *Foreign language learning: Content-based instruction in college-level curricula* (pp. 215–232). Routledge.

Douglas Fir Group. (2016). A transdisciplinary framework for SLA in a multilingual world. *The Modern Language Journal, 100*(Supplemental 2016), 19–47.

Feng, L. (1996). Democracy and elitism: The May fourth ideal of literature. *Modern China, 22*(2), 170–196.

García, O., & Li, W. (2014). *Translanguaging: Language, bilingualism and education*. Palgrave Macmillan.

Geisler, M., Kramsch, C., McGinnis, S., Patrikis, P., Pratt, M. L., Ryding, K., & Saussy, H. (2007). Foreign languages and higher education: New structures for a changed world: MLA Ad Hoc committee on Foreign languages. *Profession*, 234–245.

Goh, Y.-S. (2017). *Teaching Chinese as an international language: A Singapore perspective*. Cambridge University Press.

Hall, J. K. (2019). *Essentials of SLA for L2 teachers: A transdisciplinary framework*. Routledge.

Huang, M. W. (1998). Sentiments of desire: Thoughts on the cult of Qing in Ming-Qing. *Chinese Literature: Essays, Articles, Reviews (CLEAR), 20*, 153–184.

Klee, C. A. (2009). Internationalization and foreign languages: The resurgence of interest in languages across the curriculum. *The Modern Language Journal, 93*(4), 618–621.

Klee, C. A., & Barnes-Karol, G. (2006). A content-based approach to Spanish language study: Foreign languages across the curriculum. In B. Lafford & R. Salaberry (Eds.), *Art of teaching Spanish: Second language acquisition from research to praxis* (pp. 23–38). Georgetown University Press.

Kumagai, Y., & Kono, K. (2018). Collaborative curricular initiatives. *Japanese Language and Literature, 52*(2), 247–276.

Levy, D. J. (1999). *Ideal and actual in the story of the stone*. Columbia University Press.

Lewis, G., Jones, B., & Baker, C. (2012). Translanguaging: Origins and development from school to street and beyond. *Educational Research and Evaluation: An International Journal on Theory and Practice, 18*(7), 641–654.

Li, W. (2018). Translanguaging as a practical theory of language. *Applied Linguistics, 39*(1), 9–30.

Li, W. (2020). Introduction. In W. Li & Y. Pines (Eds.), *Keywords in Chinese culture* (pp. 169–218). The Chinese University of Hong Kong Press.

Lin, A. M. Y. (2016). *Language across the curriculum & CLIL in English as an additional language (EAL) contexts: Theory and practice*. Springer.

Looney, D., & Lusin, N. (2019). *Enrollments in languages other than English in United States institutions of higher education, summer 2016 and fall 2016: Final report*. Modern Language Association.

Norton, B. (2013). Identity and second language acquisition. In C. Chapelle (Ed.), *Encyclopedia of applied linguistics* (pp. 146–169). Wiley-Blackwell.

O'Dowd, R., & Lewis, T. (Eds.). (2016). *Online intercultural exchange: Policy, pedagogy, practice*. Routledge.

Plaks, A. H. (2007). Leaving the garden: Reflections on China's literary masterwork. *New Left Review, 47*, 109–129.

Schonebaum, A., & Lu, T. (Eds.). (2012). *Approaches to teaching the story of the stone (Dream of the Red Chamber)*. Modern Language Association.

Shanahan, D. (1997). Articulating the relationship between language, literature, and culture: Toward a new agenda for foreign language teaching and research. *The Modern Language Journal, 81*(2), 164–174.

Shanahan, D. (2008). A new view of language, emotion and the brain. *Integrative Psychological and Behavioural Science, 42*, 6–19.

Stryker, S. B., & Leaver, B. L. (Eds.). (1997). *Content-based instruction in foreign language education: Models and methods*. Georgetown University Press.

Van Rossem, K. (2006). What is a Socratic dialogue? *Filosofie, 16*(1), 48–51.

Williams, R. (1985). *Keywords: A vocabulary of culture and society*. Oxford.

Wu, C. (2006). *The monkey and the monk: An abridgment of the Journey to the West*. (A. Yu, Trans. and Ed.). University of Chicago Press. (Original work published 1592).

Yu, A. (1989). The quest of Brother Amor: Buddhist intimations in the Story of the Stone. *Harvard Journal of Asiatic Studies, 49*(1), 55–92.

Yu, A. (1997). *Rereading the stone: Desire and the making of fiction in dream of the red chamber*. Princeton.

Zheng, B. (2021). Translanguaging in a Chinese immersion classroom: An ecological examination of instructional discourses. *International Journal of Bilingual Education and Bilingualism, 24*(9), 1324–1339.

6 Promoting translingual and transcultural literacies in a collaborative content-based Japanese classroom
Audiovisual translation as pedagogy

Saori Hoshi and Ayaka Yoshimizu

Introduction

This chapter reflects on our collaborative curricular project named "Japanese media and translation," a content-based language course co-taught by two instructors with different disciplinary expertise in language and media studies. Our study responds to the gaps identified in teaching Japanese language and Japanese media as mutually independent disciplines. Although content-based instruction (CBI) has been widely recognized as a remedial approach to serve the linkage between language and content studies, its primary focus is on language learning as an instrument for understanding content knowledge; a lack of content knowledge potentially discourages language specialists from developing such a course (Chikamatsu, 2012). Meanwhile, so-called content courses that examine Japanese films and other types of media in translation offer little room to discuss linguistic and extralinguistic effects of audiovisual translation despite significantly affecting how the texts are interpreted and experienced by audiences that rely on the translation (Flynn, 2016).

To fill these gaps, we built upon the Douglas Fir Group's (DFG, 2016) transdisciplinary framework to operationalize our project. First, our instruction involved both advanced learners of Japanese and proficient Japanese speakers through a pedagogical practice of translanguaging (Li, 2018) to examine media texts in the form of translation practice between English and Japanese. DFG (2016) presented one of its themes as maximizing learners' access to any multimodal semiotic resources including learners' first, second, and any named languages. Thus, we employed the translanguaging practice in our instruction for translation processes among language users of English and Japanese with different levels of proficiencies. Second, our instruction was informed by a sociolinguistic perspective of identity construction through language (Cook, 2008; Ochs, 1990) to explore how social identities—namely, gender and sexuality in this case—are constructed and negotiated through situated uses of linguistic resources in audiovisual media texts. To examine this, we selected recent films produced in Japan and North America to provide learners with diverse linguistic contexts. To engage in translation for the films, we draw on the critical approaches to subtitles (Kapsaskis, 2008; Nornes, 2007) to discuss the implications of deconstructing the dominant ideologies that

DOI: 10.4324/9781003266976-8

exist in the source and target cultures. Both approaches are useful to increase second language (L2) learners' access to diverse semiotic resources in their target languages (DFG, 2016).

However, our transdisciplinary approach goes beyond DFG's (2016) conceptualization of transdisciplinary framework in that language acquisition is viewed as a byproduct of developing students' translingual and transcultural literacies. In other words, the mobilization of multiple languages is a vital means to perform linguistic and media analyses in a critical and creative manner as well as further question, rather than acquire and adopt, the conventional usage of the given languages. By engaging in critical subtitling and shuttling between multiple languages, students become creators of new expressions in target languages (English and Japanese) as they negotiate moments of untranslatability of the source language or choose to challenge ideological conventions of the target languages.

In this chapter we discuss the roles of critical content-based instruction (CCBI) and translanguaging and how we incorporate sociolinguistics and subtitles studies into the course content. To address how students develop translingual and transcultural literacies, including the ability to negotiate diverse semiotic resources and ideological differences to make meaning across linguistic and cultural boundaries (Canagarajah, 2013), this chapter first outlines how we bring together different disciplines to teach a critical approach to audiovisual translation in our course design and then discuss how students utilized the knowledge and skills they learned from their collaborative subtitling assignment. We conclude this chapter by providing pedagogical suggestions for language educators interested in adopting our course design.

Pedagogical and theoretical backgrounds

Critical content-based instruction (CCBI)

The field of foreign language (FL) education, since the movement of communicative language teaching (CLT) in the 1970s, has focused its instruction on developing learners' communicative abilities. This trend led to a bifurcation between language and content in the curricula of higher education, especially in North America (Geisler et al., 2007). CBI originated as an instructional and curricular approach that makes a dual commitment to language and content-learning objectives (Stoller, 2008). Various approaches to teaching content have been proposed to implement several distinct types of CBI including language for specific purposes (LSP) for the development of language skills needed for particular fields of study such as engineering and business, Foreign Languages Across the Curriculum (FLAC), and content-based language instruction (CBLI). Whereas the CBLI model allows teachers to choose thematic units relevant to learners' interests and their proficiency levels, FLAC involves a collaboration between language and content specialists teaching paired courses. The FLAC model treats language as a tool to expand students' knowledge of the respective disciplinary fields (Caldwell, 2001) and the cross-cultural knowledge (Leaver & Stryker, 2008) and skills to develop critical analysis and disposition, an approach called CCBI (cf. Sato et al., 2017).

Kumagai and Kono (2018) drew on the FLAC model to incorporate CCBI focused on a common theme—namely, ethnic minorities in Japan. The paired courses, taught by two instructors with different disciplinary expertise (language/linguistics and literature), guided students to develop their linguistic and literary analytical skills by translating the same texts in both Japanese and English. Their curriculum enhanced students' critical language awareness (Fairclough, 1992), which enabled them to further advance their linguistic proficiency, critical literacy, and cultural fluency. Chikamatsu (2022) reported on the implementation of a FLAC curriculum and reflected the collaboration between Japanese language and religious studies courses in which the students developed linguistic sensibility and critical literacy through engagement with environmental literary translation works in translanguaging settings.

Following CBI-informed pedagogical practices that have evolved over years, we developed a new Japanese language course ("Japanese media and translation") co-taught by two instructors with different disciplinary expertise: Japanese language/linguistics and media/cultural studies. Our CCBI model is situated within the construct of critical pedagogy, which emphasizes students' development of critical reflection and enactment for the transformation of knowledge, power, and ideology (e.g., Kubota & Miller, 2017). Our instruction incorporated audiovisual media (films and videos in Japanese and English) related to topics such as gender, sexuality, race, ethnicity, and Indigeneity in contemporary Japan and beyond. Students were informed by linguistics theories and subtitles studies to develop critical skills to examine and translate the audiovisual media text into subtitles. By utilizing audiovisual translation as a vital and distinct translanguaging method, our course aimed to promote students' translingual and transcultural literacies.

Pedagogical translanguaging and translation

The development of translingual and transcultural competence as the ultimate goal of language and cultural studies leads to the need for CCBI "to integrate not only language and content but also all the languages in the students' multilingual repertoires" (Cenoz, 2013, p. 393). Although translanguaging has been understood as a pedagogical practice building on students' multilingual repertoire to facilitate language development and standard academic practices, a more recent view on translanguaging extends to the concept of pedagogical translanguaging: the instructionally planned strategies that integrate two or more languages for the development of the multilingual repertoire and metalinguistic awareness as learners emerge as multilingual speakers rather than deficient speakers when evaluated against the yardstick of monolingual standards (Cenoz & Gorter, 2020).

Our practice drew on pedagogical translanguaging, which entails an explicit invitation for students to learn about sociocultural perspectives on topics such as gender, sexuality, race, and Indigeneity by shuttling between languages and cultures through the translation of audiovisual media texts. In our course, students and instructors alike utilized translanguaging in all aspects of class activities including lectures, discussions, written assignments, oral presentations, and group activities. We also view translation as a specific and vital translanguaging pedagogical tool. Our pedagogical approach supports Baynman et al. (2019), who argued for the reconceptualization of translation from an entity conceived of as a relationship between texts to one as a dynamic and creative deployment of resources within the multilingual repertoire, which embodies "cultural translation" (p. 44). In our course context, for instance, students negotiated the lack of equivalent expressions in translating gendered speech of a Japanese character into more gender-neutral English subtitles or negotiated the hyper-gendered conventions of Japanese subtitling practice when creating their original subtitles. These processes engaged students with what Kramsch (2009) called the third place, which captures intercultural and transcultural awareness of named languages (e.g., Japanese and English) including (un)translatability and (in)consistency in translation between those two languages. We aligned with this perspective—namely, how pedagogical translanguaging enables students to utilize their knowledge of multiple languages and cultures as resources for translating from one text to another. Not only is this a dynamic and creative practice, but, as discussed herein, it is also a potentially transformative act in which students critically analyze texts and potentially make intervention into the ideological conventions of the target languages.

Design and implementation

Our course, "Japanese media and translation," is a fourth-year, advanced Japanese course, which we delivered for the first time in the fall semester of 2021. Thus far, it has been offered as the only Japanese language course that also encourages the enrollment of Japanese-proficient speakers including those who would conventionally be perceived as native (L1) and heritage speakers.

Student profile

Students enrolled in the initial semester included one advanced learner of Japanese, one heritage speaker with L1 English, and seven L1 speakers of Japanese. Among those L1 speakers of Japanese, their English proficiency varied, and they included one student with native proficiency, four international students from Japan with previous experience living in English-speaking countries, and two international students from Japan without any experience of living in English-speaking countries prior to coming to Canada to attend the university. During the term, we organized students into groups of three to work on collaborative assignments in a way that ensured that these groups had comparable ranges of proficiencies in English and Japanese.

Course outline

The course contained two thematic units that focused on sociological, cultural, and sociolinguistic issues related to (a) gender and sexuality and (b) colonialism, race, and Indigeneity. Table 6.1 outlines the course content with assigned readings

Table 6.1 Course outline of "Japanese media and translation" (with assigned readings for Weeks 2–5)

Weeks, topics, and in-class activities	Audiovisual materials and related readings
Part I: Language and audiovisual media translation	
Week 1: Language and media transformation	
Week 2: Critical subtitles studies	**Readings:** • "For an abusive subtitling" (Nornes, 2007) • "Donald Richie on subtitling Japanese films" (Richie, 1991)
Part II: Gender and sexuality	
Week 3: Indexicality	**Film:** 彼らが本気で編むときは / *Karera ga honki de amutoki wa/ Close-Knit* (Ogigami, 2017) **Other audiovisual material:** A clip from ハッシュ！ / *Hush!* (Hashiguchi, 2001) **Readings:** • "Social meaning and indexicality" and "Functions of the masu form" (Cook, 2008) • "*Gengo to jendā kenkyū no arata na tenkai* [Current issues in gender and language research]" (Okamoto, 2011)
Week 4: Gender, language, and media	**Readings:** • "Transgender, non-binary genders, and intersex in Japan" (Dale, 2019) • "The formation of a sociolinguistic style in translation: cool and informal non-Japanese masculinity" (Nakamura, 2020)
Week 5: Queer language In-class presentation: Group 1 Workshop: Collaborative Learning Annotation System (CLAS)	**Film:** *Tangerine* (Baker, 2015) **Readings:** • "Queen's speech and the playful plundering of women's languages" (Abe, 2010) • "Grrrl-Queens: One-kotoba and the negotiation of heterosexist gender language norms and lesbo(homo)phobic stereotypes in Japanese" (Maree, 2008)
Week 6: Intermediality, affect, and coloniality of subtitles Workshop: Agisub (subtitle editing application) Week 7: Scene subtitles student presentations (*Tangerine*)	
Part III: Colonialism, race, and Indigeneity	
Week 8: Race and ethnicity in Japan Week 9: Dialects & よ、な／ね (*yo, na/ne*) Week 10: Contemporary Ainu culture and identities Week 11: Ainu language in transformation Week 12: Scene subtitles student presentations (*Tsuki wa docchi ni deteiru*)	

for Week 2 through Week 5. In this chapter, Gender and Sexuality (Part II: Week 3–5) is the focus of our discussion.

Course materials

Course readings are chosen from subtitles studies, sociolinguistics in both English and Japanese, and other fields that provide sociocultural contexts relevant to the specific theme of each film (see Table 6.1). In each section, we assigned students to watch two audiovisual materials (feature-length films or videos), whose primary language is either Japanese or English, prior to class sessions in which the film was first discussed. When watching subtitled audiovisual material, students watched it with the subtitles and critiqued them during class discussions. They also produced their own translations of selected lines to compare and contrast them with the existing subtitles. In addition, we also included unsubtitled materials that are less circulated beyond their primary audience so that the students needed to analyze them without the aid of subtitles and produce their own subtitles.

Course assignments

We implemented two major group assignments that involved translanguaging and peer collaboration. The first assignment was an in-class presentation in which each group selected a film of any genre based on their interests and performed a comparative analysis of its promotional materials (e.g., poster, trailer, DVD cover) and film reviews produced in Japanese and English.

The second assignment included two scene-subtitling projects where student groups created subtitles for a short segment of two course films: *Tangerine* (Baker, 2015) for English to Japanese and 月はどっちに出ている *Tsuki wa docchi ni deteiru* (Sai, 1993) for Japanese to English translation practice. Students used a shared annotation platform to work on a micro-analysis of linguistic, extralinguistic (intonation, pitch, gesture, etc.), and other audiovisual elements (mise-en-scène, cinematography, editing, sound, etc.) to examine how meaning is constructed in a multimodal manner. Based on their analysis, they translated the scene and created subtitles using a subtitle editing program. The resulting subtitles were presented to the class to discuss subtitling processes, choices, and implications. The first assignment with *Tangerine* is discussed in detail in this chapter.

Interdisciplinary translanguaging practices: Two disciplinary approaches

In the following sections, we discuss two learning activities designed based on the two disciplinary themes: one in media studies, critical approaches to subtitling, and the other in linguistics, indexical relationship to gender and sexuality. Using students' group translation samples from the fall 2021 course, we examine how such skills and knowledge built in class were applied for learners' collaborative subtitling projects.

Critical subtitles studies (Week 2)

In Week 2, we first discussed a critical approach to subtitling by drawing primarily on Abé Markus Nornes's (2007) groundbreaking writing "For an abusive subtitling" (from *Cinema Babel: Translating global cinema*). The required readings and lecture introduced students to definitions of audiovisual translation, different types and roles of audiovisual translation, and their political implications.

Drawing on critical subtitles studies (Kapsaskis, 2008; Nornes, 2007), our instruction focused on examining the political and ideological implications of subtitling and explored the following questions: To what extent does subtitling familiarize the source text, reveal its foreignness, and even defamiliarize the target language and culture? What is at stake, ideologically and politically, in each subtitling act? Nornes's (1999, 2007) influential notions of "corrupt" and "abusive" subtitling[1] are useful in discussing the tension between what Kapsaskis (2008) called "familiarizing" and "defamiliarizing" effects of subtitles. Nornes (1999) defined "corrupt" subtitling as a form of "domesticating translation" when the translator violently appropriates the source text and turns it into writing that conforms to the "rules, regulations, idioms, and frame of reference of the target language and its culture" (p. 18).

For an example of a "corrupt" subtitling, Nornes (1999) used Japanese subtitles of a short dialogue between a female and a male officer from *RoboCop* (Verhoeven, 1987):

FEMALE OFFICER: I better drive until you know your way around.
SUBTITLES: 私が運転するわ。(*Watashi ga unten suru wa*; I will drive.)
MALE OFFICER: I usually drive when I'm breaking in a new partner.
SUBTITLES: 君にはまかせられん。(*Kimi ni wa makaseraren*; I can't leave it to you.)

The Japanese translation reduces the complex power dynamics negotiated between the female and the male officers into the latter's simple domination over the former. In addition to the semantic transformation of the original dialogue, this subtitling domesticates the female officer's speech by using the soft and hyperfeminine sentence-final particle *wa* and the masculinity of the male officer's speech with the sentence ending form *-en*. Such highly gendered subtitling practice is typical in Japanese subtitles of foreign audiovisual media and literature and serves to reproduce the gender stereotypes and ideology in Japan (Nakamura, 2013, 2020; Okamoto, 2021). Here, familiarization of the source culture involves domestication of the foreign and perpetuation of the dominant ideology in the target culture.

On the other hand, "abusive" subtitling takes a more creative and experimental approach, where the resulting translation retains the foreignness of the source culture by revealing the incompleteness of the translation. Nornes (1999) used an example from Rob Young's subtitling of Yamamoto Masashi's *Tenamonya Connection* (1991), where he translates obscene expressions such as *konchikusho!* and *konoyaro!* into "!%&$#!@!!," entirely abandoning the semantic equivalence and instead creating a "sensuous" experience for the viewer through the "materiality of language" (Nornes, 2015, cited in Josephy, 2017). In Kapsaskis's (2008, pp. 42–43) words, this is subtitling's "defamiliarizing effect," which leads to an increased awareness of the foreignness of the source culture and potentially defamiliarizes the viewer's own culture. In the aforementioned *RoboCop* example, a gender-neutral translation of the original dialogue would not only bring viewers into an experience of difference of the source culture but also force them to turn their gaze back to their own culture, including the gender power dynamic, and experience its strangeness.

In class, we asked students to work in a small group to translate into Japanese the same lines of the female and male officers in *RoboCop* that Nornes (1999) discussed. After each group came up with their translation, we compared the groups' works side by side, critiquing each other's translation and discussing the differences between those variations created for viewers' understanding of the characters.

Indexical relationship to gender and sexuality (Weeks 3–5)

In Week 3, the focus of our class activity was primarily on how gender and sexuality in film are expressed, performed, negotiated, or subverted by linguistic and extralinguistic means as well as the different ways in which they have been or can be subtitled in English. Our central concern was how gender ideologies are embedded in and challenged through language use.

We adopted a sociocultural linguistic approach (Bucholtz & Hall, 2005) for the micro analysis of language and identity in discourse as it posits that speakers' language use is not a reflection of a particular social category but is instead associated with identities and personae that are interactionally negotiated and constructed in social contexts. A sociolinguistic theory of indexicality (Ochs, 1990) is particularly useful as an analytical framework with which to explore how language contributes to the social construction of gender and sexual identity of individual characters in a film. This indexical approach accounts for the diverse uses and interpretations of gendered linguistic forms in Japanese. Research on Japanese gendered language shows that few linguistic forms are directly linked to male or female speech. For example, sentence-final particles (*ne, yo, zo, ze, no, yone*, etc.), often introduced in textbooks as having gender-specific functions, are not exclusively used by one gender but rather index diverse social meanings that speakers are trying to convey in situated contexts (Cook, 2008; Matsumoto, 2002).

In the current unit, to critique the audiovisual media texts, students were encouraged to employ an indexical approach to identity construction (i.e., characters in films) in translation between the source and target languages from the following perspectives: (a) identity is a discursive social construct that emerges in situated contexts of interaction; (b) both linguistic and extralinguistic resources (e.g., gesture, intonation) can index different social meanings, such as encouragement and threat; and (c) an indexical relationship to an (extra)linguistic form in one language may or may not be available in another.

In class, students watched a short segment of the Japanese film *Hush!* (Hashiguchi, 2001), in which a gay man, Naoya, is talking to his partner Katsuhiro and their female friend Asako while preparing dinner. The clip had no English subtitles.

(a) Naoya says to Katsuhiro:
ほらもう煮たっちゃってる…。 (*hora, mou nitacchateru* "Now dinner's cooked")
(b) Naoya says to Asako, who just arrived at their place:
あ、てめえ、どこ行ってたんだよ。(*a, temee, doko ittetanda yo* "Where were you?")

While considering these two lines, students discussed how Naoya enacts different social identities depending on the individuals he is addressing. With his partner Katsuhiro, as in (a), Naoya is orienting to a gender identity often associated with female speech by speaking softly with an elongated sentence ending; with Asako, as in (b), in contrast, Naoya is using a highly vulgar second-person pronoun てめえ (*temee* "you"), which indexes masculinity and aggressiveness associated with male identity. Students further analyzed that, by using this address term toward Asako, Naoya is not necessarily expressing anger toward Asako but is rather trying to establish closeness as a token of their friendship.

Students then worked in a group to provide their own English translations of these lines without the aid of existing subtitles. In the compare-and-contrast discussion that followed, students commented that the existing subtitles were too simplistic and took almost no account of social meanings of those affective resources expressed through Naoya's speech toward Katsuhiro and Asako (e.g., vowel elongation::: and use of the address term *temee*). Some groups provided alternative translations to (b), such as "Where the hell (fuck) were you?!", which highlighted Naoya's situated and shifting gender identities that could have been lost in translation.

Another film discussed in class was 彼らが本気で編むときは (*Karera ga honki de amutoki wa* "Close-knit," Ogigami, 2017), a Japanese film that features a transgender woman, Rinko, and her struggle over gender identity and desire to become a foster mother of her partner's niece in contemporary Japanese society, where cisheteronormativity still dominates. Students watched a short clip in which Rinko and her cis colleague Yuka chat while knitting at a care home for the elderly. Rinko looks at the soon-to-be-married Yuka and speaks softly, saying, 由香ちゃん、最近きれい。なんかね、きれいさが中から溢れてる (*Yuka chan, saikin kirei. Nanka ne, kireisa ga naka kara afureteru*. "You look so pretty, Yuka. It's like your beauty is like flowing out from inside."). Yuka responds in a blunter manner: 大変なんすよ…なんせ、貧乏人同士の結婚っすからね (*taihen nan su yo . . . nanse binboo nin dooshi no kekkon su kara ne*. "It's pretty chaotic . . . cause we are getting married poor and broke.").

Students worked in a group to discuss (non)normative language use in this scene and its challenge to gender ideologies as well as ways in which Rinko and Yuka (de)construct their gender and sexual identities through their linguistic practices. Students discovered that Rinko's and Yuka's respective speeches in this particular context were indicative of crossing linguistic and ideological gender boundaries: Rinko's transgender identity is constructed through her expression of femininity (e.g., gentleness) in her gesture, gaze, and tone of voice as well as the use of *ne*, a sentence-final particle that is often found in female speech; meanwhile, Yuka, a cis woman, speaks with the sentence-ending *su*, a new polite style in Japanese that young men often adopt to meet the simultaneous demands of politeness, solidarity, and intimacy toward their superiors (Nakamura, 2021). Based on these findings, students shared their translation processes and consideration to create English subtitles for this conversation, including possibilities and challenges in translating Japanese as gendered language as well as its non-normative use, into a less gender-defined language such as English.

Another focused key linguistic feature was *onee kotoba* ("queen's language"). Maree (2008) reported that some lesbians choose to use *onee kotoba*, a parody of (hyper)feminine linguistic forms, to resist both restrictive heteronormative femininity and stereotypes of the butch lesbian. Another of Maree's (2013) studies on *onee kotoba* used among queer TV personalities illustrated its incongruent qualities as (hyper) politeness, criticism, and assertiveness to bring about comical effects induced by alternating a feminine form (*no yo*, *yone*) with exaggerated masculine speech styles (*kono yaro!*) by the same speaker. This evidence of crossing linguistic gender boundaries by socially diverse groups can be considered as both a challenge to and acceptance of the dominant ideology of heteronormativity.

We next reflect on students' applications of indexicality and subtitles studies by discussing their first subtitling assignment. With the knowledge gained from previous discussions on the intersection of gender, language, and subtitles, students tackled the task of subtitling a short segment of the American film *Tangerine* (Baker, 2015) into Japanese.

Outcomes and reflections: (Un)gendering and queering Japanese subtitles

Students watched *Tangerine* in Week 5. One of the first feature-length films shot entirely with an iPhone camera, the film gives a street-level depiction of Christmas Eve in a multiracial neighborhood of Los Angeles. The main characters are two black transgender sex workers, Sin-Dee and Alexandra. Each of the three student groups was given a clip that included dialogue in both English and Armenian (with English translation) and was asked to create Japanese subtitles for the clip. The specific scene comes from the film's climax sequence, where the two main characters are joined by their regular client, Armenian cab driver Razmik, and—unexpectedly—his mother-in-law Ashken at a little donut shop. For the purpose of comparison, our discussion focuses on the works by Groups 1 and 2, which were assigned the same segment to subtitle.

In the following scene, Alexandra, Sin-Dee, and Dinah, another character who is a cisgender woman, have a conversation in English about Ashken's dress.

Original script

ALEXANDRA: Girl, she shopped at the same store you shopped at!
(DINAH: But she wore it better, bitch!)
SIN-DEE: Nobody asked you, bitch.

Group 1 subtitles

(1.A) ALEXANDRA: ねえ、アンタのと同じトコで買ったんだわ
Nee, anta-noto onaji toko-de kattan da wa.
(1.B) SIN-DEE: 誰もアンタに聞いてないわよ、ブス
Dare-mo anta-ni kiitenai wa yo, busu.

Group 2 subtitles

(2.A) ALEXANDRA: ヤダー あの人アンタとおんなじ店で買い物したんじゃん
Yada:::, ano-hito anta-to on'naji mise-de kaimono shitan jan.
(2.B) SIN-DEE: 誰もアンタなんかに聞いてねえよ
Dare-mo anta nanka-ni kiite-nee yo.

Having studied the gendered nature of Japanese language and the overly gendered Japanese subtitles of foreign audiovisual media (Nakamura, 2020), as well as the creative and strategic use of *onee kotoba* by queer speakers (Abe, 2010; Maree, 2008), one key question students addressed was how to translate the speech of transgender and cisgender women characters. In this example, although the two student groups came up with slightly different versions of Japanese subtitles, they both used *onee kotoba* to invoke the hyperfemininity of Alexandra's and Sin-Dee's wording, tones, and gestures.

Group 1 used sentence-final particles *da wa* and *wa yo*, which typically index hyperfemininity, to translate Alexandra's and Sin-Dee's lines. "Girl" in Alexandra's original line was translated into *nee* (hey) in (1.A) or *yada::::* (oh, no) in (2.A), which are not semantically equivalent to the original word but are both often associated with women and used to initiate a conversation (1.A) or to respond to the given situation with surprise or excitement (2.A). In addition, both groups used the second-person pronoun *anta* (you), which can be used by women in a casual conversation when referring to somebody close to the speaker but is also often perceived as part of the vocabulary in *onee kotoba* (Abe, 2010). They also spelled it in *katakana* to parody and distinguish it from cis women's use of the word (Abe, 2010). Group 2 combined the feminine second-person pronoun with a masculine sentence-final form *kiite-nee yo* in (2.B) to mimic how queer TV personalities insert an exaggerated masculine form within their hyperfeminine language. During the in-class presentation, Group 1 justified their use of *onee kotoba* by explaining how it emerged not simply as an imitation of "women's language" but also in the process of queer identity-making. The deft use of *onee kotoba*, which includes hyperfeminine and occasionally masculine forms, effectively conveys the characters' negotiations of queer identities when confronted by older and conservative cis woman Ashken, who frowns on both their occupation and queerness.

The two groups approached the exchange between Razmik and Ashken in the same scene differently. In this exchange, the characters speak Armenian, and the English translation comes from the captions.

Original script

RAZMIK: What are you doing here?
ASHKEN: What are you doing here?

Group 1 subtitles

(3.A) RAZMIK: ここで何を
Koko-de nani wo
(3.B) ASHKEN: あなたがここで何してるのよ
Anata ga koko-de nani shiteru no yo

Group 2 subtitles

(4.A) RAZMIK: お義母さんここで何をしてるの？
Okaasan koko-de nani shiteru no?
(4.B) ASHKEN: あんたこそ！
Antakoso!

First, both groups decided to translate the repeated line "What are you doing here?" differently for Razmik and Ashken. Group 1 used a brief, incomplete, and gender-neutral sentence, *Koko-de nani wo* ("What are you . . .") to translate Razmik's line in (3.A) and used a longer and complete sentence that ends with the feminine particle compound *no yo* to translate Asken's line in (3.B). In this case, Asken's femininity, formality, and politeness are highlighted. During the in-class presentation, Group 1 explained that they assigned a typical hyperfeminine form seen in Japanese subtitles to Ashken to express her conservative attitude toward gender, sexuality, and family. In this manner, they clarified that their decision was intentional and distinguished their subtitling from the "corrupt" subtitling that Nornes (2007) identifies in the subtitling of *RoboCop*. On the other hand, Group 2 avoided assigning overly feminine language to the cisgender woman character to make an intervention into existing ideological convention in Japanese subtitling. Instead, this group used a complete sentence with a soft sentence-final particle *no* to translate Razmik's line and the very brief phrase *Antakoso!* ("And you!?") to translate Ashken's line. In this translation, they also used the casual second-person pronoun *anta* in (4.B) as opposed to a more formal variation *anata* in (3.B) used in the translation by Group 1. Although *anta* is more frequently used in female and queer speech, as previously mentioned, its vulgarity defies the invocation of politeness and softness often presented in Japanese translations of women's speech (Nakamura, 2013; Okamoto, 2021).

In summary, students explored an indexical approach to analyze characters' identities as constructed and negotiated through linguistic interaction. A close reading of the texts was most effectively conducted through translation processes. As in the examples of students' subtitling works, students encountered the absence of equivalent expressions when translating the original dialogue into a different language; they also learned to critique existing conventions of subtitling practices that often reproduce gender ideologies in the target linguistic and cultural community. Whatever subtitling decisions they made, students had to consider the ideological implications of their translation choices and the potential impact on the viewer's interpretations. In many cases, instead of unconsciously reinforcing binary gender norms and expectations of what is "feminine" or "masculine," students opened up the "third place" (Kramsch, 2009), a new linguistic and cultural space that emerged as a result of simultaneously reflecting upon multiple languages and cultures, including their own, while defamiliarizing and making a critical intervention into existing ideologies of the source and target cultures.

Whatever final product each group created, the processes of translation and discussion that were observed in class activities were crucial. During the in-class presentations, students compared multiple versions of subtitling and different justifications for their translation choices; they also discussed the ideological implications of their decisions. The exposure to multiple variations of subtitling was particularly impactful as it pointed to yet other possible ways in which the film could be translated and experienced by viewers.

Conclusion

This chapter discussed how we have brought together our backgrounds in linguistics and media studies into the implementation of CCBI in an advanced Japanese language course. By utilizing translanguaging and audiovisual translation as a pedagogical framework, our transdisciplinary approach facilitated students' language learning through the active mobilization of multimodal semiotic resources. What is unique about our approach, however, is that language acquisition is not necessarily the ultimate goal in our teaching; it is the use of multiple languages as a method to enhance students' translingual and transcultural literacies. Their critical subtitling often produced unconventional and even subversive expressions in both English and Japanese. What can be learned from this is that interdisciplinary collaboration in a language course can turn students from language learners to active language users and, even further, language creators.

DFG (2016) expresses concerns that "negative language ideologies, often in conjunction with other ideologies of difference, function to create unfavorable social, academic, cognitive and personal evaluation of . . . speakers of minority varieties" (p. 34). For example, research concerning learners of diverse genders and sexualities in Japanese language education is still in its infancy (Arimori, 2020). This reflects Japanese teaching materials such as textbooks, which provide very limited or no resources about language varieties like alternative and non-normative usage of gendered language that could expand learners' linguistic repertoires. As evident in our current analysis, a closer observation of everyday language use enables us to ruminate upon the social constructivist concept of language resource with which speakers detach themselves from an imposed social category or gender norms and orient to their desired identities in a given situation. This concept indeed leads us educators to reconceptualize language pedagogy in terms of how we negotiate and challenge oppressive language ideologies that exist behind it and guide learners to develop criticality in learning and using their new language as who they are and who they want to become.

One possible direction can be considered for future instruction. Many students in this course commented about how they had benefited from having group members with different linguistic backgrounds and how they complemented each other in deciding on translation choices in their subtitling assignments. However, from the perspective of second or additional language acquisition, the relationship between the role of translanguaging and the micro analysis of language learning is still inconclusive in this project. Language educators need to keep exploring how desired language learning occurs during the translanguaging practice among individual students engaging in group class discussion and collaborative assignments.

Note

1 In response to the criticism of the word "abusive" being violent and potentially misleading, Nornes (1999) later replaced "abusive" with "sensuous" (and "corrupt" with "sensible") in a talk he delivered in 2015 (Josephy, 2017). We use the original words as they have been widely cited and continue to be used by other scholars.

References

Abe, H. (2010). *Queer language: Gender and sexual identities through linguistic practices*. Palgrave Macmillan.

Arimori, J. (2020). Toward more inclusive Japanese language education: Incorporating an awareness of gender and sexual diversity among students. *Japanese Language and Literature, 54*(2), 359–371.

Baker, S. (Director). (2015). *Tangerine* [Film]. Duplass Brothers Productions; Through Films.

Baynman, M., Cronin, M., & Lee, T. K. (2019). *Translation and translanguaging*. Routledge.

Bucholtz, M., & Hall, K. (2005). Identity and interaction: A sociocultural linguistic approach. *Discourse Studies, 7*(4–5), 585–614.

Caldwell, A. M. (2001). A FLAC model for increasing enrollment in foreign language classes. *The French Review, 74*(6), 1125–1137.

Canagarajah, S. (2013). *Translingual practice: Global English and cosmopolitan relations*. Routledge.

Cenoz, J. (2013). Towards a plurilingual approach in English language teaching: Softening the boundaries between languages. *TESOL Quarterly, 47*, 591–599.

Cenoz, J., & Gorter, D. (2020). Teaching English through pedagogical translanguaging. *World Englishes, 39*, 300–311.

Chikamatsu, N. (2012). Communication with community: Connecting an individual to the world through Japanese content-based instruction of Japanese-American history. *Japanese Language and Literature, 46*, 171–199.

Chikamatsu, N. (2022). Translanguaging in language and area-studies curriculum: A Japanese FLAC course of Minamata and Fukushima in environmental humanities. In M. J. de la Fuente (Ed.), *Education for sustainable development in foreign language learning: Content-based instruction in college-level curricula* (pp. 215–232). Routledge.

Cook, H. M. (2008). *Socializing identities through speech style: Learners of Japanese as a foreign language*. Multilingual Matters.

Dale, S. P. F. (2019). Transgender, non-binary genders, and intersex in Japan. In J. Coates, L. Fraser, & M. Pendleton (Eds.), *The Routledge companion to gender and Japanese culture* (pp. 60–68). Routledge.

Douglas Fir Group. (2016). A transdisciplinary framework for SLA in a multilingual world. *Modern Language Journal, 100*(Supplement 2016), 19–47.

Fairclough, N. (1992). *Critical language awareness*. Longman.

Flynn, N. (2016). An intimate encounter: Negotiating subtitled cinema. *Open Library of Humanities, 2*(1). http://dx.doi.org/10.16995/olh.14

Geisler, M., Kramsch, C., McGinnis, S., Patrikis, P., Pratt, M. L., Ryding, K., & Saussy, H. (2007). Foreign languages and higher education: New structures for a changed world: MLA Ad Hoc committee on Foreign languages. *Profession*, 234–245.

Hashiguchi, R. (Director). (2001). *Hush!* [Film]. T. Yamagami et al. [Producer].

Josephy, D. E. (2017). *Reflection on the subtitling and dubbing of anime: The translation of gender in Perfect Blue, a film by Kon Satoshi* [Unpublished doctoral dissertation]. School of Translation and Interpretation, University of Ottawa.

Kapsaskis, D. (2008). Translation and film: On the defamiliarizing effect of subtitles. *New Voices in Translation Studies, 4*, 42–52.

Kramsch, C. (2009). Third culture and language education. In V. Cook & L. Wei (Eds.), *Contemporary applied linguistics* (pp. 233–254). Continuum.

Kubota, R., & Miller, E. (2017). Re-thinking and re-envisioning criticality in language studies: Theories and praxis. *Critical Inquiry in Language Studies, 14*(2–3), 129–157.

Kumagai, Y., & Kono, K. (2018). Collaborative curricular initiatives: Linking language and literature courses for critical and cultural literacies. *Japanese Language and Literature, 52*(2), 247–276.

Leaver, B. L., & Stryker, S. B. (2008). Content-based instruction for foreign language classrooms. *Foreign Language Annals, 22*(3), 269–275.

Li, W. (2018). Translanguaging as a practical theory of language. *Applied Linguistics, 39*(1), 9–30.

Maree, C. (2008). Grrrl-Queens: One-kotoba and the negotiation of heterosexist gender language norms and lesbo(homo)phobic stereotypes in Japanese. In F. Martin & P. Jackson (Eds.), *AsiaPacifQueer: Rethinking genders and sexuality* (pp. 67–84). Routledge.

Maree, C. (2013). Writing Onê: Deviant orthography and heteronormativity in contemporary Japanese lifestyle culture. *Media International Australia Incorporating Culture and Policy, 147*, 98–110.

Matsumoto, Y. (2002). Gender identity and the presentation of self in Japanese. In S. Benor, M. Rose, D. Sharma, J. Sweetland, & Q. Zhang (Eds.), *Gendered practice in language* (pp. 339–354). CSLI.

Nakamura, M. (2013). *Honyaku ga tsukuru nihongo: Hiroin wa onna kotoba o hanashi tsuzukeru* [Translation and Japanese: Heroines speak women's language]. Hakutakusha.

Nakamura, M. (2020). The formation of a sociolinguistic style in translation: Cool and informal non-Japanese masculinity. *Gender and Language*, *14*(3), 244–262.

Nakamura, M. (2021). The indexical regimentation of a male youth style in Japanese: Two approaches of metapragmatic discourse on a Q&A website. *East Asian Pragmatics*, *6*(1), 219–237.

Nornes, A. M. (1999). For an abusive subtitling. *Film Quarterly*, *52*(3), 17–34.

Nornes, A. M. (2007). *Cinema Babel: Translating global cinema*. University of Minnesota Press.

Nornes, A. M. (2015). *Afterthoughts on 'For an Abusive Subtitling'* [Keynote address]. Subtitle and Translation and Foreign Communication. Rikkyo University.

Ochs, E. (1990). Indexicality and socialization. In G. Herdt, R. Shweder, & J. Stigler (Eds.), *Cultural psychology: Essay on comparative human development* (pp. 287–307). Cambridge University Press.

Ogigami, N. (Director). (2017). *Karera ga honki de amu toki wa [Close-knit]* [Film]. Paradise Cafe.

Okamoto, S. (2011). Gengo to jendā kenkyū no arata na tenkai [Current issues in gender and language research]. *Nihongogaku*, *30*(14), 232–243.

Okamoto, S. (2021). How do female and male characters speak in the Japanese translation of English Crime Novels? *Contrastive Pragmatics*, 1–28.

Richie, D. (1991). Donald Richie on subtitling Japanese films. *Mangajin*, *10*, 16–17.

Sai, Yo. (Director). (1993). *Tsuki wa docchi ni deteiru* [All under the moon] [Film]. Cinequanon.

Sato, S., Hasegawa, A., Kumagai, Y., & Kamiyoshi, U. (2017). Content-based instruction (CBI) for the social future: A recommendation for critical content-based language instruction (CCBI). *L2 Journal*, *9*(3), 50–69.

Stoller, F. L. (2008). Content-based instruction. In N. H. Hornberger (Ed.), *Encyclopedia of language and education* (pp. 1163–1174). Springer.

Verhoeven, P. (Director). (1987). *RoboCop* [Film]. Orion Pictures.

7 Wellbeing and Chinese language study
A case of cross-disciplinary teaching

Chieh Li, Ann Cai, and Dongying Liu

Introduction

Recent years have witnessed increasing collaboration between language educators and experts in other disciplines (de la Fuente, 2022). Whether the purpose is to increase enrollment in language classes or enhance the quality of language education, content-based instruction (CBI) has been increasingly adopted in foreign language teaching so that language learners can not only develop language proficiency but also gain knowledge about concepts in non-language disciplines such as art, literature, history, and religious studies (Chikamatsu, 2019; Stryker & Leaver, 1997). According to Stryker and Leaver (1997), there are a myriad of CBI models and strategies ranging from language instructors independently designing and integrating specific content in a foreign language class to language instructors offering a course to help students learn and use a foreign language as a research tool for another content course offered concurrently.

This chapter reports on two projects carried out during the Summer China Dialogue of Civilization Program (Dialogue Program, hereafter), which was embedded as a cultural learning component designed for North American undergraduate students in a language immersion program at a regional university in Yunnan province, China. Aiming to develop students' Chinese language proficiency while enhancing their understanding of wellbeing as a cultural and interdisciplinary concept, the two projects featured curricular collaboration among faculty in four distinct disciplines: Chinese as a foreign language education, evolutionary psychology, Buddhism philosophy, and quantum physics. We first introduce the theoretical frameworks guiding the project design and implementation and then share how the cross-disciplinary collaboration was initiated and evolved. Next, we describe how each project was implemented in 2019, which is followed with respective data on student feedback. Finally, we reflect on students' language learning in both projects from a transdisciplinary perspective and offer pedagogical suggestions for colleagues interested in replicating or emulating the projects in their own language programs.

DOI: 10.4324/9781003266976-9

Theoretical frameworks

Integral education

The interdisciplinary collaboration between the authors was primarily inspired by the principals of integral education (Adams & Bell, 2016; Esbjörn-Hargens et al., 2010; Ferrer et al., 2005), an emerging educational approach that encourages accepting different conceptualizations of reality and expanding learners' inquiry by crossing disciplinary boundaries. Integral education promotes four dimensions of learning: experience, culture, behavior, and learning system (Wilber, 2000), with a focus on students' self-awareness through the development of the physical, emotional, mental, and spiritual domains. It also recommends "individual and collective social practices" to better understand ethnographic issues nationally and globally (Weis & Fine, 2012, p. 185). Both projects reported in this chapter focus on the central theme of wellbeing, which is a concept that can be understood from diverse cultural and disciplinary perspectives. By following the principals of integral education, students participating in the projects were expected to develop a deep understanding of wellbeing by reading interdisciplinary interpretations of its one or more aspects while conducting cross-cultural comparison.

Transdisciplinary approach to second language acquisition (SLA)

As the focus of both projects was Chinese language learning, the transdisciplinary approach to second language acquisition (SLA) provides additional theoretical guidance for the design and implementation of both projects (Douglas Fir Group, 2016; Hall, 2019). The transdisciplinary framework is a new and problem-oriented approach to understanding multiple dimensions of learning additional languages. Viewing language learning as a complex and dynamic process, this framework seeks to transcend the boundaries of academic disciplines, such as linguistics, anthropology, cognitive science, psychology, and sociology, and generate understanding by unifying multiple layers of SLA (Hall, 2019). Based on this framework, language learning involves three mutually dependent levels of social activity: micro, meso, and macro levels. At the micro level, language learners draw on their cognitive and emotional capacities to process diverse semiotic resources around them and form their multilingual repertoires. According to Hall (2019), "the more extensive and complex the contexts of interaction become over time and the more enduring L2 learners' participation is in them, the more complex and enduring their multilingual repertoires will be" (p. 7). At the meso level, language learners' relationships with people and interactions in diverse social contexts shape the semiotic resources accessible to them as well as their reactions to these resources, which eventually influences their L2 development. At the macro level, how learners approach language learning and how resources are provided to them are also shaped by larger ideological structures at the institution and society levels. It is important to note that these levels of social activity coexist and constantly interact with one another.

Background of the cross-discipline collaboration

The cross-discipline collaboration was initiated by a language expert who has been exploring ways to reduce students' anxiety when taking Mandarin Chinese language classes (Fallah, 2017; McCown et al., 2011). Inspired by her personal experience with meditation, which helped reduce stress and anxiety, she reached out to a psychology professor specializing in school psychology. In their joint research, the two professors recognized the positive psychological and academic effects of meditation (Edwards, 1991; Miller et al., 1995; Shapiro & Walsh, 2003), which sparked their interest in developing students' awareness of cultural practices and understanding of wellbeing. They codesigned the first project, the Bilingual Guided Meditation project, which featured guided meditation practices in both Chinese and English language in a foreign language class. The project was launched in 2013, received multiple rounds of revisions based on students' feedback, and was then integrated into campus-based language classes as well as a study abroad program.

Driven by the first project's success, the language professor reached out to two additional experts, one in quantum physics and the other in Buddhist philosophy, to develop the new course "Understanding Natural Reality as a Path to Wellbeing," which aimed to help students develop a comparative understanding of the concept of wellbeing from three distinct disciplines. First, Buddhism is primarily concerned with the nature of the mind and the alleviation of human suffering (Wallace, 2003). Some of its key concepts are emptiness, interconnectivity/oneness, and reality as a projection of the mind, which is deeply ingrained in Chinese cultural practices and belief systems (Chu, 2019; Wright, 2017). Second, quantum physics explores physical properties of nature on an atomic scale with certain key concepts explaining our physical reality such as quantum field, entanglement, and double slit experiments (wave/particle) (Chu, 2019; Kohl, 2007). Finally, evolutionary psychology attempts to explain useful mental traits (such as memory, perception, languages) as adaptation from an evolutionary perspective (e.g., natural selection; Wright, 2017). The commonality of all three fields constitutes a potential road to achieve inner peace (Chu, 2019; Kohl, 2007; Wright, 2017). The course was first offered as a bilingual cultural comparison project in a summer study abroad program in 2019 (i.e., the Dialogue Program).

Cross-disciplinary projects

Bilingual guided meditation (BGM) project

The BGM project combines bilingual positive suggestions with guided meditation and relaxing background music, which is a contemplative practice designed to reduce college students' anxiety while learning a foreign language (Li et al., 2019). With the combined expertise of the language professor and the psychology professor, the team designed the BGM materials and conducted pilot studies in 2013 and 2014 to test its effectiveness. The project has been practiced in both regular Chinese language classrooms on a U.S. campus and as part of the Dialogue Program in China since 2015 (Cai, 2017; Li & Cai, 2018).

Project description

The BGM project has three versions. The short version, designed for regular second language (L2) classes on a college campus, has two sessions and lasts 5 minutes: 3 minutes at the beginning of the class and 2 minutes at the end of the class. Each session has nine lines, with a music break between line 3 and line 4 (see Appendix I for BGM scripts). The long versions, which last 20 or 30 minutes, are designed for L2 classes in the Dialogue Program. The Northeastern website (https://web.northeastern.edu/bilingualguidedmeditation/) has a sample of BGM in action.

Before starting the very first BGM meditation session in this project, a few steps were taken to help students understand the Chinese sentences used in the session. First, the language instructor shared a handout of the scripts and explained the content, line by line, to the class. All the Chinese characters in the handout were marked with pinyin. Depending on students' language proficiency, select key words were explained, such as 放松*relax*, 身体*body*, and 头脑*mind*. Second, students practiced reading the pinyin version out loud. Finally, students were required to record their own reading of the scripts and submit their recordings as an oral assignment. Once all students were familiar with the lines in the scripts, the language instructor led the bilingual meditation practices. During the practice, each line was said in English first and then in Mandarin Chinese. For instance, "Gently close your eyes" was followed by "轻轻地闭上你的眼睛."

Student feedback

After practicing a few sessions, students in the beginning Chinese courses started to greet the teacher with "*qing qing de*" ("gently") as opposed to "*nihao*" ("hello"). "*Qing qing de*" is the opening line of the BGM practice and is a more advanced phrase typically not covered in a beginning-level course. Some students even naturally memorized and recited the whole Chinese script by the end of the semester. In addition, the students approached the teacher with a big hug and positive sentiments after finishing the final exam for the academic term. It appeared that the environment created by BGM was conducive to developing a closer bond between the students and the instructor.

On the end-of-the-term questionnaire, students overwhelmingly reported that the BGM project was helpful for their language study. Themes of student feedback included (a) greater relaxation and calmness; (b) stress/anxiety reduction; (c) increased confidence in their performance in the Chinese class; and (d) enhanced concentration and learning in the classroom. Half of the students reported improved learning in their speaking, pronunciation, and listening skills. One student said, "It was a really good and useful experience listening to a native speaker pronounce Chinese words. It really helped me with my pronunciation." Another student learned the meaning and sound of *qing song* ("relaxed") during the practice: "If it weren't for the bilingual meditation, I wouldn't have known that '*qing song*' is 'relaxed'. I think it is super effective, personally." Students also reported enhanced concentration and mind-sharpness. One student shared, "It positively impacts performance as afterwards I feel myself more focused and alert." Students also enjoyed the general psychological benefits gained from experiential meditation practice. One student explained, "We practiced different guided meditations a few times a week and I was surprised by the results after each session. I was more relaxed, driven, motivated in life and optimistic through meditation." Another student reflected, "I think it [meditation] does help relieve stress and it gives you time to think about life in general; reflect; and develop awareness."

Bilingual cultural comparison (BCC) project

Project description

The BCC project was designed to help students develop interdisciplinary and cross-cultural understandings of wellbeing. It was embedded as a culture course in a study abroad program. Due to the focus on language learning during the study abroad program, part of the culture course was offered for the duration of 5 weeks before the study abroad trip, and students' presentations were delivered during the study abroad trip. The culture course was codesigned by the four aforementioned experts, although only the language professor was able to join students' on-site presentations during the trip.

During the 5-week pre-trip study, students were assigned weekly tasks with a focus on developing their final cultural comparison project. In each of the first 3 weeks, students were required to conduct weekly readings and participate in online class discussions via an online learning management system. The reading materials included selected articles, documentary clips, and interview recordings, which were mainly from the three chosen disciplines of thought and discoveries—that is, quantum physics, evolutionary psychology, and Buddhist philosophy. The faculty team selected and posted bilingual learning materials on each topic as starting points and encouraged students to research additional resources independently. As for the weekly online postings, students were required to post their main threads on the online discussion board by midweek. The posts reflect students' digestion of the materials they learned and their views on the topic they chose to discuss. As part of the assignment, they had to ask two follow-up questions under two other students' main posts by Friday, which the instructor responded to before Sunday. In their quiz design task, students were asked to include true/false, multiple choice, and short essay questions in their quizzes. The detailed weekly tasks are listed in Table 7.1.

During the study abroad program, students were required to complete three tasks. First, they were required to submit a weekly reflective journal on activities and interactions in China and focus in particular on how their BCC projects influenced their daily life. Second, they presented their own BCC projects on each

Table 7.1 Pre-trip weekly tasks

	Task instructions
Week 1	Students read the definitions of 11 themes based on both materials provided by the professors and additional resources they find. Among the 11 themes, some consist of two complementary concepts from two distinct disciplines whereas some focus on one major concept from one discipline. The 11 themes are quantum field vs. emptiness (空性), quantum entanglement vs. interconnectivity/oneness (万法相通), double slit experiment (wave/particle) vs. reality as a projection of the mind (相由心生), evolutionary psychology (natural selection) vs. first noble truth (sense of unsatisfactoriness) (苦谛), evolutionary psychology vs. second noble truth (impermanence of things) (无常), Buddhist philosophy, similarities between Western psychology and Buddhist philosophy, differences between Western psychology and Buddhist philosophy, mindfulness-based stress reduction, concentration meditation, and guided meditation.
Week 2	Students compare complementary concepts from different disciplines and understand benefits and real-life implications of each major concept.
Week 3	Students discuss the daily life implications of the concept(s) they have researched in the first 2 weeks.
Week 4	Students design their final presentations (to be presented in China).
Week 5	Students create their post-presentation quizzes (to be administered in China).

Tuesday and Thursday (see Appendix II for the weekly presentation schedule and topics). Third, after each student presentation, the rest of the class took a post-presentation quiz created by the presenter, which was then graded by the language professor who was also the faculty director of the study abroad program. Students earned their final project presentation scores from the sum of two components: the average score on the quizzes designed by their classmates and the average score of classmates on the quiz they designed. This approach aimed to encourage students to understand what each classmate presented and to learn how to help their classmates understand their presentation.

During the study abroad program, each student was paired with a Chinese student from the local university as a language partner, with whom they met for 2 hours each weekday afternoon. Students were encouraged to discuss with their Chinese language partners the themes covered in the BCC project and seek their input on the cultural understanding of each concept. They could also ask their language partners to help research authentic materials in Chinese on each concept and expand their Chinese vocabulary. In addition to presentations and class discussions, students also sampled a variety of meditation types consisting of mindfulness meditation, concentration meditation, and guided meditation chosen by a different student for each session.

Student feedback

Students were asked to submit a reflective essay after completing the BCC project. In general, students reported participating in this project facilitated a positive and receptive learning environment that helped expand their linguistic learning and cultural understanding of various concepts related to wellbeing. In particular, three types of benefits emerged in students' reflections. First, students reported that the BCC project increased their Chinese language proficiency by stimulating them to utilize and explore abstract concepts in Chinese. For instance, one student reflected that "my language abilities have improved as well from learning about the culture, the different aspects, and the different projects that all students did." For example, this student learned the meaning of 无常 ("impermanence") as a Buddhist concept through another student's presentation.

Second, students reported heightened and expanded cultural awareness by discovering and comparing Eastern and Western cultures. The deeper understanding in turn challenged their previous beliefs about wellbeing. One student shared,

> I had to research and present on the Buddhist idea of Emptiness and its Western counterpart, the Quantum Field. I was met with lots of new information I had never known. It was also quite surprising to see so many correlations between two subjects that seem drastically different.

Another student further elaborated,

> Through this research, I found that Western psychology and Buddhist psychology were actually similar. After listening to everyone's presentation, I found most fascinating that there were such similar and overlapping concepts in posts, both Eastern and Western ways of thinking.

Reflecting on the changes they experienced after learning the new concepts, one student shared, "Emptiness can remind me that I have many choices and I should not limit my thinking to one correct answer. Being more flexible will lead to better outcomes and more happiness."

Third, students reported enhanced wellbeing, personal growth, and inner peace through the interplay between learning about the concepts and engaging in the meditation practices. One student shared,

> I think the project between evolutionary psychology and the second noble truth of Buddhism (the impermanence of thing) was really cool. The Second Noble Truth states that humans tend to cling to things that do not last. This is incredibly relevant to me because I have anxiety, and frequently scared of change. I find that if I am able to recognize that all things change, I can work out of anxiety.

Pedagogical reflections

Inspired by the integral education approach, our team initially attempted to integrate students' academic development with increasing their understanding and practice of psychological wellbeing in the Dialogue Program. Given the bilingual and bicultural focus of the two projects included in the Dialogue Program, students' linguistic and cultural learning during the projects can be analyzed from a transdisciplinary perspective of SLA (Douglas Fir Group, 2016; Hall, 2019).

According to the transdisciplinary approach to SLA, language learning is a complex and dynamic process that engages learners' cognitive and emotional mechanisms and takes place in diverse social contexts affording a myriad of multilingual semiotic resources shaped by and shaping each learner's learning and living experience. The Douglas Fir Group (2016) claimed that "emotional and cognitive processes overlap in brain functioning and are therefore highly integrated" and "mutual influences (of cognition and emotion) are not fleeting but can be lingering, which suggests cognition and emotion interact at multiple time scales" (p. 36) in learning. Thus, integrating the BGM program's meditation practices into Chinese language classes clearly provided a positive and low-stress environment in which students felt emotionally supported when learning Chinese. The bond forged between the language instructor and the students also indicates that students developed rapport with the language instructor through the meditation practices.

In addition, both explicitly explaining the meanings of the Chinese phrases in the meditation scripts and practicing meditation following the Chinese instructions helped students develop a meaningful understanding of the phrases in appropriate contexts, as shown in the examples shared earlier. Students started to use *qing qing de* ("quietly") as a Chinese greeting before each meditation session instead of *nihao* ("hello"), which is a greeting phrase in common social interactions. Moreover, in order to make all the preselected resources accessible to students in both projects, the faculty team provided English translations and pinyin for all Chinese characters in the BGM scripts and included video clips in addition to bilingual reading materials in the BCC project. Students were also required to reflect on daily life implications of the concepts based on their real-life experiences during their sojourn abroad. Despite students' limited experiences as foreign students living for a short term in China, having language partners who were peer students from the target culture provided additional access to semiotic resources that may only be available to permanent community members in the context.

Last but not least, the wellbeing theme in the cultural learning from an interdisciplinary perspective provides meaningful contexts for students to learn complex concepts that expanded their understanding of the self and others. By analyzing the overlapping concepts in three distinct disciplines (i.e., quantum physics, evolutionary psychology, Buddhist philosophy) and exploring the real-life implications of these concepts during their study abroad trip, students recognized the limitations of their preconceptions of wellbeing and discovered the connections and uniqueness between Western and Chinese cultures. For instance, by exploring the Buddhist concept of emptiness (空性), some students learned to become more flexible, which they started to believe would "lead to better outcomes and more happiness." In other words, the content-based learning (Stryker & Leaver, 1997) afforded in the BCC project prompted students to reflect on who they are, what their relationships with the rest of the world are, and what they need to do to maintain individual wellbeing. This self-reflection and self-discovery process is important for L2 learning as it could help motivate students' executive agency, moving from an actual L2 self to an ideal L2 self (Dörnyei, 2009).

Conclusion

An increasing number of schools are searching for innovative ways to meet the academic, social-emotional, and behavioral needs of students (Wisner et al., 2010). The lessons and tools developed from our projects might be helpful to other language educators in supporting their efforts to integrate the nurturing of the wellbeing of the whole student with L2 learning. However, a few caveats need to be brought to educators' attention. Time limitations posed the greatest challenge to the implementation of the projects. At one point in the BGM project, the university administrators hesitated to authorize the language instructor to use 5 minutes of precious instruction time to do meditation in class. They believed that the language class was for teaching students language skills and, therefore, should not be used for non-language activities such as meditation (which was viewed as a non-language teaching activity). In addition, due to time and format limitations, the components of the BGM (i.e., directions, music) were not individualized to fit each student's preference to optimize engagement during the meditation process. Another challenge stemmed from time demand for implementing the two projects. Both projects complement each other if implemented in a study abroad program. However, if only the BGM project is adopted in a regular classroom, there is usually not enough time to provide additional background information on meditation and its benefits, which may impede the opportunity to stimulate a deep understanding and interest among students. Foreign language educators interested in adopting one or both projects in their own teaching may need to consider the time-related challenges highlighted here and make appropriate adjustments according to their local administrative and curricular contexts.

As we summarized in a previous paper,

> Our approach begins with one individual, in one program, in one university, but the effect can ripple into something much greater than we imagined. We hope the soft melody from our hearts can join with the collective choir of the growing development of consciousness that promotes the wellbeing of all.
>
> (Li et al., 2019, p. 11)

We hope the cross-disciplinary projects we reported in this chapter can stimulate more foreign or second language educators to integrate meaningful content and enrich language teaching and learning.

References

Adams, M., & Bell, L. A. (2016). Theoretical foundations for social justice education. In *Teaching for diversity and social justice* (pp. 21–44). Routledge.

Cai, Q. (2017). *Acceptability and preliminary outcomes of bilingual guided meditation (BGM®) in the college foreign language classroom* [Unpublished doctoral dissertation]. Northeastern University.

Chikamatsu, N. (2019). Collaborative teaching of a Japanese content-based course: 3.11 and nuclear power crisis. In C. A. Melin (Ed.), *Foreign language teaching and the environment: Theory, curricula, institutional structures* (pp. 146–160). The Modern Language Association of America.

Chu, E. L. (2019). A dialogue between Buddhism and quantum physics. In *Exploring curriculum as an experience of consciousness transformation* (pp. 41–76). Palgrave Macmillan. https://doi.org/10.1007/978-3-030-17701-0_3

de la Fuente, M. (Ed.). (2022). *Education for sustainable development in foreign language learning: Content-based instruction in college-level curricula*. Routledge.

Dörnyei, Z. (2009). Individual differences: Interplay of learner characteristics and learning environment. *Language Learning, 59*, 230–248.

Douglas Fir Group. (2016). A transdisciplinary framework for SLA in a multilingual world. *The Modern Language Journal, 100*(Supplemental 2016), 19–47.

Edwards, D. L. (1991). A meta-analysis of the effects of meditation and hypnosis on measures of anxiety. *Dissertation Abstracts International, 52*(2—B), 1039–1040.

Esbjörn-Hargens, S., Reams, J., & Gunnlaugson, O. (Eds.). (2010). *Integral education: New directions for higher learning*. Sunny Press.

Fallah, N. (2017). Mindfulness, coping self-efficacy and foreign language anxiety: A mediation analysis. *Educational Psychology, 37*(6), 745–756.

Ferrer, J. N., Romero, M. T., & Albareda, R. V. (2005). Integral transformative education: A participatory proposal. *Journal of Transformative Education, 3*(4), 306–330. doi:10.1177/1541344605279175

Hall, J. K. (2019). *Essentials of SLA for L2 teachers: A transdisciplinary framework*. Routledge.

Kohl, T. C. (2007). Buddhism and quantum physics: A strange parallelism of two concepts of reality. *Contemporary Buddhism, 8*(1), 69–82. https://doi.org/10.1080/14639940701295328

Li, C., & Cai, Q. A. (2018, August). *Mindful in two tongues: Enhancing second-language learning using bilingual guided meditation* [Paper presentation]. 2018 Annual Convention of the American Psychological Association (APA).

Li, C., Cai, Q. A., Elias, S., & Wilson-Jones, L. (2019). Mindfulness and well-being: A mixed methods study of bilingual guided meditation in higher education. *Journal of Research Initiatives, 5*(1), 3.

McCown, D., Reibel, D., & Micozzi, M. S. (2011). *Teaching mindfulness: A practical guide for clinicians and educators*. Springer.

Miller, J., Fletcher, K., & Kabat-Zinn, J. (1995). Three-year follow-up and clinical implication of a mindfulness-based intervention in the treatment of anxiety disorders. *General Hospital Psychiatry, 17*, 192–200.

Shapiro, S. L., & Walsh, R. (2003). An analysis of recent meditation research and suggestions for future directions. *The Humanistic Psychologist, 31*(2–3), 86–114.

Stryker, S. B., & Leaver, B. L. (Eds.). (1997). *Content-based instruction in foreign language education: Models and methods*. Georgetown University Press.

Wallace, B. A. (Ed.). (2003). *Buddhism & science: Breaking new ground*. Columbia University Press.

Weis, L., & Fine, M. (2012). Critical bifocality and circuits of privilege: Expanding critical ethnographic theory and design. *Harvard Educational Review, 82*(2), 173–201.

Wilber, K. (2000). *Integral psychology: Consciousness, spirit, psychology, therapy.* Shambhala Publications.

Wisner, B. L., Jones, B., & Gwin, D. (2010). School-based meditation practices for adolescents: A resource for strengthening self-regulation, emotional coping, and self-esteem. *Children & Schools, 32*(3), 150–159.

Wright, R. (2017). *Why Buddhism is true: The science and philosophy of meditation and enlightenment.* Simon and Schuster.

Appendix I
BGM materials

The 3-minute BGM script (beginning of class)

Part 1

1. Gently close your eyes. 轻轻地闭上你的眼睛。
2. Enjoy the flow of the music for a few minutes. 在接下来的几分钟里享受美好的音乐。
3. The music will relax your body and mind. 这段音乐会帮助你放松你的身体和头脑。

Part 2

4. Now your body is relaxed and your mind is alert. 现在你的身体已经完全放松,你的头脑变的非常清晰。
5. We are going to start our Chinese learning. 我们马上就要开始我们的汉语学习了。
6. Our Chinese learning will be interesting and easy. 汉语学习很有意思也很容易。
7. In this class you will naturally begin tapping into your reserved potentials. 在这堂课里,你会自然地开启你的潜能。
8. We will have a joyful learning time together today. 今天我们会有愉快的学习时光。
9. Now gently open your eyes. 现在轻轻地睁开你的眼睛。

The 2-minute BGM script (end of class)

Part 1

1. Gently close your eyes. 轻轻地闭上你的眼睛。
2. Enjoy the flow of the music for two minutes. 在接下来的两分钟里,享受美好的音乐。
3. The music will relax your body and mind. 这段音乐会帮助你放松你的身体和头脑。

Part 2

4. Now your body is relaxed and your mind is alert. 现在你的身体已经完全放松了，你的头脑变得非常清晰。
5. We are going to complete our Chinese learning today. 我们马上就要完成我们今天的汉语学习了。
6. Our Chinese learning is interesting and easy. 汉语学习很有意思也很容易。
7. What you have learned today will naturally stay in your mind. 今天你学的汉语会自然地留在你的头脑里。
8. We are looking forward to our next happy Chinese learning. 我们期待下一次愉快的学习时光。
9. Now gently open your eyes, and quietly leave the classroom. 现在轻轻地睁开你的眼睛，安静地离开教室。

Appendix II
2019 Summer cultural comparison project

Final presentation	Quantum Physics	Buddhism	Pre-trip tasks	Starting points
5/21 (T)	Quantum Field	Emptiness	1. **Definition** of the two concepts (April 5). 2. **Comparison** of the two concepts (April 12). 3. **Implication** of the correlation of the two concepts in our daily life (April 19). 4. PowerPoint Presentations (April 26). 5. Post-presentation quiz (May 3).	Video 1
5/23 (Th)	Quantum Entanglement	Interconnectivity/ Oneness		
5/28 (T)	Double Slit Experiment (Wave/Particle)	Reality is a Projection of the Mind		
	Evolutionary Psychology	**Buddhism**		
5/30 (Th)	Mindfulness-based Stress Reduction		1. **Definition** of this meditation (What–April 5). 2. **Benefits** of this meditation? (Why–April 12). 3. **Application and Practice** (How–April 19). 4. PowerPoint Presentations (April 26). 5. Post-presentation quiz (May 3).	Video 2
6/4 (T)	Concentration Meditation			Video 3
6/6 (Th)	Guided Meditation			Reading Material
	Evolutionary Psychology	**Buddhism**		
6/11 (T)	Evolutionary Psychology (Natural Selection)	First Noble Truth: Sense of Unsatisfactoriness	1. **Definition** of the two concepts (April 5). 2. **Comparison** the two concepts (April 12). 3. **Implication** of the correlation of the two concepts in our daily life (April 19). 4. PowerPoint Presentations (April 26). 5. Post-presentation quiz (May 3).	Videos 7, 8 & 9
6/13 (Th)	Evolutionary Psychology (Natural Selection)	Second Noble Truth: Impermanence of Things		
	Western Psychology	**Buddhism**		
6/18 (T)	Similarities between Western Psychology and Buddhism		1. **Definition** of the two concepts (April 5). 2. **Comparison** the two concepts (April 12). 3. **Implication** of the correlation of the two concepts in our daily life (April 19). 4. PowerPoint Presentations (April 26). 5. Post-presentation quiz (May 3).	Videos 4 & 5
6/20 (Th)	Differences between Western Psychology and Buddhism			
6/25 (T)	Introduction of Applied Buddhist Thought			Video 6

Section 3

Across communities

Language and community partner collaboration

8 Negotiating C2 expectation and Third-Space personae in transdisciplinary L2 learning

Collaboration with Chinese professionals in advanced Chinese language curricula

Xin Zhang

Introduction

Moving into the third decade of the 21st century, foreign language learners live, study, and work in an ever-expanding global market where national economies coexist in close interdependence and international organizations and multinational companies and institutions proliferate. The field of Chinese as a second language (CSL), especially CSL programs with advanced curricula, face the challenge of readjusting their program goals to accommodate learners' needs to function successfully in the current global economic market.

In the field of CSL, there has been a concerted effort among a group of Chinese language educators and scholars (Walker & Jian, 2016; Zhang & Jian, 2020) to propose the use of Third Space as a new framework for CSL pedagogy. The Third Space perspective aligns with key themes of the transdisciplinary framework (Douglas Fir Group, 2016; Hall, 2019; Ortega, 2019). Following recent thinking in the field, this chapter advocates for a shift in the focus from language proficiency to communicative performance in CSL programs for those learners with a long-term commitment to and a vision of becoming multilingual professionals in the Chinese workplace. Specifically, CSL programs should train such learners to recognize and negotiate what is culturally expected of them at the most sophisticated level to best achieve their own communicative intentions and agenda in the multilingual workplace. Showcasing the pedagogical manifestation of this proposal, this chapter discusses the collaboration between a Chinese language instructor and a Chinese professional expert in an advanced CSL course at a Sino-U.S. joint-venture university.

Theoretical rationale: a shift of focus in CSL from a transdisciplinary Third Space lens

The concept of Third Space has attracted attention in language and intercultural studies as a powerful metaphorical framework of conceptualizing and analyzing the in-betweenness, hybridity, and transformability of human encounters

DOI: 10.4324/9781003266976-11

across languages and cultures (Zhou & Pilcher, 2019). This chapter is theoretically grounded in a transdisciplinary Third Space framework for foreign language pedagogy (Walker & Jian, 2016; Zhang & Jian, 2020). Instead of presuming the existence of a static and bounded first and second culture as objective realities, a Third Space lens draws our focus beyond a monolingual/monocultural and essentialist view of what constitutes each culture and their differences toward how multilingual speakers dynamically converge, contest, and cooperate to transcend the perceived cultural divisions.

> Cross-lingual and intercultural interaction should and can open up a new field [a Third Space], where different cultures converge, contest and cooperate; where expectations for the actors and interpretations of their actions do not entirely or constantly conform to the assumptions and norms of one culture but are dynamic and fluid, motivated by specific goals of the interaction in question and negotiated among involved actors; and where the cooperative interactions of the actors' emerging multilingual and transcultural personae are made possible by, and in turn, continue to co-construct the multilingual and transcultural Third Space that is continuously becoming.
>
> (Jian, 2020, p. 8)

Such a Third Space perspective is fundamentally transdisciplinary. First and foremost, both view second language (L2) learning and, consequently, the learning of the target culture (C2) as learning to socialize in L2—specifically how to "negotiate social and linguistic action in the face of minimal common ground and maximal semiotic demands" (Douglas Fir Group, 2016, p. 23). Furthermore, both adopt a nonessential view of L2 learning with an emphasis on the openness of language in the meaning-making process. In other words, the complex meaning-making process between L2 learners and their interlocutors in the C2 is jointly construed and negotiated via multilingual and multilayered semiotic resources (Hall, 2019; Ortega, 2019). Therefore, meaning making in the Third Space is highly situated and constantly contested as the multilingual speakers and interlocutors negotiate intentions, interpretations, and expectations during the moment-by-moment unfolding of the communicative event. Lastly, both criticize viewing nativeness, or native likeness, as the ultimate goal of L2 learning. L2 learning is redefined as "successful late-time multilingualism" (Ortega, 2019, p. 25) in the sense that L2 learners should instead aim at functioning well in a new language in a variety of sophisticated life and work contexts in the C2.

Guided by the transdisciplinary Third Space framework outlined herein, this chapter advocates for a shift in the focus of foreign language program goals in the 21st century to help L2 learners develop capacities of expertly and productively negotiating intentions and expectations in the multilingual and transcultural space. L2 learners should develop capacities to co-construct successful interactions in the Third Space and move beyond a monolingual and monocultural position of "cultural gazing" to a multilingual and transcultural need of productively working together with the other (Zhang & Jian, 2020,

p. 1). The following sections introduce the rationale of highlighting learners' capacities of negotiating C2 expectations and Third-Space personae in CSL pedagogy.

Negotiate C2 expectations

L2 learning is driven by communicative needs and is situated in meaning-making interactions with others in various social contexts (Hall, 2019). Therefore, L2 learning occurs as L2 learners develop linguistic and behavior knowledge about situated social norms in the C2 as they socialize with speakers of the L2. However, simply following the situated C2 norms is not sufficient for many L2 learners. As Agar (1994) pointed out, as non-native speakers are consciously or subconsciously perceived differently by interlocutors in the C2, the nature of the L2 socialization activities in which they participate also drastically changes. Many L2 learners are immediately subject to an additional layer of aggregated C2 expectations based on how they are often stereotypically perceived. One common set of C2 expectations based on L2 learners' perceived nativeness is described by Zhang (2020) as aggregated expectations toward the imagined foreigner with regard to how well they can and should function linguistically and culturally in Chinese.

Although foreign language educators should problematize the ideologies that subscribe to such a binary opposition of natives and non-natives and the assumed uneven power relationship, it is equally important to recognize that such prejudicial ideologies are real in the sense that they have a concrete real-life impact on people's linguistic practices and their perception of others. In China, for example, the typical assumption that a foreigner is not likely to have equal or better Chinese linguistic skills than Chinese natives has been demonstrated by many foreigners living in China who are treated as culturally and linguistically incompetent outsiders regardless of their individual experience and actual capacities (Liu & Self, 2019). In contrast, Chinese heritage speakers often encounter C2 expectations that, as members of the in-group, they are obligated to speak Chinese well and perform "Chineseness" properly. Unfortunately, L2 learners who are uninformed of and unprepared to handle such divergent C2 expectations based on their racial-ethnic identities often experience frustration and, in some cases, severe identity dissonance.

In Chinese language teaching and learning, there has not been sufficient attention and efforts to orient the learners toward such C2 expectations beyond the C2 norms. Mainstream practices adopted in most CSL classrooms still predominately center around linguistic accuracy and pragmatic competence leading towards nativeness or native-likeness while learners are left to figure out strategies on their own after encountering stereotyping based on their varied social identities. This project seeks to offer an alternative pedagogical approach that treats the multiple social identities, both transportable ones (such as race, gender, nationality) and situated ones (such as student, intern, foreigner), as important resources that mediate L2 learning (Hall, 2019).

Negotiate Third-Space personae

Personae refers to ways of being or performing ideologized character types identifiable in certain (imagined) communities (D'Onofrio, 2019; Johnstone, 2017). Unlike a social identity or psychological sense of self, the appeal of persona is self-explanatory: Personae can vary from one situation to another in a moment-by-moment manner as communicative events unfold. Moreover, it draws our attention away from the multiple identity categories individuals are conceivably locked into. Persona instead highlights the co-constructed and emergent process of acting and embodying certain character types recognizable by others in the community. That is the personae one enacts are in nature co-constructed by speaker and audience on both sides of the interaction.

Speaking a second or foreign language inevitably involves making choices of linguistic codes and styles to shape desired Third-Space personae intended in given moments, which are mediated by L2 speakers' varying positions in the society (e.g., a professional, a Westerner, a woman) and the C2 expectations of them foregrounded in Third Space encounters. Zhang (2020) argued that "a Third-Space persona is most effective in resulting in fruitful intercultural engagement if it emerges from a proper recognition of situated C2 expectations and participation in negotiating various levels of expectation . . . leading toward a shared goal" (p. 38). Therefore, CSL education should aim to prepare Chinese learners for the successful enactment of desirable and effective Third-Space personae oriented toward negotiating and reaching situated communicative goals. In forming and enacting successful Third-Space personae, learners can and should make conscious use of their multilingual and diverse semiotic resources they are afforded in negotiating who they intend to be and not just who they are allowed to be.

Pedagogical manifestation

Broad teaching context

The collaborative instruction design was integral to the advanced CSL course "Professional Networking in China" offered at a Sino-U.S. joint-venture university. Located in the Jiangnan region in China, the English-medium university offers a globalized liberal arts education experience to its undergraduate students. Roughly 70% of the undergraduate student population consists of Chinese students while the remaining 30% are international students from across the globe. Since early 2020, due to the influence of the COVID pandemic on international travel, the majority of international students have been displaced outside of China and have been taking courses remotely via Zoom. The 7-week advanced CSL course is designed for CSL learners who have completed or were placed above the regular 400-level Chinese course sequence. The collaboration between a Chinese language instructor and a Chinese human resources professional was implemented in the fall semester of 2020 and then again in fall 2021. During said semesters, diverse student groups were represented in terms of both linguistic and cultural backgrounds (including heritage and non-heritage students from Europe, North America, and Asia) and classmanship (including first-year, sophomore, junior, and senior students).

The advanced CSL course "Professional Networking in China" aims to equip CSL learners with the knowledge and skills necessary to build effective personal and professional relationships. In other words, the goal is to prepare CSL learners for socializing in various groups and activities in the Chinese workplace. Although an actual internship is not a required component of this course, during the class students observe, analyze, and perform in scenarios that involve students as foreign interns or professionals in a range of Chinese professional contexts spanning from settling into a new Chinese professional environment to socializing with supervisors, colleagues, and business partners and maintaining long-term, mutually beneficial relationships. Table 8.1 presents a full list of themes covered and sample scenarios students analyzes and practiced in class, which is based on the textbook *Negotiating the Chinese workplace: An integrated course to construct learner vision of a professional persona* (Jia & Zeng, in press).

For example, in Week 1, students first read and analyze the dialogue in the textbook when a new American employee 罗杰明 (James Rogers) was introduced by the marketing manager to the team in a Chinese tech company in Beijing. Class discussion highlighted the context of the social interaction and how it indexes the cultural expectations of humbleness and collegiality from a new employee as well as demonstrable Chinese skills, experience, and/or interests in China from a foreigner. Students were then put into groups and took turns to practice performing the roles of the new employee and Chinese colleagues in contexts that involve

Table 8.1 Themes and sample workplace scenarios

Weeks	Themes	Sample workplace scenarios
W1	初来乍到 Settling down in a new Chinese workplace	Introduce yourself as a new employee in a Chinese workplace
W2	企业文化 Understanding Chinese corporate culture	Make strategic reference to humanist corporate value "以人为本" when requesting a family leave from your supervisor
W3	君子和而不同：与领导与同事的说话之道 Handling disagreement with leadership and colleagues	Express a different opinion about employee promotion to your supervisor
W4	面子、协商与妥协 Negotiation and compromise in the workplace	Negotiate a contract with an old business partner (service provider)
W5	人情往来：接风洗尘 Hosting guests and business partners	Invite an important business partner who visits your company to dinner as a local host
W6	来而不往非礼也 Maintaining relationships over time	Return favors to a colleague who has been helping you with daily tasks
W7	外籍职场人士在中国 Perception and persona: Foreign professionals in China	Politely negotiate languages used at work with Chinese colleagues

self-introduction in a new Chinese workplace. They were encouraged to make use of target expressions introduced in the textbook and supplementary materials (e.g., social etiquette video clips).

Collaborative project with a human resources professional: Chinese resume and mock job interview

The collaboration with the Chinese human resources (HR) professional is a core aspect of the curriculum collaboratively designed and carried out to help students prepare a Chinese resume and conduct a mock job interview.

Collaborator

The collaboration was between the Chinese language instructor and a career services manager Jingjing Wang (pseudonym) at the joint-venture university. With a master's degree in developmental and educational psychology, Jingjing has more than 10 years of experience in HR development in China. Before her tenure at the university, she had served as a senior HR manager, a talent assessment consultant, a headhunter, and a career counselor in various Chinese industries. The Career Services Office in which she currently works hosts English-medium career skills workshops and advising sessions on topics such as resume preparation, interview skills, internship and job searches, and professional etiquette. As an HR expert, she has expertise in preparing students for professional career development in both English and Chinese contexts and is privy to the relevant internship resources and policies.

Planning stage

The collaboration was initiated by the CSL instructor who emailed the Career Services Office in summer 2020 to set up an in-person consultation about offering a training session for resume building and interview skills for the CSL students in the professional networking class. The goals of setting up this initial conversation were two-fold: (a) introduce the course and clarify the type of support needed from the Career Services Office, including resources and information on job searches in China, a Chinese resume-building workshop, and potentially a mock job interview organized at the end of the session; and (b) establish a connection with colleagues who have expertise in HR and human development in the Chinese context and who would be interested in the collaboration. Jingjing responded to the request and expressed interest in contributing her previous experience as an HR manager in a Chinese state-owned company and her expertise as a career services manager to help the students in this course.

Overall timeline

Throughout the 7-week session, a series of tasks and assignments were designed around the two main collaborative activities: the Chinese resume workshop in

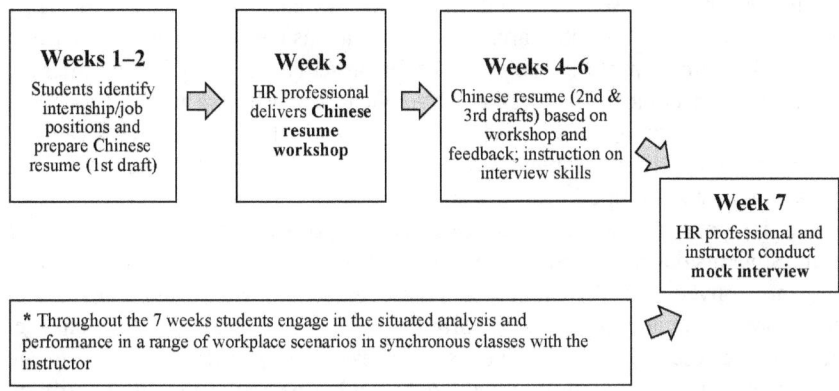

Figure 8.1 Collaboration timeline

Week 3 and the final mock interview in Week 7. The CSL faculty member took the lead in setting up the overall learning goals, scheduling activities, and designing tasks and assignments that prepared students for the workshop and mock interview; whereas the career services expert's direct involvement included providing the most updated information and resources (e.g., recommending Chinese websites for internship and job positions and the mentor-mentee matching program on LinkedIn China), preparing and giving a workshop on how to build a Chinese resume as a non-Chinese job applicant, and serving as the interviewer in the mock job interview. The flow chart in Figure 8.1 illustrates the 7-week timeline of the collaboration.

Resume workshop: Recognizing situated C2 norms and C2 expectations

The resume workshop was designed to assist CSL students to recognize and make sense of the C2 norms mediated by their individual transportable and situated identities (i.e., a foreign college student of a particular social class, gender, race, ethnicity, and nationality from a Sino-foreign university in China applying for a particular intern position). Prior to the workshop, each student was asked to identify a real internship position in China via Chinese job-search websites according to their major and future career plans. They were required to prepare a first draft of their Chinese resume based on the position they chose. Although none of the students had written a Chinese resume in the past, they had varying degrees of experience in resume writing in English or other languages. This preparatory task prompted students who had already been socialized into resume-writing activities in their first language (L1) to hypothesize ways of transferring that L1 knowledge and experience to resume writing in Chinese.

In Week 3, Jingjing gave a Zoom-based workshop to students about Chinese resume writing. The workshop was carried out in Chinese and covered the functions of a resume in the job search as well as the basic elements and format of a resume for Chinese professional purposes. In particular, the workshop highlighted the covert expectations for foreign job applicants in Chinese workplaces (e.g., linguistic and cultural skills and global perspectives Chinese employers value in a foreign job applicant). Table 8.2 lists key topics covered in the resume-writing workshop hosted by Jingjing.

Jingjing gave feedback as an experienced HR professional on the first resume drafts students developed. She primarily offered top-down feedback with a focus on genre conventions of a Chinese resume (e.g., style, layout, and other ways of better presenting and categorizing information and experiences in different sections of the resume) and effectiveness of presenting experience tailored to the specific position (e.g., describing actions taken by the applicant and quantifying outcomes of the actions with concrete numbers). The second round of feedback focused on the linguistic accuracy and style in addition to the global-level issues. Prior to the final mock job interview, students had a finalized Chinese resume ready.

Table 8.3 shows a sample section from a first draft of a resume that focused on students' designing skills and experiences, which were reorganized and elaborated on in the final draft after two rounds of feedback and revision. The example shows major improvements at three interwoven levels: genre conventions, linguistic style, and content. In terms of genre convention, what was lumped into a section named 设计与创作能力 ("Design and Creativity Skills") in the first draft was rearranged into three sections in the final draft typical for a Chinese resume: 设计经历 "Design Experience," 实习经历 "Internship Experience," and 个人技能 "Personal Skills." The Design Experience section was highlighted and listed as a separate section from the other internship experiences to be tailored to the designer position the student was targeting. One example of the improvement in both linguistic and content aspects is the elaboration of the student's graphic design experience. Translated from a bulleted item in the student's English resume, the short description 做过面向儿童教育市场的平面设计 ("Had graphic design experience for children's education industry") in the first draft was vague and insufficient to demonstrate the student's actual skills and involvement. The final draft included a detailed description of the project to outline the time, hosting organization, as well as the student's title (宣传/平面设计 "publicist/graphic designer"), responsibilities (采用绘画软件 "Office Publisher, Adobe Photoshop" 画出引人注目的海报, 帮忙宣传XX会的培训班 "Created eye-catching flyers using Office Publisher and Adobe Photoshop to promote the organization's training program"), and outcomes achieved (活动完成后英语班、备考班与报税班报名人数新增40 "Led to 40 new enrollments in the English, Test Prep, and Tax programs"). The student also highlighted their multilingual skills in the Personal Skills section of the finalized resume, which was not included in the first draft.

Table 8.2 Topics covered in the Chinese resume workshop

Topic	Tasks

Composing an effective resume
 	
简历撰写的要点
	• 与岗位匹配
	  Match the position
	• 简洁明了
	  Be concise
	• 强调行动和成果
	  Highlight actions and outcomes
	• 用数字量化成果
	  Quantify the outcomes with numbers
	• 识别技能并加以呈现
	  Identify demonstrable skills

Basic elements in Chinese resume in a Chinese workplace (vs. English resume)
 	
中文工作环境下简历的基本要素 (区别于英文简历)
	• 个人信息: 姓名、联系方式
	  Personal information: name, contact information
	• 可选个人信息：性别、年龄、政治面貌、籍贯、民族、照片
	  Optional information: gender, age, political affiliation, place of household registration, ethnicity, photo
	• 求职意向/自我评价/背景综述
	  Position applied/self-evaluation/summary of background
	• 教育背景
	  Education background
	• 工作实习经历
	  Work and internship
	• 社会实践/社团工作经历
	  Involvement in experiential learning/student organization
	• 其他信息
	  Other information

What skills and experiences do Chinese employers value in a foreign job applicant?
 	
对于国际求职者中国雇主还关注什么？
	• 中文能力 Chinese language capacities
	• 对本国语言文化的理解和传播
	  Knowledge and competency in their first language and base culture
	• 对中国文化的理解、尊重和融入
	  Willingness to respect and socialize into Chinese culture
	• 国际化的视野
	  Global perspectives

Mock interview: Negotiating multilingual Third-Space personae while navigating C2 expectations

During Weeks 2–6, students were guided first to watch and discuss selected job interview excerpts from a popular reality show 令人心动的Offer ("The Exciting Offer") about eight young Chinese interns' experiences seeking a final offer at a law firm in Shanghai. The selected excerpts highlighted the performance of these young people during the interview with live commentary made by a group

Table 8.3 Sample sections in a student resume: 1st draft and final draft

1st draft	设计与创作能力 Design and Creativity • 做过面向儿童教育市场的平面设计 • 为尚舞艺舞蹈学校设计销售方案、在微信和 Instagram 上推广舞蹈课程 • 精通Photoshop, Premiere Pro软件；懂基础Python编程语言
Final draft	**设计经历 Designing Experience** 2017年7月–2018年 7月　　XX项目：宣传/平面设计 July 2017–July 2018　　　XX Project: Event Promotion/Design 项目描述 Project Description： 1、采用绘画软件（Office Publisher, Adobe Photoshop）画出引人注目的海报,帮忙宣传多华会的培训班。 2、活动完成后英语班、备考班与报税班报名人数新增40。 **实习经历 Intern Experience** 2019年7月–2020年7月　　尚舞艺舞蹈学校：媒体协调员/前台 July 2019–July 2022　　　Shangwuyi Dancing School: Media Coordinator/Receptionist 1、使用SaaS管理会员账户、每星期写关于学员数目的报告。 2、设计销售方案，在Instagram上推广舞蹈课程；Instagram账号每月平均新增关注人数80。 **个人技能 Personal Skills** 软件：精通Photoshop, Premiere Pro软件；熟悉基础Python, HTML5, CSS3编程语言 语言：英语（母语）、中文普通话（熟练）、法语（基础）

of celebrities and law professionals as special observers of the interns. These concrete cases analyzed in class offered students an opportunity to learn about not just the general procedure and principles of job interviews in the Chinese workplace but also how linguistic and other semiotic resources were used in the situated meaning-making process between the individual interviewers and interviewees in a well-defined interview context. Simultaneously, in class the students analyzed and practiced a series of transferrable communicative strategies that could be applied to an interview context (e.g., self-introduction on the first day of work, expressing interests in and knowledge about a position, responding to compliments, politely negotiating with superiors). In doing so, they learned how one negotiate professional persona in these specific workplace contexts. These curricular designs led to the final mock job interview for a specific job or internship position that each student chose based on their vision of their future career.

The mock interview was scheduled for the last week of class. Before the interview, the instructor and career services expert worked together to develop the mock interview script including a list of interview questions and corresponding C2 expectations—that is, responses considered appropriate and desirable by Chinese HR experts and employers (see Table 8.4 for a few sample questions). In designing the interview script, it was crucial to combine expertise from both the CSL faculty and career services expert to ensure that

Table 8.4 Sample interview questions and corresponding C2 expectations[1]

Interviewer questions	Situated C2 expectations (linguistically and culturally appropriate behaviors)
1、XX同学你好，我是今天的面试官。谢谢你来参加今天的面试。 Hi, [name of the student]. I am the interviewer today. Thank you for participating in the interview today.	• Greet and address the interviewer properly • Show appreciation for the interview opportunity and interest in the position/organization • Demonstrate confidence (linguistically and kinesthetically)
2. 能不能请你先做个两到三分钟的自我介绍，如果在相关领域里有过一些实践的经历，也请给我们讲一讲。 Could you give up a quick 2- or 3-minute self-instruction? Tell us about your experience, if any, in relevant fields.	• Give formal self-introduction to demonstrate domain-specific expertise
3. 你的中文说得可真不错啊！看你的简历也这么优秀，还会说多种语言！为什么申请我们公司的这个职位呢？ You speak Chinese well! Your resume is impressive, and you speak multiple languages! Why are you interested in this position at our company?	• Respond to compliment and show humbleness • Demonstrate multilingual/multicultural background and global perspectives • Elaborate on your interests in the position and the company

the general interview questions aligned with interview strategies and social scenarios practiced in class (so that the students were not ambushed by entirely unexpected questions) and that the specific questions and procedure for each student were individualized to resemble real-life job interviews in Chinese professional contexts.

For the mock interview, Jingjing performed the role of an HR manager from the hiring company who was the main interviewer asking questions during the interview. The CSL instructor performed the role of an HR officer (Rita) from the hiring company who set up the interview and collected the resume from students via email. This work division also freed up the instructor during the interview to observe and take detailed notes on each student's performance for inclusion in individual feedback. The mock interview supported students by offering opportunities to socialize in Chinese workplaces through the job interview event. The following sections offer a case analysis of one student's performance during the mock interview that revealed the intended learning outcomes of this course—namely, to help students develop awareness of and strategies for navigating the covert C2 expectations and social norms in situated professional contexts and, while doing so, to negotiate a Third-Space persona appreciated by Chinese professionals in a specific disciplinary domain or industry.

A case of student performance: navigating C2 expectations and negotiating an effective and desirable Third Space persona in the mock interview

Analysis of the recorded interactions during the mock interview revealed that students employed individualized strategies to navigate the situated C2 expectations manifested in the moment-by-moment unfolding of the conversation between the interviewer and themselves. Excerpt 1 and Excerpt 2 showcase how a student negotiated a desirable persona as a multilingual speaker with the interviewer without conforming entirely to the C2 norms. The student is a male junior student from a European country who started learning Chinese in high school.

Excerpt 1

面试官： 你的中文说得这么好，是不是你们学校中文最好的学生？

Interviewer: You speak Chinese so well. Is your Chinese the best among students at your university?

学生： 哪里哪里（微笑），我还要学习很多。但是，对，我在高中就开始学中文了。

Student: It's nothing (smiled), I have a lot to learn. But yes, I started learning Chinese in high school.

面试官： 嗯（赞许地点头）。

Interviewer: Em (nodded with smile).

学生： 我妈妈也教了我，她是30年前在复旦大学学习中文的，所以....

Student: My mother also taught me. Thirty years ago, she studied Chinese at Fudan University, so . . .

Excerpt 2

面试官： 你的中文英文都很棒，还会很多别的语言对吧。今后有机会我们员工也要跟你请教一下怎么学外语，请你分享一下经验。

Interviewer: Your Chinese and English are both great, and you speak many other languages, right? In the future when there's a chance, our employees should learn from you about how to learn foreign languages. You should share your experiences.

学生： （微笑）我，对对，就是我很喜欢学语言。现在正在学习俄语和法语，但是我觉得就是，我还没有，就是没有那么大的经历[值得分享]。我学中文和英文特别棒，其他的语言还要学习很多。

Student: (Smile) I, right, right, I really enjoy learning languages. I'm currently learning Russian and French, but I think I haven't, haven't got that many experiences [to share]. My Chinese and English are great, but other languages I still have so much to learn.

面试官： 好，也很谦虚。

Interviewer: Well, you are very humble, too.

In response to a compliment on his Chinese in Excerpt 1, the student first answered with the phrase 哪里哪里 ("It's nothing"), which is a conventional way of expressing humbleness. However, instead of sticking to the humble persona, he continued to highlight his Chinese learning history and the fact that he was influenced by his mother who studied Chinese at Fudan University 30 years ago, presenting himself as an experienced and confident CSL speaker. Excerpt 2 offers another example of how a humble, yet confident foreigner persona was enacted and co-constructed. The student's response to the interviewer's compliment on his multilingual competency was twofold. The first message was an explicit acceptance of the compliment by confirming his passion for language learning. The second—and what he intended to emphasize—was that he still has a long way to go as a multilingual speaker. At the linguistic level, the student's utterance 我的中文和英文特别棒 ("My Chinese and English are very good") could be interpreted as the opposite of humbleness in Chinese. But the context helped clarify the intended meaning. The statement was followed by a modest statement: 其他的语言还要学习很多 ("but other languages I still have so much to learn"). The student's response was taken up by the interviewer as an enactment of confidence as opposed to arrogance and, thus, did not contradict the established humble persona. If anything, the foreignness embodied in the sometimes unconventional and ungrammatical use of Chinese probably prompted the interviewer to be more lenient when interpreting the student's intention. This analysis is supported by the fact that, in both exchanges, the humble and confident multilingual foreigner persona was picked up and accepted by the interviewer, as indicated by the interviewer's explicit verbal comment 也很谦虚 ("very humble too") and nonverbal cues such as nodding and smiling. In both excerpts, the student recognized the situated C2 expectation mediated by his social roles as an (imagined) interviewee in China. He played along by embodying both humbleness and confidence, which is appreciated and often interpreted as elite globalism in a foreign employee in the Chinese workplace.

Discussion and conclusion

As shown in the analysis of students' actual performances in resume writing and the mock interview, students made noticeable progress in recognizing and employing individualized strategies to negotiate, comply, and contest the situated C2 norms and expectations in meaning-making processes with a Chinese professional. The sample student performance showed that the student deployed multilingual and diverse semiotic resources in co-constructing a desirable humble and confident foreigner persona with the interviewer. Through the process of negotiating the Third Space persona, which is neither entirely native nor non-native, the students engaged in effective Chinese learning and socializing events that oriented them toward functioning well in the Chinese workplace as multilingual professionals. The promising learning outcomes are a testament to the proposed shift of CSL program goals and the effectiveness of the pedagogical practices implemented in the advanced CSL curriculum and the collaborative instruction.

This chapter concludes by offering the following summary and reflection for foreign language teachers and program designers who wish to prepare students for handling real-life C2 expectations in the long term. First, to situate L2 learners in appropriate social contexts, teaching practices and pedagogical materials should be grounded in concrete real-life encounters between the L2 learners and their interlocutors. Within the curriculum, we should embrace opportunities of collaboration with L2 speakers from the C2 communities such as Chinese professionals and language partners. The more routine and frequent learners' socializing experiences are with a variety of interlocutors in L2, the more likely they will develop stable situated linguistic and behavioral knowledge in their repertoires (Hall, 2019).

Second, L2 learners should not just learn to follow the C2 norms and become "L2 natives." Instead, our teaching practices should afford them with opportunities to engage in L2 learning from their varied positionalities (e.g., as a Chinese-speaking foreigner, an intern, a female student) and provide strategies that help them draw from their multilingual and diverse semiotic resources to navigate complex sets of situated C2 expectations. The CSL instructor made great efforts to emphasize the CSL learner's identity and agency in the mock interview task, which is a pedagogical adaption at the meso level from the transdisciplinary perspective.

Finally, when assessing student performance from a transdisciplinary Third-Space perspective, a dynamic and individualized rubric should be developed that considers the use of diverse semiotic resources beyond linguistic accuracy defined in a monolingual sense. Mutual intelligibility and effectiveness in negotiating intentions and expectations in the Third Space should be considered instead. If we see student performance as a meaning-making process in L2, then the meaning remains "ambiguous and contested" (Ortega, 2019, p. 30) as different interlocutors could perceive the same utterance in a positive or negative way. As language teachers, we should put less weight on assessing the utterance itself and put more weight on assessing how successful individual learners are in negotiating the meaning.

Note

1 The questions of the mock interview are adapted from the Chinese course "21st century China" (体演中国职场文化) offered at University of Mississippi in 2020 by Zhini Zeng.

References

Agar, M. (1994). *Language shock: Understanding the culture of conversation*. William Morrow.

D'Onofrio, A. (2019). Complicating categories: Personae mediate racialized expectations of non-native speech. *Journal of Sociolinguistics*, *23*(4), 346–366. https://doi.org/10.1111/josl.12368

Douglas Fir Group. (2016). A transdisciplinary framework for SLA in a multilingual world. *The Modern Language Journal*, *100*(Supplement 2106), 19–47.

Hall, J. K. (2019). *Essentials of SLA for L2 teachers: A transdisciplinary framework*. Routledge.

Jia, J., & Zeng, Z. (in press). *Negotiating the Chinese workplace: An integrated course to construct learner vision of a professional persona* [field test version]. Foreign Lanuage Publications.

Jian, X. (2020). Negotiating a co-constructed multilingual and transcultural third space. In X. Zhang & X. Jian (Eds.), *The third space and Chinese language pedagogy* (pp. 7–25). Routledge.

Johnstone, B. (2017). Characterological figures and expressive style in the enregisterment of linguistic variety. In C. Montgomery & E. Moore (Eds.), *Language and a sense of place* (pp. 208–300). Cambridge University Press.

Liu, Y., & Self, C. C. (2019). Laowai as a discourse of othering: Unnoticed stereotyping of American expatriates in Mainland China. *Identities*, 1–19. https://doi.org/10.1080/1070289X.2019.1589158

Ortega, L. (2019). SLA and the study of equitable multilingualism. *The Modern Language Journal, 103*, 23–38.

Walker, G., & Jian, X. (2016). *A Chinese language pedagogy for the 21st century: Basic assumptions* [Video]. YouTube. www.youtube.com/watch?v=ApNFVYHKIeU

Zhang, X. (2020) Native speaker effects, C2 receptivity of learner and co-construction of Third-Space personae: A pedagogy of target culture expectation. In X. Zhang & X. Jian (Eds.), *The third space and Chinese language pedagogy* (pp. 26–44). Routledge.

Zhang, X., & Jian, X. (Eds.). (2020). *The third space and Chinese language pedagogy: Negotiating intentions and expectations in another culture*. Routledge, Taylor & Francis Group.

Zhou, V., & Pilcher, N. (2019). Revisiting the "third space" in language and intercultural studies. *Language and Intercultural Communication, 19*(1), 1–8.

9 Internships at Japanese orphanages

A case study of a first-year Japanese language student's growth

Nobuko Koyama

Introduction

Interactions are key to successful second language (L2) learning. Communities can enable L2 learners to interact with others in different settings, contexts, and activities. From this perspective, overseas internships provide a unique opportunity for L2 learners to experience their target language communities, while gaining hands-on work experience, reshaping one's identity, and building agentive powers for personal and linguistic growth.

Overseas internships differ significantly from study abroad programs and domestic internships as experiential learning opportunities. The effects and benefits of these overseas internships are extensive and include gaining linguistic and intercultural competence, learning the values and worldviews of people from different cultures, exploring one's potential career interests, and developing one's overall personal growth (He & Qin, 2017; Kolb & Kolb, 2005; Koyama, 2020; Toncar & Cudmore, 2000; Twombly et al., 2012).

This chapter examines how overseas internships foster L2 learners' holistic growth and, in particular, how this contributes to their language development. To that end, we first describe a unique overseas internship program called the Japan Children's Home Internship Program (JCHIP) and present a case study involving a first-year Japanese language student. After his internship, his language growth was so exceptional that he managed to pass all second-year language courses. The analysis of his experience allows us to understand how his language growth was enabled through the internship.

Japan Children's Home Internship Program (JCHIP)

Unlike other internships and study abroad programs, in the JCHIP interns cannot resort to nonparticipation (Norton, 2001) or language avoidance (Pellegrino Aveni, 2005). JCHIP interns are placed in a "no-way-out situation" by living in onsite quarters, which reinforces an immersion setting from breakfast until bedtime while performing their daily chores and tasks, thereby forcing them to interact with others in Japanese, regardless of their language skills. Furthermore, throughout the history of the JCHIP, most interns often end up forming special relationships and a strong rapport with some of the children, if not all of them. Through their interactions with these children, the interns gain a unique insight into Japanese culture in addition to improving their language skills (Koyama, 2020).

The JCHIP was established in 1993 as a nonacademic internship program by the late Eiko Taylor, a Japanese language lecturer at the University of California, Davis (UCD). One summer, Taylor volunteered at a children's home in Kyoto after which she expressed her strong appreciation for this particular experience. This volunteer experience prompted her to launch the JCHIP for UCD students to experience full immersion learning opportunities. Since then, 13 to 15 UCD students have been selected every summer to be JCHIP interns who volunteer at affiliated children's homes in Japan for a 10-week period.

Children's homes are a combination of orphanages and group homes (termed orphanages hereafter). This summer internship program is affiliated with eight orphanages across Japan from the northernmost Aomori, Fukushima, Saitama, Tokyo, Yokohama, Aichi, and Kyoto regions to the southernmost Kumamoto. These orphanages each home 40 to 90 children, 2 to 18 years old, with no on-site English-speaking supervisors. They provide shelter for underprivileged children for various reasons including those who are wards to these orphanages after being orphaned, victims of domestic abuse, and victims of their legal guardians' financial hardships. Many of these children have emotional scars and psychological difficulties, which interferes with interns' efforts to develop good rapport with them. It takes more than simple language skills to be able to communicate effectively with them.

To be eligible for the program, prospective interns must have completed at least 1 year of university-level Japanese language courses, although their language proficiency still varies from beginner to near-native levels. Because most orphanages request two interns, students are paired based on their proficiency levels. When possible, a student with a lower proficiency is paired with another with a higher proficiency to ensure that they can support each other and communicate with the supervisors overseeing interns at the orphanages. Their volunteer work includes basic housekeeping chores, daily activities with the children (e.g., playing with them, helping them with their homework), and assisting the Japanese staff who work around-the-clock to help manage the orphanages in terms of housekeeping, supervising children, and serving as social counsellors. JCHIP interns also participate in summer events, including local summer festivals, camping, and various field trips with children and staff. As cultural ambassadors of UCD, they are tasked with hosting English language lessons and cultural events at their respective orphanages. The cultural events reflect the diversity of JCHIP interns, varying from American to Vietnamese culture, as many interns are multicultural and multilingual.

In exchange for their volunteer work, the orphanages provide the interns with room and board wherein they spend their time alongside the children and staff (Koyama, 2020). Upon completion of their internships, the participating students can claim a transcription notation to have their internship officially recorded on their university transcript (Internship and Career Center at the University of California, Davis, 2021), although no academic units are awarded.

Interactions and communities

Language learning on an overseas internship site such as the JCHIP can be interpreted from theories on communities, interaction, and language learning. The unique aspects of the relationship between communities and learning have been delineated in Lave and Wenger's (1991) theory on communities of practice. They examined how apprenticeship learning occurred through participation and viewed learning as a "situated activity" (p. 29) that "involves the whole person" (p. 53)—that is, "becoming a different person with respect to the possibilities enabled" through participation and engagement in communities (p. 53). This holistic learning process leads to the establishment of new identities as participants further develop their affiliations with their communities (Wenger, 1998). Lave and Wenger's (1991) notion of situated learning has been extended to examine "how learners' affiliation with imagined communities might affect their learning trajectories" (Kanno & Norton, 2003, p. 242). According to Kanno and Norton (2003), language learning will occur or be accelerated (or even discouraged) when we engage in establishing personal connections with our target language communities. As a case in point, L2 learners may inhabit their imagined target language communities where they connect and interact with the native speakers of their target language. Their imagination could motivate them, incentivize their learning, and advance their L2. They may simultaneously develop their imagined L2 identities, which in turn affect their learning (Kanno & Norton, 2003; Norton, 2000, 2001; Trentman, 2013; Wenger, 1998).

As a Japanese language teacher, I have encountered many learners who first dabbled in Japanese because of their affinity with Japanese pop culture (e.g., anime, manga, video games, and J-Pops). Many aspired to travel to Japan someday. In some cases, their prior sojourn stimulated their imagination and enabled them to develop their version of Japan or an imagined Japan. Regardless, their imagined Japan was often positive and full of wonder. Thus, unsurprisingly, some JCHIP interns augmented their imagined Japan while others experienced a clash between their imagined Japan and their realities once they visited Japan. However, this clash is sometimes viewed as a strength and a challenge in JCHIP as it can serve as a catalyst for a participant's personal and linguistic growth (Koyama, 2020).

The Douglas Fir Group's (DFG, 2016) transdisciplinary framework guided us in understanding the mechanism of the multilayered interactions needed for language learning to occur in a given community. Herein, three levels of social activities that are crucial to the transdisciplinary framework of L2 learning—the micro, meso, and macro levels (DFG, 2016; Hall, 2019)—could help illustrate how language learning is enabled when a learner experiences a clash between their imagined community and the real community.

At the micro level, L2 learners interact with others in various social contexts from texting and chatting with others via various media and learning within "more formal contexts" like schools or workplace to experiencing unfamiliar cultures and communities by "traveling to different geographical regions" (Hall, 2019, p. 6). Through these diverse experiences, L2 learners are then able to gain and develop their semiotic resources that include multilingual and multimodal linguistic or paralinguistic repertoires (Blommaert & Backus, 2013; DFG, 2016; Hall, 2019; Hall et al., 2006). Access to semiotic resources is often determined by learners' affective state, as DFG stressed that "the more they experience emotionally and motivationally positive evaluations of their anticipated and real interactions, the more effort they will make to participate in them and affiliate with others" (p. 28).

The meso level refers to a wide range of small to large social contexts and communities, including families, schools, and workplaces, such as "clubs, sports leagues, political parties, various online contexts, and so on" (Hall, 2019, p. 7). When situated in any given social context, L2 learners adopt certain roles or identities as required or assigned to them by the situation, which influences their degree of participation and learning (Lave & Wenger, 1991). DFG (2016) claimed that such identities are "aspects of L2 learners' personhoods that are defined in terms of ways in which individuals understand their relationship to the world" (p. 31). Through interactions, learners can "refashion their relationships with others by taking on alternative identities" (p. 33), thereby accessing new sets of semiotic resources. Throughout this process, learners can exert their agency and take charge of their own learning.

These different levels interact and are interrelated with the learners' roles, identities, degrees of learning, and participation, which all then interact with larger-scale ideological structures. The macro level shapes and influences both societal and individual beliefs, values, and expectations. The ideological structures "about language use and language learning are especially significant to SLA endeavors" (Hall, 2019, p. 9). The macro level also determines the opportunities and their accessibility for L2 learners' engagement in using their target languages.

The communities of practice and the transdisciplinary framework can be used to examine situated learning for L2 learners, which helps us better understand how they can grow and participate in their target language communities through overseas internships. More importantly, these approaches explicate the detailed workings of one student's JCHIP experience and growth at the orphanage. Tom (pseudonym) was a first-year Japanese language student who was among the youngest internship participants.

Case study: a first-year Japanese language student's holistic growth

This case study examines Tom's JCHIP internship experience by drawing upon semi-structured interviews I conducted with Tom prior to and following the internship. Before delving into Tom's case study, some of my background information needs to be outlined. I joined the JCHIP in 2014 as an advisor and liaison between the UCD and orphanages in Japan. As a Japanese language pedagogy expert, I (hereafter referred to as advisor) was placed in charge of training new interns every year by providing two to three language and culture training sessions (lasting 2 hours each) and individual consultations to help prepare new interns.

I conducted a 1-hour interview with Tom 2 months prior to his internship. I subsequently conducted an interview 1 month after he completed his internship.

Tom's background as a JCHIP applicant

In the summer of 2018, Tom was a first-year student at UCD; he was 19 years old, male, Caucasian, and a cognitive science major (with a minor in education), although he indicated an intention to switch to Japanese as his major. He had just completed his first-year Japanese courses; however, he had initially begun learning Japanese with a private tutor while he was babysitting the tutor's children. At this time, he was a multilingual speaker (native fluency in both English and French) and was fascinated with learning other languages (Japanese, Mandarin Chinese, and Spanish).

The selection for the JCHIP includes two processes: (a) the initial screening of application packets (including an application form, a statement of purpose, and two letters of recommendation) and (b) group interviews of the finalists. The participating judges include two faculty members (the JCHIP director and the advisor) as well as former interns from the previous year as representatives of the affiliated orphanages.

Tom's statement of purpose highlighted his extensive childcare and tutoring experiences including babysitting two bilingual children (English-Japanese). As a multilingual speaker, Tom also tutored Spanish-speaking children in his community who were "at a disadvantage because of a language barrier" (JCHIP, 2018). During the group interview session, the judges were impressed by Tom's communicative skills, maturity, and professional demeanor. He successfully demonstrated his Japanese skills, which were stronger than the judges' initial assessment of his low proficiency as a first-year student. The judges also favorably considered his multilingual/multicultural background and his relatively high understanding of underprivileged children. As a result, Tom was selected as the youngest intern among the 2018 cohort. Tom's internship began in late June and ended in early September 2018.

Language and culture training and preparation for an "imagined community"

Prior to Tom's first interview, he completed a predeparture orientation and two language and culture training lessons, as shown in Table 9.1.

The initial interview took place after Tom had one office visit and email correspondence with the advisor to explain the progress of his preparations with enthusiasm. During this interview, the advisor asked basic questions to find out about Tom's mindset during his preparation period. The questions focused on his (a)

Table 9.1 Internship preparations

Timeline predeparture	Events	Notes
4 months prior	Predeparture orientation (2 hours), hosted by the director	• The JCHIP Guidebook and a lecture to discuss useful resources and code of conduct. • Small group discussions with former interns on what to expect.
2 months prior	Language-Culture Training Workshop: Session 1 (2 hours), hosted by the advisor	• "From your departure to arrival in Japan" lecture (decorum/dress code, regulations and transportation systems in Japan, etc.). • Language and culture lesson (conversation practice, vocabulary list, roleplay practice).
1 month prior	Language-Culture Training Workshop: Session 2 (2 hours), hosted by the advisor	• Language and culture lesson (proprietary and work-related language, vocabulary for daily commands, and expressions to use in interactions with staff).

motivation (e.g., reasons to apply for the internship), (b) language background (e.g., proficiency in Japanese and other languages), (c) preparedness (e.g., understanding and feelings about underprivileged children, orphanages, good interns), and (d) personal experience and goals (e.g., expectations from internship and future career).

In the following discussion, all quoted conversations are by Tom, unless specifically stated otherwise.

Tom's goals and roles in his imagined community

Tom considered the JCHIP to be a perfect opportunity to "go to Japan without being a complete tourist" and experience the Japanese working culture that would allow him to determine whether he might wish to live in Japan later in life. In sum, the "JCHIP checked all the boxes" for Tom.

At the start of the interview, Tom jokingly referred to the training sessions (Table 9.1) as a "brainwashing process" that helped him shift his focus from going to Japan for fun to going there for the children at the orphanage. His view of orphanages seemed to be conceptualized through the training sessions that had consistently emphasized the importance of interns' active engagement and participation while striving to maintain the qualities of patience, understanding, punctuality, and maturity and being hardworking, proactive, and polite at the orphanages. These descriptions were repeatedly used by Tom in explaining what he thought made up a good intern.

Several aspects stood out at his initial interview, forming a striking contrast to Tom's subsequent interview. For example, in answering the motivation and preparedness questions, Tom inserted "I don't know" 16 times. This general extender suggested that Tom felt a degree of uncertainty. In fact, Tom hesitantly admitted that he became "nervous," "overwhelmed," and "worried" when he thought about potential encounters with violence at the orphanage. Furthermore, he tended to have long pauses before giving well-thought-out answers, which was the mirror image of what was presented during the training sessions. Although much remained unknown to him, Tom concluded the interview with his outlook on his JCHIP experience providing him with "three big things": gaining greater fluency in Japanese, meeting new people, and learning how to work with underprivileged children. In addition, at the end of the interview, both Tom and the advisor optimistically anticipated that new interns would be supported by the Japanese staff members. At this stage, Japanese staff members were perceived to be the primary agents that would affect Tom's looming internship.

Soon after the interview, Tom sent the following first contact email to his orphanage in late May, 1 month before his departure:

初めまして。

XXと申します。YY(Tom's internship partner)と申します。どうぞよろしくお願いいたします。今度の夏休みにカリフォルニア大学デービス校から来るインターン生なんです。よく準備することと自己紹介のためこの最初の連絡をしたいんです。いつもこんなプログラムに参加したかったですが全然できると思わなかったです。だから、どうもありがとうございます。そして、一所懸命頑張るの約束を守るつもりなんです。

子供達とスタッフの毎日の生活に参加できることを本当に楽しみにしています。

私達は何かお土産を準備しておきたいですが、子供とスタッフは何人だか分かっていません。もしよければ、おしえていただけませんか。最終的に、私達は一緒に最高の準備をするつもりです。そして、ZZ先生(Advisor)にたくさんのいい提案をもらいました。でも、子供の家の皆様からもっと提案があれば、お知らせくださいませ。

どうぞよろしくお願いいたします。本当に感謝して、楽しみにしています。

XXとYY

How do you do?

My name is XX. My name is YY (Tom's internship partner). Nice to meet you all. We are interns from the University of California, Davis coming to you this summer. We wish to contact you regarding good preparations and self-introductions for the first time. We have always wanted to participate in programs like this, but never dreamed of having this opportunity at all. So, thank you very much. And we promise to do our best. We are looking forward to participating in the daily life of children and staff every day.

We want to prepare some souvenirs for you, but we do not know how many children and staff members are there. If it is okay, will you please let us know? Lastly, we will make the best preparations. And Professor ZZ (advisor) gave us many good suggestions. But please let us know if everyone at the orphanage can share more suggestions with us.

Very pleased to meet you! We are really grateful and looking forward to meeting you.
From XX and YY

Despite using a few pragmatically awkward expressions, Tom managed to write this message on his own based on the advisor's feedback, which also demonstrated his Japanese proficiency at that point. In the message, Tom expressed his enthusiasm and commitment to serve as an active member of the community as evident in 一生懸命頑張るの約束 ("promise to do the best"), 最高の準備 ("the best preparations"), and 子供の家の皆様からの提案 ("suggestions from everyone at the orphanage"). He presumed and imagined his role and identity as a responsible member of the community in his upcoming experience with great enthusiasm.

Buzz words, retorts, and being a foreigner in a Japanese community

The 2-hour long interview conducted after the internship was different from the initial interview as Tom's internship partner, June (pseudonym), joined him even though she had not participated in the first interview. They expressed their willingness to participate in the interview together as they could compare notes that would help them shed more light on their internship experiences. Because we focused on Tom's internship experience in this chapter, data extracted from June is minimized, except as necessary, in the following sections.

The questions in the second interview focused on three categories: obstacles and difficulties, growth and improvement, and career trajectories. These categories covered the themes asked in the initial interview—namely, motivation (Was his motivation met with any difficulties?), preparedness (Was he prepared to encounter any obstacles and new experiences?), and goals (Has he gained and learned anything as he hoped/expected?). A good portion of this second interview was spent on the discussion of the detailed and emotionally loaded accounts of memorable episodes and events as well as their reflections on the internship.

Tom's first obstacles at the orphanage

An orphanage presents a microcosm of Japanese society. It is a shelter for underprivileged children with supervisors and experienced staff members who operate within strict legal guidelines and regulations to protect their wards. Each member has a designated role and function in performing their duties. For Tom, an orphanage further resembled a community of practice (Lave & Wenger, 1991) where, he believed, he was placed as a novice intern to perform his duties with assistance from the experienced Japanese staff and supervisor. Thus, he arrived at the orphanage with a clear intention to fully participate in this community organization. However, his expectations quickly changed as he started feeling unsure of his role as an intern due to the lack of clear instructions.

First, to his disappointment, Tom was excluded from an orientation for new domestic interns during which they were taught what their chores and duties were and how to perform them. Although he was still hoping to be given a separate orientation (for international interns), he was left with no specific guidance. This was the first clash between his imagined community and real communities at the meso level, as the orphanage clearly restricted Tom's access to new and potential semiotic resources including proprietary information about the orphanage (DFG, 2016, p. 24). Second, he felt that he was treated like "a foreign object" throughout his internship. This particular treatment reflects people's belief and attitudes toward Tom's transportable identity as a foreigner (Hall, 2019), which mirrors part of Japan's longstanding ideological structures firmly anchored in the dichotomy between *uchi* (inside) and *soto* (outside), which deems non-Japanese entities outsiders by default (e.g., Arudou, 2013; Bachnik & Quinne, 1994; Kubota, 1998). In other words, Tom's identity as a foreigner superseded all his other identities (e.g., a novice intern, an ardent learner of Japanese) at the outset of this internship.

The community automatically deemed Tom a foreigner and this treatment then subsequently limited his involvement in the activities designated by the organization. Furthermore, Tom's learning opportunities were provided as "an improvised practice" (Lave & Wenger, 1991, p. 93) when unexpected situations unfolded. As a result, Tom was left alone as a peripheral participant at the orphanage, which led him to experience a general sense of "community neglect" (Lave & Wenger, 1991, p. 93).

Tom's agency and language growth with identity shifts

At the start of his internship, Tom immediately experienced the clash between his imagined community and real communities, which manifested as people's identification of him as a foreigner, rather than an intern. However, Tom overcame all the hindrances to his full participation as an intern, as he "got through [by] trial and error and observed others to figure out" what his work was and how to carry it out for the first three weeks. During those weeks, he felt that staff members "had very low expectations" of him. As he continued making an extra effort to fully function as an intern, Tom encountered the children's serious behavioral and emotional issues and learned of their traumatic experiences firsthand (e.g., he was accidentally punched by a 17-year-old boy and was reprimanded by the staff members because he did not know how to intervene between two teenagers who had started quarrelling). Furthermore, he gained more critical views of the staff and the overall work environment.

Tom was scared of the staff members for various reasons, primarily because of their passive-aggressiveness toward him. Tom explained that "they never corrected" his Japanese and lamented that they "talked [about] a lot of messes from the past (JCHIP) interns. They were really harsh." Meanwhile, Tom became critical of the questionable judgments and behaviors of certain staff members at various social events. For instance, during a camping trip for elementary school-age children, Tom observed potentially dangerous behaviors being performed by small children and then asked the supervisor whether it was safe to let the children use a cooking knife unsupervised. In response, the supervisor said 子供たちに任せます *Kodomotachini makasemasu* ("I will leave it up to the children"), to which Tom immediately thought to himself 任せないほうがいいと思いますけど *Makasenaihooga iitoomoimasukedo* ("I do not think you should leave it to them"). Tom's internal dialogue displays not only his criticism and retort, but is also an expansion of his linguistic repertoire as part of his semiotic resources (DFG, 2016; Hall, 2019). This type of retort—negating the addressee's statement—is often observed when native Japanese speakers display their cynicism.

Throughout his internship, Tom noticed a lack of clarity about his role(s) at the orphanage that resulted from a sense of "community neglect" (Lave & Wenger, 1991, p. 93), with no instructions or guidance provided. He was also concerned about the staff's laissez-faire attitude toward the children's behavioral issues. All of these issues are accurately summarized by two buzz words that Tom constantly heard: 適当 *tekitoo* ("do as it fits") and しょうがない *shooganai* ("it cannot be helped"). When Tom asked for specific instructions, such as how to prepare the cultural events, the supervisor and other staff members told him to 適当. When he reported the children's behavioral issues to the supervisor, Tom was told しょうがない. In return, however, he mentally responded しょうがあります *shoogaarimasu* ("it can be helped"), which is another retort often observed among native speakers. More importantly, his response signifies his creativity as a language learner and agency with critical thinking.

Interestingly, the orphanage's "community neglect" (Lave & Wenger, 1991, p. 93) was compensated by the young children's willingness to teach Tom as well as his unwavering motivation to achieve "high levels of proficiency and community engagement" (Duff, 2014, p. 566). Tom developed a close rapport with some of the children and these relationships became increasingly significant and meaningful to him. In fact, Tom believed that his language improvement was enabled by the young children, in general, but especially the 17-year-old boy who had accidentally punched him earlier in the internship.

Tom and the 17-year-old boy began talking every night after dinner; their topics of conversation varying from daily chitchat to their personal experiences and expanded to politics, history, social issues in Japan, and philosophy. Due to the similarity in age between Tom (19) and this boy (17), Tom felt that he "was old enough to make a friend connection" and they "really got super close." Tom acquired new vocabulary and managed to train his listening skills with the 17-year-old's assistance. In particular, he appreciated how patient the boy was and how he would speak slowly with Tom for their first few conversations until Tom felt comfortable with the normal speed of a native speaker's speech. Meanwhile, Tom learned about his newfound friend's hardships and traumas as he emotionally bonded with the 17-year-old; he was shocked to learn of the "rough" life the boy had endured.

Tom's emotional bonding with the 17-year-old became one of the highlights of his internship, which exemplifies the importance of interactional instincts that occur at the micro level of social activities (DFG, 2016; Hall, 2019; Lee et al.,

2009; Schumann, 2013). In Tom's case, his friendship with the boy compelled him "to seek out emotionally rewarding, motivating relationships," not only with the boy, but also with others in the orphanage, proving that "the more they [L2 learners] experience emotionally and motivationally positive evaluations of their anticipated and real interactions, the more effort they will make to participate in them and affiliate with others" (DFG, 2016, p. 28). Following his interactions with the 17-year-old, instead of being fixated on being "a good intern," Tom began to shift his identities from a friend to the boy to a big brother to the small children, as needed. The fluidity of these identity shifts was positively fostered as the influence of the Japanese staff quickly diminished, leading to them lose their power over Tom. Furthermore, he gradually began embracing his identity as a foreigner as he strengthened his personal connections with the children. He began viewing his foreignness as a license to make mistakes freely. As a foreigner, Tom began to believe that he would be naturally prone to making mistakes. In fact, everyone "laughed with" Tom but never "laughed at" him when he made mistakes in Japanese. When he was unaware of the house rules, the young children were happy to teach him. All these experiences expanded his social circle within the orphanage and eventually helped alleviate his fear of making mistakes, encouraged him to speak more freely with everyone at the orphanage, and led him to embrace his foreignness as one of his identities during the internship.

Tom's overall growth

Tom experienced significant linguistic improvements throughout his internship, which enabled him to advance forward to the third-year Japanese language course upon his return. He summarized his overall personal and linguistic growth at the end of the second interview by saying 別人みたいに違った *betsujin mitaini chigatta* ("I am different and grown now"), as he had become both more mature and professional. In fact, June, Tom's internship partner, described Tom's attitude as "always going for it! Just speaking and going for it."

Tom felt strongly that his internship experience had solidified his future trajectories by strengthening his interest in education and in pursuing a Japanese major. His hands-on work experience "provided an opportunity to test the waters" (Koyama, 2020, p. 72) and yielded positive results. However, his journey was neither smooth nor easy. His initial motivation and expectations were met with clashes at multiple levels of social activities at the orphanage that were intricately related, sometimes even working against one another. Tom's agency as an intern and a dedicated L2 learner was grounded in his resilience and unwavering determination to function holistically as a member, and, as a result, he developed a close rapport with the children (micro) and ended up with a renewed awareness and identification as a foreigner (macro) (DFG, 2016; Hall, 2019).

At the orphanage (meso), people's attitudes initially discouraged Tom's motivation and expectations. In fact, throughout the internship, Tom did not believe that his role as an intern was acknowledged or legitimized, as he was often left without any instructions and was not provided with any legitimate access (King, 2008; Lave & Wenger, 1991; Norton, 2000). However, that did not stop him. Through his interactions with the children (micro), Tom gained his own access to learning. At this micro level, he "refashion(ed)" his "relationships with others by taking on alternative identities" and roles, such as a big brother and a friend to children, rather than a good intern to supervisors and staff (DFG, 2016, p. 33). Moreover, as he strengthened his friendship with the 17-year-old boy at a very personal level, Tom made explosive linguistic and personal growth. His identity as a friend reinforced his agency as an L2 learner by giving him such transformative power and helping him reinterpret his initial dismay as "a foreign object." Ultimately, Tom embraced this identity as a license to freely make mistakes and used it as means to further his L2 learning. Tom continually focused on nurturing his meaningful interactions with the children over improving his Japanese, despite clashes he encountered at the meso and micro levels at the orphanage. His language growth was then a byproduct of his "interactional instinct" (Hall, 2019; Lee et al., 2009; Schumann, 2013) through which the Japanese language was incarnated within him and eventually became an integral part of his linguistic repertoires, enriching his semiotic resources. This further indicates the importance of an environment or community (meso) wherein language learners must live their language by interacting with others (micro), working, solving problems, or simply surviving, instead of focusing on learning a language in isolation. The multifaceted nature of a community enables L2 learners to live and experience their languages.

Conclusion

The JCHIP is often considered a life-changing experience that has a lasting impact on students' Japanese language development, personal lives, and career trajectories (Koyama, 2020). Nonetheless, each student's journey and experience are uniquely different and not always the rosy picture they desired.

Tom's internship experience and ensuing personal and linguistic growth were gravely affected by specific constructs of his assigned orphanage (i.e., the meso level) while these constructs reflected the prejudices and ideological issues in Japanese society (i.e., the macro level). Faced with obstacles, Tom deliberately stepped outside of his comfort zone to exert himself to develop a close rapport with some children and expand his access to multilingual resources (i.e., the micro level), which all resulted in his newfound awareness and identity shifts after the internship (i.e., the macro level; DFG, 2016; Hall, 2019).

This case study suggests that providing a unique internship opportunity, such as the JCHIP, can afford a powerful learning opportunity for students, which leads to their holistic growth. As the transdisciplinary framework encourages educators to reevaluate social, affective, and psychological aspects of learning beyond the conventional approach, international internships could serve as an optimized setting via collaborations among educators, school administrators, and communities across borders.

Lastly, Tom's overall experience suggests that there are some instructional interventions we can provide as educators to facilitate and ease a transition for prospective students. In implementing similar projects, instructors may explicate the potential gap between the imagined and real communities before the students embark on a study abroad or international internship trip. Clearly, it is impossible to cover every aspect or issue, but the students will be made aware of potential identity clashes they might encounter and prepared in terms of how to react to them. In this way, the students can be prepared for their identity work ahead as part of their L2 learning—negotiating, reshaping, reinterpreting, and/or embracing their identities (DFG, 2016, p. 31).

Acknowledgments

This study was financially supported by Small Grant In Aid of Research by the University of California, Davis. My thanks to Tom and June and to Professor Joseph Sorensen, Director of JCHIP-UCD, whose vision and dedication made the JCHIP what it is today.

References

Arudou, D. (2013). An introduction to Japanese society's attitudes toward race and skin color. In R. Hall (Ed.), *The melanin millennium: Skin color as 21st century international discourse* (pp. 49–70). Springer. doi:10.1007/978-94-007-4608-4

Bachnik, J. M., & Quinne, C. J. (Eds.). (1994). *Situated meaning: Inside and outside in Japanese self, society and language*. Princeton University Press.

Blommaert, J., & Backus, A. (2013). Superdiverse repertoires and the individual. In I. de Saint-Georges & J. Weber (Eds.), *Multilingualism and multimodality* (pp. 9–32). Sense Publishers.

Douglas Fir Group. (2016). A transdisciplinary framework for SLA in a multilingual world. *The Modern Language Journal*, *100*(Supplement 2016), 19–47.

Duff, P. A. (2014). Second language socialization. In A. Duranti, E. Ochs, & B. B. Schieffeling (Eds.), *The handbook of language socialization* (pp. 564–586). Wiley Blackwell.

Hall, J. K. (2019). *Essentials of SLA for L2 teachers*. Routledge.

Hall, J. K., Cheng, A., & Carlson, M. T. (2006). Reconceptualizing multicompetence as a theory of language knowledge. *Applied Linguistics*, *27*, 220–240.

He, Y., & Qin, X. (2017). Students' perceptions of an internship experience in China: A pilot study. *Foreign Language Annals*, *50*(1), 57–70.

Internship and Career Center at the University of California, Davis. (2021). *Transcription notation for students*. https://icc.ucdavis.edu/find/internships/tn

JCHIP. (2018). *Tom's application packet file* [Unpublished data file].

Kanno, Y., & Norton, B. (2003). Imagined communities and educational possibilities: Introduction. *Journal of Language, Identity, and Education*, *2*(4), 241–249.

King, B. W. (2008). "Being gay guy, that is the advantage": Queer Korean language learning and identity construction. *Journal of Language, Identity, and Education*, *7*(3–4), 230–252. doi:10.1080/15348450802237855

Kolb, A. Y., & Kolb, D. A. (2005). Learning styles and learning spaces: Enhancing experiential learning in higher education. *Academy of Management Learning and Education*, *4*(2), 193–212.

Koyama, N. (2020). Challenges and gains through internships in Japan. *Applied Language Learning*, *30*(1–2), 60–78.

Kubota, R. (1998). Ideologies of English in Japan. *World Englishes*, *17*(7), 295–306.

Lave, J., & Wenger, E. (1991). *Situated learning: Legitimate peripheral participation*. Cambridge University Press.

Lee, N., Mikesell, L., Joaquin, A. D. L., Mates, A. W., & Schumann, J. H. (2009). *The interactional instinct: The evolution and acquisition of language*. Oxford University Press.

Norton, B. (2000). *Identity and language learning: Gender, ethnicity and educational change*. Pearson Education.

Norton, B. (2001). Non-participation, imagined communities, and the language classroom. In M. Breen (Ed.), *Learning contributions to language learning: New directions in research* (pp. 159–171). Pearson Education.

Pellegrino Aveni, V. A. (2005). *Study abroad and second language use: Constructing the self*. Cambridge University Press.

Schumann, J. H. (2013). Societal responses to adult difficulties in L2 acquisition: Toward an evolutionary perspective on language acquisition. *Language Learning*, *63*(2), 190–209.

Toncar, M. F., & Cudmore, B. V. (2000). The overseas internship experience. *Journal of Marketing Education*, *22*(1), 54–63.

Trentman, E. (2013). Imagined communities and language learning during study abroad: Arabic learners in Egypt. *Foreign Language Annals*, *46*(4), 545–564. doi:10.1111/flan.12054

Twombly, S. B., Salisbury, M. H., Tumanut, S. D., & Klute, P. (2012). *Study abroad in a new global century: Renewing the promise, refining the purpose*. Wiley Periodicals.

Wenger, E. (1998). *Communities of practice: Learning, meaning, and identity*. Cambridge University Press.

Section 4
Across languages
Chinese-Japanese and multi-language collaboration

10 An experiment of cross-language and cross-disciplinary collaboration

Integrating Xu Bing's text-based arts into Chinese and Japanese classrooms

Noriko Sugimori and Leihua Weng

Introduction

Hanzi, the logographic characters in China, was introduced to Japan in the fifth century or earlier and has been referred to as kanji (meaning "Han characters") in Modern Japanese. During the indigenization of hanzi, supplementary native writing systems were developed for the current Japanese language along with the natively derived syllabic scripts of hiragana and katakana (Coulmas, 1991). However, despite the genealogical connection between hanzi and kanji, most Chinese and Japanese L2 learners and instructors have little experience connecting hanzi and kanji in their Chinese and Japanese language classrooms.

The prevalent ideology in linguistics places more emphasis on spoken rather than written language (Meletis, 2021), which has greatly influenced pedagogical approaches in world language teaching. Despite being a rich semiotic repertoire worthy of exploration, learning hanzi/kanji does not often constitute a significant activity in Chinese and Japanese classrooms that tend to focus on developing oral communicative skills. Instead, hanzi/kanji learning often takes place outside the classroom as part of students' homework or self-study. Hanzi/kanji is usually treated as something for rote memorization for learners (Mori, 2020). The repetition of practicing writing hanzi/kanji is emphasized in related learning exercises, although educators have recently started to explore learners' creativity more (Hamakawa, 2010; Wang, 2009). In addition, very few classroom activities pay attention to the roles that technology, institution, and community play in the meaning productions of hanzi/kanji. Even more rare are discussions and reflections—if any occur at all—on the prevalent language pedagogy that emphasizes accuracy and memorization in hanzi/kanji learning rather than learners' agency and creativity or on the dominant ideologies that uphold language standardization and reject plurilinguistic views (Beacco & Byram, 2007; Oyama, 2014).

This chapter presents an experiment of incorporating text-based arts into Chinese and Japanese L2 courses as a cross-language and cross-disciplinary course project aimed to engage both Chinese and Japanese learners in a shared discursive space built upon their knowledge of hanzi/kanji and upon their creative use of hanzi/kanji. More specifically, this joint project was designed to help both Chinese and Japanese L2 students reflect collectively on their hanzi/kanji learning while encouraging them to contextualize hanzi/kanji within and beyond their own communities. Through this collective exploration, these L2 students were expected to discover and reflect upon the language ideologies that they were previously unaware of, such as monolingualism (Heinrich, 2012). In addition, this project aimed to develop a new learning community among the Chinese and Japanese L2 learners by including Xu Bing's text-based arts, which are readily accessible to L2 learners of East Asian languages. In this chapter, "sinograph" is used as the cover term referring to characters used in China as well as those introduced to other regions, including kanji in Japan.

This chapter first introduces the theoretical framework employed in this joint project and then moves on to its description and learning outcomes, with a concluding discussion of its implications and suggestions for future implementation. Samples of students' work and feedback are included to illustrate how this cross-language and cross-disciplinary project helped Chinese and Japanese L2 learners develop their critical and creative thinking skills in addition to enhancing their hanzi/kanji learning.

Rationales

As the Douglas Fir Group (DFG, 2016) discussed in the SLA transdisciplinary framework, language learning in the contemporary world is seen as an "emergent, dynamic, unpredictable, open ended, and intersubjectively negotiated" (p. 19) process due to today's globalization and digitalization. In this project, we applied the transdisciplinary framework that proposes three mutually dependent levels of social activity in order to capture L2 language use and learning: the micro level of social activity to enhance linguistic skills and metalinguistic awareness; the meso level of social interactions at certain institutions and communities that shape the resources accessible to learners, as well as their motivation, investment, and agency in L2 learning; and the macro level of ideological structures that mold views of language learning (DFG, 2016). The transdisciplinary framework pays attention to learners' multifaceted meaning-making processes in their multilingual worlds. It also helps instructors foster a profound awareness of the cultural, social, and institutional factors influencing L2 learners' as well as the users' own dynamic participatory roles in the meaning-making interactions and intersubjective negotiations.

Our objectives in this project were delineated at the micro, meso, and macro levels in the framework (DFG, 2016; Hall, 2019). At the micro level, we expected Chinese and Japanese L2 learners to improve their hanzi/kanji writing by observing the structure and composition of hanzi/kanji characters, practicing the strokes and radicals, and understanding the connections and disconnections between the forms and meanings. At the meso level, Chinese and Japanese L2 learners were expected to be able to identify meanings of hanzi/kanji in their daily settings and in their communities. Finally—and most importantly—we hoped learners would have opportunities to reflect upon stereotypes of perceiving hanzi/kanji as one whole set of static entities and start perceiving hanzi/kanji as dynamic, ever-emergent graphemic components that constantly interact with various factors in their regional and interregional contexts. The framework guided us, as instructors and project designers, in outlining our expectations and assessing the outcomes of this project.

Cross-language collaboration in recent years has been more active and visible than ever, partly due to the wide adoption of remote teaching and learning in language classrooms during the pandemic. Various practices of online international collaboration, such as collaborative online international learning (COIL), have been introduced between institutions across regions. Those practices in the United States typically involve collaborations between English and other languages, such as between Chinese language classes in the United States and English language classes in China or Japanese language classes in the United States and English language classes in Japan (Luo, 2021; Mori et al., 2020). There is increasing cross-disciplinary interdepartmental collaboration between language classes and nonlanguage classes in literature or other disciplines in social science and humanities. This approach is known as Cultures and Languages Across the Curriculum (CLAC) or Foreign Languages Across the Curriculum (FLAC; Chikamatsu, 2019, 2022; Hartfield-Méndez et al., 2019; Kisselev & Corner, 2019; Reisinger et al., 2022). In CLAC practices, language instructors and nonlanguage instructors work closely in curricular design and implementation. Those practices often require funding support to accommodate special curricular needs. As is always the case, both the interinstitutional collaboration of COIL and the interdepartmental practices of CLAC involve many adjustments in both course scheduling and content, and almost all of them inevitably entail a much heavier workload for participating instructors (Chikamatsu, 2019). In addition, these projects are mostly limited to participation among advanced language students.

Our project adopted a unique cross-language (Chinese and Japanese) and cross-disciplinary (language and arts) approach by integrating Xu Bing's text-based artworks into Chinese and Japanese language classrooms. It engaged both Chinese and Japanese L2 learners in creatively using hanzi/kanji that constituted a shared and important part of their respective L2 learning. It also encouraged them to explore the cultural and historical diversities in hanzi/kanji in a collective space created in groups and between classes. Unlike most COIL or FLAC courses, this project did not require any joint international or interdepartmental collaboration or any major curricular adjustment in language courses. In addition, it accommodated students at various proficiency levels across target languages as our project paired novice learners in one language and advanced learners in another. Xu Bing's text-based artworks can be integrated in language teaching with flexibility in a wide range of educational settings, which made our project uniquely cross-language and cross-disciplinary.

Xu Bing's text-based artworks

Xu Bing (1955–), a contemporary Chinese artist, is internationally renowned for his conceptual and installation arts. He started his text-based art installations in the 1990s and has held exhibitions throughout China, Europe, and North America. His arts, many of which are based on texts, evoke questions on the conventional perceptions of meaning production and meaning indeterminacy (Fraser & Li, 2020; Tsao & Ames, 2011).

Xu Bing's text-based artworks contain rich and diverse semiotic signs that are present in history and in contemporary realities. The *Living Word* installation (Xu, 2001) includes a work that references the ideographic evolution of pictographic language (see Figure 10.1). It is assembled with more than 400 pictographs of "bird." It starts with the modern simplified character, 鸟, to the traditional form of hanzi/kanji 鳥 on the left, and then flows upward and outward (toward an outdoor space) through various historical pictograms of the same word; the more ancient they are, the more vivid these ideograms look in terms of both shape and color.

Another major recurrent component of Xu Bing's text-based artworks is his square word calligraphy, in which artificial ideographs are created in an imitation of hanzi/kanji—sometimes to convey the incomprehensibility of hanzi/kanji as textual language, as in his *Book from the Sky* (1987–1991), and sometimes to communicate the meaning of Roman alphabetic letters in hanzi/kanji form, as in

Figure 10.1 Xu Bing's *Living Word*

his exhibition *Art for the People for the Met* (2020). In addition, Xu Bing's artworks draw from an extremely rich repertoire of semiotics in various media. His installations of *Book from the Ground* (2003–ongoing) are composed of various signs from public urban settings such as the subway, coffee shops, and train stations. His recent *Art for the People for the Met* (2020) is a creative compilation of multiple forms of textual, visual, and digital media. The work is a six-color lithograph and relief print. It contains square word calligraphy, the Roman letters for "art for the people" in hanzi/kanji form, and red traditional seals that are QR codes for the audience to scan and to read more about the exhibition on the website of the Metropolitan Museum of Art. Being rich in materiality, this work *Art for the People for the Met* (2020) challenges conventional notions of the form and media of textual language as well as the traditional dichotomy and hierarchy in the identity of the author and the reader as well as the owner and the user (see Figure 10.2).

As Chinese and Japanese L2 language instructors, we find in Xu Bing's text-based arts a rare opportunity to bring Chinese and Japanese L2 learners and instructors together to discover and reflect upon the cultural aspects of language transformations and upon language ideologies such as certain monolinguistic concepts associated with or embedded in hanzi/kanji. In particular, we value the role of Xu Bing's artwork for the following reasons. It (a) evokes questions on ownership of language by pointing to its untraceable origin; (b) questions the perception of language as a static system and challenges a conventional belief that sinographs are one static system; and (c) serves as a catalyst for further intellectual inquiry in Chinese and Japanese as two orthographically rich languages. Above all, the project was expected to help learners build their own agency in language learning.

Figure 10.2 Xu Bing's *Art for the People for the Met*

Project description

This project of integrating Xu Bing's text-based arts into Chinese and Japanese language teaching was carried out as an experiment in the winter term of 2021 at a small liberal arts college in the Midwest region of the United States. The Department of East Asian Studies of this college encourages students to learn both Chinese and Japanese, the two East Asian languages offered at the college, but only a few students take courses in both languages. Two faculty members, one in the Chinese program and the other in the Japanese, decided to collaborate on a joint project to increase communication and exchanges between Chinese and Japanese L2 learners.

The instructor of Chinese is a specialist in Chinese literature. The instructor of Japanese is a linguist whose interests include historical sociolinguistics, language ideology, and language pedagogy. Both had previously incorporated Xu Bing's works into language classrooms on a small scale, and the instructor of Japanese has an academic interest in Xu Bing's works, specifically the sociolinguistic implications of his arts (Jaworski, 2018). In this collaborative project, the instructor of Chinese took the task of introducing Xu Bing's artworks to L2 learners in both language classes. Both instructors worked together to design activities and directed students' attention to the social historical backgrounds and significance of hanzi/kanji.

This project included two participating courses: CHIN102 (the second-quarter Chinese class in the first-year sequence) and JAPN302 (the second-quarter class in the third-year sequence and also the highest level of Japanese class offered in the Japanese program). Both classes met three times per week, and each session lasted 75 minutes. Most of the students in CHIN102 were in their first year of college, while JAPN302 included mostly juniors. This project involved all the students in the two courses with the exception that five of the 13 students in CHIN102 made their class visits to JAPN302 for their project final presentations. Both courses were taught online during the pandemic; thus, students participated across geographical distance from various regions in the United States and overseas.

By the time the project started, the first six lessons of *Integrated Chinese, Level 1, Part 1* (Liu et al., 2009) had been taught in CHIN102. In JAPN302, Chapter 4 and part of Chapter 5 of the textbook *Jokyu eno Tobira: Gateway to advanced Japanese* (Oka et al., 2009) were concurrently covered with this project. The students in CHIN102 had learned about 260 Chinese characters and those in JAPN302 had learned about 540 kanji prior to the project. Students in both CHIN102 and JAPN302 were expected to have already had adequate exposure to hanzi/kanji and basic grammar to compose at least formulaic sentences in their respective L2. We expected that the differences in L2 proficiency levels between the two classes would matter very little in this hanzi/kanji-based project, which turned out to be true.

The project started in the second week of the term. It consisted of four major steps and altogether lasted approximately 4 weeks, as shown in Steps 1 to 4 in Table 10.1.

Table 10.1 Project steps

Step	CHIN102		JAPN302
1 (in class)	Lecture (20 minutes)		Lecture (20 minutes)
2 (in class)	Square word practice (20 minutes)		Square word practice (20 minutes)
3 (after-class activities)	Writing a greeting letter Decoding letters Replying to letters	⇒ ⇐	Writing a greeting letter Decoding letters Replying to letters
4 (in class)	Presentations (75 minutes)		

Step one: introductory lecture of Xu Bing's artworks (20 minutes)

The instructor of Chinese delivered an introductory lecture on Xu Bing's text-based artworks in English in both CHIN102 and JAPN302 separately. The lecture focused on several art installations and exhibitions by Xu Bing including *The Living Word* (2001), *Book from the Sky* (1987–1991), and *Book from the Ground* (2003). During the lecture, much attention was given to the square word calligraphy components in these installations. The lecture was situated in the language transformations and diversities of hanzi/kanji as well as the contemporary social environments of globalization and digital technology. It highlighted the historical transformation of sinographs in their diversified East Asian contexts and drew attention to the new linguistic phenomena of emerging hybrid texts in East Asia in digital communications. The lecture concluded with an explication of Xu Bing's artworks in contemporary methods of meaning production such as the use of emojis and certain characters that acquire their new meanings in online media platforms.

Step two: Creating one's own square words (20 minutes)

After the lecture, students were asked to create their own square words out of their name-spellings in their respective classes and as homework. They were encouraged to experiment and render the Roman alphabetic letters of their names into the hanzi/kanji style of square words (Xu, 2020).

Step three: between-class correspondences (after-class assignment)

Following the exercises of creating one's own square words, students in each class were advised to form groups of three to four, and each group worked together to compose a greeting letter addressing the other class. They were instructed to include two parts in their letters: one part in their target language and the other part in the square words they created. CHIN102 sent out their group greeting letters first to JAPN302, and JAPN302 replied with their own letters to CHIN102 within 1 week. Each class was asked to read or decipher the letter from the other class. In the final step, they were encouraged to use external digital learning tools such as Google Translate to access any multilingual multimodal resources in cross-language communication.

Step four: student presentations (75 minutes)

Due to time conflicts, only five of the 13 students in CHIN102 joined the six students in JAPN302 for the in-class presentations. The student presenters from CHIN102 chose their own topics on hanzi/kanji in consultation with the instructor. Altogether, these five students from CHIN102 made one individual presentation and two paired ones. The JAPN302 students were provided with Eve Kushner's (2009) *Crazy for Kanji* as one resource book, from which they each chose a topic on their own and developed a presentation individually. The presentations were intended to reflect L2 learners' interest in and understanding of their target languages and the social-political-cultural factors in language transformations. Students were also encouraged to explore and reflect upon the related language ideologies.

Student learning outcomes and pedagogical reflections

Overall, students in both classes positively rated their participation on a survey after the project. Furthermore, as reported in the course evaluations 2 months later, many students described their experience in this project as the most significant part of these classes.

Letter correspondence and square words

After the lecture introducing the works of Xu Bing, students in CHIN102 and JAPN302 separately composed their letter correspondences and square words. Students in CHIN102 worked in groups to compose greeting letters to JAPN302 students, including a short message "Nice to meet you all!" rewritten in the self-created square words (see Figure 10.3). Prior to letter composition,

From：方爱努，周美，和昇铭

日文课，你们今天好吗？我们很高兴认识你们啊。 我们叫周美，方爱努，和昇铭。你们叫什么名字？我们都很喜欢喝茶，听音乐。你们喜欢做什么？要是你们想，我们一起应该去吃晚饭。再见！

Figure 10.3 Greeting letter from CHIN102 students

Experiment: cross-language & cross-disciplinary collaboration 153

during the process of creating the square words, CHIN102 students observed and examined how well balanced their own square words looked and whether or not they were composed of regular strokes. The practices of creating their own English-hanzi/kanji square word calligraphy prepared them to create their greeting letters in the Xu Bing style.

JAPN302 students warmly responded to these greeting letters, as Figure 10.4 demonstrates. They tried to read and decipher the letters sent from the other class using their L2 Japanese knowledge; they were encouraged to discuss the similarities and differences between hanzi and kanji. It is interesting to note that the letters composed by JAPN302 students contained no square words (see Figure 10.4). Some JAPN302 students explained that they experienced difficulties in writing square words without adequate in-class practice and discussion.

Project final presentations

Students displayed their understanding of hanzi/kanji most fully on their presentation day, either in their own presentations or in their responses to other student presenters. Their presentations covered a variety of topics. The five students from CHIN102 presented on the developments and transformations of Chinese pictographic writing systems in Mainland China, the pronunciation system in Taiwan, and text-based arts in the Hong Kong pro-independence movement. These presentations showed a keen interest in exploring the historical transformations of hanzi in the Chinese-speaking regions.

JAPN302 students explored the topics related to kanji, such as how hanzi in Japan gave rise to Japanese native graphs, hiragana and katakana, as well as the challenges in learning different pronunciations of kanji and the kanji-based country names. In addition, one student explored hanja (traditional writing system of sinograph) in North Korea and investigated the basic classifications of the sinographs used there. These presentations displayed students' interest in exploring

こんにちはみんなさん、

私はアネクシーです。よろしくおねがいします。私は音楽を聞くが好きです。

こんにちは。私の名前はマイルです。私は緑茶と日本のビデオゲームが大好きです。

たくさん日本の映画を見ているので、日本語を習いたいと思いました。

こんにちは。私の名前はJiazhenです。你们知道这句话什么意思吗？"どんな食べ物が好きですか？"。

Figure 10.4 Greeting letter from JAPN302 students

the transformations of hanzi through history and the current forms the characters take now in Japan and other East Asian areas.

Pedagogical reflections

At the micro level, students in this project had the opportunity to observe how hanzi/kanji are structured with strokes and radicals, and they developed metalinguistic awareness through lectures and hands-on practice with various semiotic resources made available by the instructors. One student in CHIN102, whose last name included "c" and "u," commented,

> When making my name [in square words], I was happy with how my first name came out because I was able to use Chinese radicals and strokes to make the letters. I want to find a way to make my last name, especially the "c" and "u," using either radicals or other characters.

At the meso level, students became more aware of the presence of hanzi/kanji in and outside of their own communities. Their correspondences displayed a strong interest in communicating with one another with their shared knowledge of hanzi/kanji as well as a willingness to recognize the lingual similarities in their L2 learning. One student in JAPN302 noted, "I really liked the discussion with the Chinese 102 students because we interacted more with them to the point of talking and sharing new things." Another student in JAPN302 from China initially made a negative comment on the language skills of the students in CHIN102 when he read the group letter in Chinese from them. However, in the survey after the project, the same student wrote,

> The letter from CHIN102 is pretty well [written], since they studied Chinese for only several months. It is great that they can know so many Chinese characters in such a short time. . . . In response to CHIN102, I spoke Chinese to say "good job" to them.

Such a change in his attitude and perspective may show that the project helped him experience empathy—an important component of intercultural skills (Bennett, 1998) as a member of a newly formed language learning community. We found these signs of mutual recognition and appreciation encouraging. We also took them as signs of an emerging learning community in the Department of East Asian Studies.

At the macro level, students explored the hanzi/kanji with its geographic and historical variations in East Asia, not only in Mainland China and Japan, but also in Korea and Taiwan. These geographic variations in East Asian regions, in both forms and meanings, helped them reevaluate a long-held view of perceiving Chinese characters as a static whole. By learning Xu Bing's artworks and practicing square words, many students in both classes developed a new view of the ownership of language. For example, one JAPN302 student wrote that she had found great agency in the roles as language learner and global citizen: "In being language learners, we are inherently language creators, helping to shape the evolution of both spoken and written word." Through the activities in this project, students obtained a better understanding that sinographic East Asian languages are living and borderless phenomena and that they can be transposed into another language system and then evolve into various forms based on the needs of people who use them. In turn, students in CHIN102 and JAPN302 developed a new understanding of their identities as learners and users of hanzi/kanji and of the interactions between languages in active use.

Furthermore, this project provided instructors with insights into the students' language learning ideology. As mentioned above, Japanese L2 students had previously been instructed to direct a great amount of attention to the "correct" stroke order and minute details such as how a stroke starts, pauses, and ends. They had been under such strict and rigorous writing training for more than 2 years, unlike the CHIN102 students who started handwriting about 3 months before this project. We therefore interpret JAPN302's resistance as an indicator of the existing influence of a language-learning ideology that upholds predetermined guidelines on "correct" character writing in an East Asian language classroom. In future implementations, we would provide Xu Bing's recent guideline sheet as scaffolding and reference and would make it clear to students that there is no correct or incorrect way of writing square word characters as an artistic experiment, even when there are certain references made available to them.

After the project: students' paths

Throughout the project, students were encouraged to discover and build their own agency in identifying, using, transforming, and discovering hanzi/kanji in their classrooms and their living environments. This experiment of incorporating Xu Bing's text-based arts into Chinese and Japanese classrooms did not directly involve any practice of speaking and listening in L2, but the agency that was enhanced in the students as language users and owners kept motivating them in further L2 learning. These students showed a continuing interest in exploring cultural aspects of hanzi/kanji. One student studied gender pronouns in Chinese language in the following year. Another student who presented on Taiwan's pronunciation system continues to be interested in the material culture of texts and book productions in East Asia. At the time of this writing, this student had just completed another project on the book bindings of Buddhist scripts and had applied some of her knowledge to her job in the antique department of the school library. One JAPN302 student enrolled in the beginning Chinese class in his senior year due to his new interest in Chinese language; he took this Chinese class in the fall after finishing all the requirements for his Japanese minor. One year after the project, students still expressed their fond memories of the activities of this project. One student told us that she has kept her square words hanging in her bedroom as a precious piece of artwork. We consider that their continued interest and inquiries displayed the agency that the project strengthened in these students.

Conclusion

The project we have presented here is experimental. We have seen positive signs of its outcomes in students' understanding of East Asian languages and new signs of a learning community forming among Chinese and Japanese L2 learners in our institution. We instructors are also encouraged by the students' renewed interest in exploring cultural contexts of linguistic diversities inherent in their L2 learning. We consider such a cross-language and interdisciplinary collaboration of integrating arts into language classrooms to be worthy of further explorations.

The project was designed to be flexible in terms of timeframe, students' proficiency levels, and activity format. The experiment introduced and discussed in this chapter was carried out as a 4-week project between CHIN102 and JAPN302. It could also take place in about 2 weeks or be extended beyond 4 weeks, with each step measured out according to the schedule and learning objectives of a course. It could be conducted as part of course requirements or as an extracurricular activity. East Asian language instructors can also include additional activities from Xu Bing's text-based arts. The lecture, as well as some of the follow-up activities, could be conducted in other classes in the Department of East Asian Studies or in nonlanguage classrooms to reach out to more students. For instance, we recently included Xu Bing's square word calligraphy as part of the school's outreach campaign for prospective students. A school-wide competition could be held on creating new square characters on certain designated themes to draw interest in East Asian languages within the college or as an interinstitutional activity. For instance, participants of such a competition could create new square words to denote social distancing on the theme of learning and teaching during the pandemic, as previously discussed by some scholars (Noda, 2020). We hope many ideas that are incipient in this project will be developed more fully in diverse teaching and learning settings.

References

Beacco, J., & Byram, M. (2007). *From linguistic diversity to plurilingual education: Guide for the development of language education policies in Europe*. Council of Europe. https://rm.coe.int/CoERMPublicCommonSearchServices/DisplayDCTMContent?documentId=09000016802fc1c4

Bennett, M. (Ed.). (1998). *Basic concepts of intercultural communication: Selected readings*. Intercultural Press.

Chikamatsu, N. (2019). Collaborative teaching of a Japanese content-based course: 3.11 and nuclear power crisis. In C. Melin (Ed.), *Foreign language teaching and the environment: Theory, curricula, institutional strategies* (pp. 146–160). The Modern Language Association of America.

Chikamatsu, N. (2022). Translanguaging in language and area-studies curriculum: A Japanese FLAC course of Minamata and Fukushima in environmental studies. In M. J. de la Fuente (Ed.), *Education for sustainable development in foreign language learning: Content-based instruction in college-level curricula* (pp. 215–232). Routledge.

Coulmas, F. (1991). *The writing systems of the world*. Blackwell.

Douglas Fir Group. (2016). A transdisciplinary framework for SLA in a multilingual world. *The Modern Language Journal, 100*(Supplement 2016), 19–47.

Fraser, S., & Li, Y. (Eds.). (2020). *Xu Bing: Beyond the book from the sky*. Springer.

Hall, J. K. (2019). *Essentials of SLA for L2 teachers: A transdisciplinary framework*. Routledge. https://doi.org/10.4324/9781315181271

Hamakawa, Y. (Ed.). (2010). *Nihongo kyoshi no tame no jissen kanji shido* [Practical kanji teaching for teachers of Japanese]. Kuroshio Shuppan.

Hartfield-Méndez, V., Stolley, K., & Hong, L. (2019). When sustainability means understanding: Modern languages and Emory University's Piedmont Project. In C. Melin (Ed.), *Foreign language teaching and the environment: Theory, curricula, institutional strategies* (pp. 272–288). The Modern Language Association of America.

Heinrich, P. (2012). *The making of monolingual Japan: Language ideology and Japanese modernity*. Multilingual Matters. http://dx.doi.org/10.21832/9781847696588

Jaworski, A. (2018). Language ideologies in the text-based art of Xu Bing: Implications for language policy and planning. In J. Tollefson & M. Milans (Eds.), *The Oxford handbook of language policy and planning* (pp. 677–703). Oxford University Press. doi:10.1093/oxfordhb/9780190458898.013.34

Kisselev, O., & Corner, W. (2019). Interdepartmental collaboration and curriculum design: Creating a Russian environmental sustainability course for advanced students. In C. Melin (Ed.), *Foreign language teaching and the environment: Theory, curricula, institutional strategies* (pp. 180–196). The Modern Language Association of America.

Kushner, E. (2009). *Crazy for kanji: A student's guide to the wonderful world of Japanese characters*. Stone Bridge Press.

Liu, Y., Yao, T., Bi, N.-P., Ge, L., & Shi, Y. (Eds.). (2009). *Integrated Chinese. Level 1, part 1* (3rd ed.). Cheng & Tsui.

Luo, H. (2021, February 20). *Teaching behavioral culture through Chinese-American telecollaboration [Abstract]*. 2021 Symposium on Teaching China and Japan: Pedagogical Collaboration Across Languages, Disciplines, Communities and Borders. https://las.depaul.edu/Documents/Luo%20Abstract%20&%20Bio.pdf

Meletis, D. (2021). On being a grapholinguist. In Y. Haralambous (Ed.), *Grapholinguistics in the 21st century—2020* (pp. 125–141). Fluxus Editions.

Mori, Y. (2020). Perceptual differences about kanji instruction: Native versus nonnative, and secondary versus postsecondary instructors of Japanese. *Foreign Language Annals, 53*(3), 550–575. https://doi.org/10.1111/flan.12480

Mori, Y., Omori, M., & Sato, K. (2020). Challenges of online collaborative learning between the USA and Japan: From the perspective of students participating in a COIL project. In *Proceedings of Princeton Japanese Pedagogy Forum* (pp. 121–134). Princeton. https://pjpf.princeton.edu/sites/g/files/toruqfl151/files/media/pjpf2020_proceedings-part2.pdf

Noda, M. (2020). Singata korona uirusu kansensyo ni tomonau aratana pikutoguramu no syutugen to sono kadai [Emerging new pictograms with COVID-19 and their challenges]. *Syakaigengogaku* [Sociolinguistics], *20*, 83–100.

Oka, M., Tsutsui, M., Kondo, J., Emori, S., Hanai, Y., & Ishikawa, S. (2009). *Jokyu eno Tobira: Gateway to advanced Japanese, learning through content and multimedia.* Kuroshio Shuppan.

Oyama, M. (2014). Gengo eno mezame katsudo no hatten to fuku-gengo kyoiku [Development of "awakening to languages" and its relevance to plurilingual education]. *Gengo Seisaku* [Language Policy], *10*, 47–71.

Reisinger, D., Quammen, V., Liu, Y., & Virgüez, E. (2022). Sustainability across the curriculum: A multilingual and intercultural approach. In M. J. de la Fuente (Ed.), *Education for sustainable development in foreign language learning: Content-based instruction in college-level curricula* (pp. 197–214). Taylor & Francis Group.

Tsao, H., & Ames, R. (2011). A dilemma in contemporary Chinese art: An introduction. In H. Tsao & R. T. Ames (Eds.), *Xu Bing and contemporary Chinese art* (pp. xiii–xxiv). State University of New York.

Wang, X. (2009). *Amazing characters & magic brushwork* (English and Chinese ed.). Beijing Language and Culture University Press.

Xu, B. (1987–1991). *Book from the sky* [Mixed media installation]. http://xubing.com/en/work/details/206

Xu, B. (2001). *Living word* [Mixed media installation]. http://xubing.com/en/work/details/186?type=project#186

Xu, B. (2003—ongoing). *Book from the ground* [Mixed media installation]. http://xubing.com/en/work/details/188?type=project#188

Xu, B. (2020). *Art for the people for the Met* [Mixed media installation]. www.xubing.com/en/work/details/615?year=2020&type=year#615

11 Cross-language and cross-disciplinary collaborations in a Mandarin CLAC course

Yan Liu

Introduction

The Modern Language Association (MLA) published its report "Foreign Languages and Higher Education: New Structures for a Changed World" in 2007; they proposed that foreign language education should develop students' translingual and transcultural competence. These two competencies can respectively help students "function as informed and capable interlocutors with educated native speakers in the target language" and "reflect on the world and themselves through the lens of another language and culture" (MLA, 2007). To achieve this goal, the committee called for an integrated curriculum to overcome the division between language and content and between tenure-track content-area faculty and non-tenure-track language faculty (MLA, 2007).

Regardless of this call for curriculum reform in foreign language departments, Lomicka and Lord (2018) found that only 39.1% of respondents indicated any reform attempts 10 years after the MLA's 2007 report. Despite some changes being made (e.g., engaging with the community and developing interdisciplinary initiatives), the progress was slow because of obstacles "ranging from lack of time, training, and knowledge to lack of institutional or administrative support" (p. 118). Consequently, Lomicka and Lord echoed the suggestion put forward by Porter (2009) that collaborations with colleagues across language departments, disciplines, and institutions are needed to initiate widespread change.

Similarly, according to a survey conducted by the Chinese Language Teachers Association in 2012, the long-standing separation between language teaching and content teaching still exists in Chinese programs at American universities (Li et al., 2014). Lower-level courses focus on language learning and are taught by non-tenure-track faculty or graduate students. In contrast, higher-level courses focus on content learning and are taught by tenure-track faculty. The researchers concluded that Chinese language teachers should develop an interdisciplinary curriculum and expand their teaching content beyond literary studies.

Nevertheless, current interdisciplinary courses are typically taught in English. The MLA suggested that foreign language teachers offer a credit-bearing discussion module in the target language through Foreign Language Across the Curriculum (FLAC) programs (MLA, 2007). FLAC programs first emerged in the 1980s

DOI: 10.4324/9781003266976-15

as a new initiative aiming to provide students with opportunities to practice their foreign language skills in courses outside language and literature departments (Klee & Barnes-Karol, 2006). Later, such programs were renamed Languages Across the Curriculum (LAC) and, more recently, Cultures and Languages Across the Curriculum (CLAC) to highlight the importance of culture. This curricular framework "focuses less on bringing disciplinary content or culture into the language classroom than on assimilating languages and cultures into instruction and research across a wide range of disciplinary and interdisciplinary contexts" (CLAC Consortium, n.d.). It requires collaborations across language departments and disciplines.

However, how should collaborative pedagogy be designed and implemented in CLAC courses? This chapter aims to answer this question through a case study of various pedagogical collaborations in a Mandarin CLAC course offered at a private research university in the southeastern United States. The pedagogical reflections shared in this chapter are expected to shed some light on future Chinese interdisciplinary course development. This chapter first introduces the theoretical frameworks guiding the course design. It then describes the Mandarin CLAC course and demonstrates different types of collaborations involved in developing and teaching this course. The benefits of these collaborations are discussed in the analysis of student learning and pedagogical reflections. Finally, the chapter offers some suggestions for future interdisciplinary Chinese course development and instruction.

Theoretical and pedagogical foundations

Transdisciplinary framework of second language acquisition (SLA)

To understand second language acquisition (SLA) in the context of globalization, technologization, and large-scale migration, the Douglas Fir Group (DFG, 2016) proposed the transdisciplinary framework, which calls for SLA researchers and practitioners to cross disciplinary boundaries in research and pedagogy. According to this framework, L2 learning is a complex and dynamic process involving three levels of social activity: micro level, meso level, and macro level. These levels of social activity are interrelated, constantly interact with each other, and are all essential to understanding SLA.

Based on this framework, Hall (2019) suggested that L2 teachers should expand students' opportunities to access various semiotic resources (i.e., multilingual and multimodal resources for meaning making) at the micro level and create increasingly complex meaning-making contexts for students to use newly gained resources to engage with others in classrooms, social institutions, and communities at the meso level. Moreover, L2 teachers need to be aware that what we teach and how we teach will impact students' development of L2 repertoires and their motivations, investment, and agency for L2 learning at the macro level. Therefore, teachers need to adopt a variety of instructional approaches (such as task-based approaches, pedagogy of multiliteracies, and content-based instruction) that can "facilitate communication, collaboration, critical thinking, and problem-solving" (p. 139). Given that both L2 learning and L2 teaching are complex and face many real-world challenges, teachers should work together to "respond to and develop sustainable solutions" (p. 139).

FLAC/CLAC framework

CLAC, initially known as FLAC, first emerged in American higher education in the 1980s. It has been viewed as one facet of content-based instruction (CBI) for languages (Straight, 1997). Discipline-specific content and multicultural awareness are the two essential components of CLAC programs, and language and culture are integrated to facilitate content area learning (Zilmer, 2018). Different models of integrating language and culture with content learning have been identified in CLAC programs such as dual degree, immersion, linked, modularized, infused, and empowered/independent study (Zilmer, 2018). The Mandarin CLAC course discussed in this chapter was developed using the linked model in which parallel courses are offered in the content area and the foreign languages. Existing research has found that CLAC is a useful model for internationalizing postsecondary curriculum (Bettencourt, 2011; Davies & Gonzales, 2017; Klee, 2009; Plough, 2016; Reisinger et al., 2015) and promoting students' linguistic and cultural competences (Plough, 2016; Reisinger, 2018; Reisinger et al., 2022) as well as global learning skills (Reisinger et al., 2022).

In addition, this interdisciplinary collaboration has proven to be mutually beneficial to language faculty and faculty in other disciplines (Chikamatsu, 2019, 2022; Kisselev & Comer, 2019; Reisinger, 2018; Reisinger et al., 2022). Chikamatsu (2019) described how the Japanese language faculty integrated lectures given by three bilingual specialists in the disciplines of ethics, history, and literature into a content-based course designed for advanced Japanese learners. The interdisciplinary collaboration encouraged both language and area studies instructors to "acquire interdisciplinary knowledge across fields well beyond their specializations" and transformed the language classroom into "a setting for language learners from various academic programs" (p. 159).

Successful collaborations between content area and language faculty have also been illustrated in developing a FLAC/CLAC course on environmental sustainability for advanced learners of Russian (Kisselev & Comer, 2019) and high intermediate and advanced learners of Chinese, French, and Spanish (Reisinger et al., 2022). All these courses were paired with a course taught in English by a professor in the discipline, and pedagogical collaborations mainly occurred in developing the FLAC/CLAC courses. The content area faculty members shared the detailed curricula, activities, and assignments they designed for their courses with the language faculty members, who then selected relevant materials in the target language and designed their FLAC/CLAC courses accordingly.

However, unlike Russian, French, and Spanish, Category IV languages like Japanese and Chinese are very hard for native English speakers to achieve adequate proficiency in discussing complex topics in content-based courses.

To address this problem, Chikamatsu (2022) used translanguaging practices (like translation activities and fluid usage of both English and Japanese) in a Japanese FLAC course on environmental ethics. According to García and Li (2014), translanguaging refers to "the multiple language interactions and other linguistic interrelationships that take place on different scales and spaces among multilingual speakers" (p. 51). It is beneficial for developing L2 proficiency (García & Li, 2014), accommodating students with different proficiency levels in one class (Kanō, 2016, as cited in Chikamatsu, 2022), and integrating language and content learning in FLAC courses (Chikamatsu, 2022; Kumagai & Kono, 2018).

Pedagogical collaborations in a Mandarin CLAC course

Background

The Mandarin CLAC course discussed in this chapter is offered at a private research university in the southeastern United States. This university attaches great importance to interdisciplinarity. Since its establishment in 2014, the CLAC program at this university has offered 45 half-credit tutorials in nine languages (including Arabic, French, German, Hindi, Italian, Mandarin, Portuguese, Spanish, Swahili) to more than 460 students (Reisinger et al., 2022). This CLAC program has paired core courses in the schools of global health, public policy, and environmental sciences with tutorials that provide complementary content in languages other than English. These tutorials provide students with diverse perspectives of the discipline and opportunities for continued use and development of their linguistic and cultural proficiencies (Reisinger et al., 2022).

All the CLAC tutorials were designed as half-credit courses and cross-listed in these schools and the language departments. All tutorials were titled "Voices in [a discipline, like global health, public policy, or the environment]" to highlight the importance of listening to and valuing the perspectives of the target language communities. Moreover, they were defined based on four characteristics: "1) meaningful engagement with local and global populations; 2) exploration of culturally specific solutions to real-world issues; 3) development of discourse competence for subject-specific use; and 4) critical reflection about how language and culture impact worldview" (Reisinger et al., 2022, p. 199).

The gateway course "Integrating environmental science and policy" (hereafter, ENVIRON 201) is a full-credit, 3-hour/week course that meets the environmental sciences and policy major requirements. This course is structured around four core modules, each representing a complex problem in environmental science, referring to those pressing environmental problems that are hard to resolve. In the fall 2020 course, students explored four complex problems: environmental justice, climate change and wildfires, hydropolitics, and biodiversity. Each module was covered in 2.5 weeks.

The current Mandarin CLAC course, entitled "Voices in the environment: Mandarin tutorial," meets for 75 minutes a week. Overseen by the CLAC program director, this tutorial, together with the French and Spanish tutorials, was paired with ENVIRON 201 taught in English by a professor in the school of the environmental sciences in fall 2020. Seven undergraduate students (including two Chinese heritage learners and five nonheritage learners) enrolled in the Mandarin CLAC tutorial. Six of them had a major or a minor in Chinese, and one had a minor in environmental science and policy. All students had taken at least one third-year Chinese language course before enrolling in this course, which was a prerequisite for the course. None of them enrolled in ENVIRON 201 even though concurrent enrollment in the two courses was encouraged.

The CLAC course included a variety of multimodal materials collected by the instructor. The instructor considered both the linguistic complexity and the diversity of perspectives or voices when selecting materials. The materials included images, social media posts, advertisements, oral or written interviews, news reports, research articles, government documents, and movie clips, mainly in Chinese but some in English. Before each class, students needed to study the assigned materials (usually one or two readings and at least one video or audio), compose a list of essential concepts or terminology related to the topic, and prepare for the class discussions. All class discussions and activities were conducted in Chinese. A typical class consisted of a warm-up (either a discussion of news or a current event related to the focal theme or a game or activity of the keywords about the theme), a group discussion of the materials assigned before class, a class discussion of new materials provided by the instructor, and a wrap-up activity (such as a Kahoot game, a writing activity on Padlet or Google Jamboard, or a reflection on the topic).

Developing and teaching the Mandarin CLAC course involved different pedagogical collaborations including partnerships across languages and disciplines. Student-led class discussions and student-student teamwork were also intentionally designed class activities. The following sections discuss these collaborations in detail.

Collaborations among faculty members across languages and disciplines

At the beginning of the 2020 summer, the professor of environmental science met with the three CLAC instructors and the CLAC program director. During this meeting, she explained her syllabus and course plan for ENVIRON 201 and shared her observations of students and the potential challenges of teaching this course. The CLAC program director introduced the CLAC framework and shared her experience designing and teaching CLAC courses.

After this meeting, the three tutorial instructors had multiple meetings discussing course details like course goals, course themes, and major instructional components. The Spanish instructor also shared his previous CLAC teaching experience while the French and Mandarin instructors shared their language and culture teaching expertise. The instructors thus put their different expertise together, which laid the foundation for the successful integration of the content and language instructions in the CLAC tutorials.

Developing course goals and course themes

Through the discussion, the three CLAC instructors decided to set similar course goals that took inspiration from the Global Learning benchmarks detailed in the Association of American Colleges & Universities (AAC&U) Valid Assessment of Learning in Undergraduate Education (VALUE) rubrics (AAC&U, 2014). The Mandarin CLAC tutorial set the following goals for students:

- Identify environmental challenges in China
- Discuss the issues with relative ease and confidence in Chinese
- Understand the factors underlying sustainability-related issues and relevant environmental policies in China
- Identify relevant and reliable resources beyond the conclusion of this course
- Create public-facing documents that are thematically relevant and culturally appropriate.

To align the tutorials with ENVIRON 201, the three instructors decided to focus on the same core modules covered in ENVIRON 201. However, as wildfires were not a pressing issue in China, the Mandarin instructor decided to focus on flood risks and food security, two urgent problems related to climate change in China. Furthermore, the Mandarin Chinese tutorial included culturally unique themes like traditional Chinese thoughts about environmental sustainability, the current government's advocacy for environmental protection, and challenges and opportunities in international collaborations on environmental issues related to the Belt & Road Initiative. Table 11.1 summarizes the course structure and course themes of ENVIRON201 and the Mandarin CLAC courses.

Identifying major instructional components

After finalizing the course goals and themes, the instructors collectively identified three major instructional components for their concurrent CLAC tutorials: case studies, project-based learning, and community-based learning. The instructors agreed to use one or two case studies for each core module. Through case studies, students could learn basic facts and concepts about the complex problem in the target culture and identify the specific linguistic and cultural factors at play.

For example, for the environmental justice module, students in the Mandarin Chinese CLAC tutorial explored the broad question of how history, language, and culture inform environmental justice via a case study of cancer villages in rural China. Before the class, students were asked to complete three activities: (a) select a village on the map of cancer villages in China[1] and investigate what kind of cancer people in this village got, why they got it, and the current situation of the village; (b) read a written interview in Chinese of a person who has visited 20 cancer villages in 20 provinces at his own expense; and (c) watch a short video (in Chinese but with English subtitles) featuring how a non-governmental organization (NGO) named Friends of Nature helped people in a cancer village in

Table 11.1 Course outline of ENVIRON 201 and Mandarin CLAC courses

Week	ENVIRON 201 (Two 75-minute classes per week)	Mandarin CLAC course (One 75-minute class per week)
1	Course Introduction	Course Introduction
2	Science Diplomacy	Environment Sustainability: Traditional Chinese Thoughts & Current Government's Advocacy
3	Module 1: Environmental Justice	Module 1: Environmental Justice
4		• Cancer villages
		• Environmental activism and activists in China (Student-led Discussion 1)
5		Module 2 Climate Change
	Module 2: Climate Change and Wildfires	• Climate change and flood risks in the Yangtze River Delta
6		• Climate change and food security in China (Student-led Discussion 2)
7		Midterm Project Presentation: PSA topics in Chinese
8	No class	Science Diplomacy:
		• Challenges and opportunities in international collaborations on environmental issues related to the Belt & Road Initiative (Guest Lecture 1)
	Module 3: Hydropolitics	
9		Module 3: Hydropolitics
10		• Three Gorges Dam and hydropower in China
		• Drinking water crisis in China (Guest Lecture 2)
11	Module 4: Biodiversity	Module 4: Biodiversity
12		• Panda conservation and biodiversity in Southwest China (Guest Lecture 3)
		• Biodiversity conservation and ecological tourism in ethnic minority populated areas in China (Student-led Discussion 3)
13		Final PSA Project Presentation in Chinese
	Conclusion	
14	Working on final project	Joint session in English with the French and Spanish tutorials: Students' final projects in different cultures

Southern China's Yunnan province file a lawsuit against the factory that polluted the area with chemical wastes.

During class discussions, students were first guided to synthesize their knowledge gained from the assigned materials and their own research. Students then identified different stakeholders' positions and perspectives (from villagers and local enterprises to NGOs, health experts, and the government), traced the roots of the problem, and compared the situations of the problem in the past and present in China. Finally, they were asked to compare the public health problems resulting from the environmental pollution in China and the United States and brainstorm possible interventions and solutions to the environmental injustice in rural China.

In addition to case studies, project-based learning (PBL) was identified as the second primary instructional approach to teaching the CLAC tutorials because PBL facilitates "academic discourse socialization, decision-making, critical thinking, and collaborative work skills while providing deep engagement with subject matter content through the use of language as medium" (Beckett et al., 2019, p. 8).

After consulting with the CLAC program director, the three CLAC instructors designed two projects for students to complete: a midterm project and a final project. For the midterm project, students needed to identify a specific environmental challenge related to the four complex problems in a target-language-speaking community, do a case study, and then present the case study to their classmates and lead a discussion about it. Students needed to analyze various factors (e.g., geography, history, culture, and ideology) underlying this environmental issue and proposed some possible policies/solutions to the problem.

For the final project, the instructors asked students to create a two-part public service campaign to address the problem identified in their midterm projects: a bilingual public service announcement (PSA) poster and a short video (in the target language but with English subtitles). The final project of ENVIRON 201 was to create a community-based social marketing campaign for a real or imagined organization to address a problem/issue related to the four complex problems. Students needed to write a description of the campaign (2000–2500 words in length) and make a video of 2–3 minutes about the need for this campaign. Therefore, the final projects of the parent course and the tutorials were not identical but were highly related.

To help students complete the final project, the tutorial instructors asked students to examine authentic PSAs in the target culture through which students could learn the linguistic features and conventions of the genre. They also designed the following areas for students to think about when creating their PSAs: (a) who their target audience is; (b) whom they represent; (c) what cultural and linguistic issues relate to the problem; and (d) how they should present the message in a culturally appropriate and easily accessible way to the target audience.

The third instructional component that the three CLAC instructors identified was community-based learning, which is defined as "any pedagogical tool in which the community becomes a partner in the learning process" (Mooney & Edwards, 2001, p. 182). Due to the COVID-19 pandemic, all courses had to be conducted online in the fall semester of 2020. Therefore, the instructors decided to connect the students, who were in different locations and time zones, with professionals or experts in the local or international communities via Zoom, which they believed would allow students to engage with different perspectives and voices.

The Mandarin instructor invited three specialists in the discipline of environmental studies (see Table 11.2). Before each lecture, students were asked to complete the readings (including newspaper articles, research reports, or scholarly papers) provided by the guest speaker and then prepare a few questions they would like to ask the speaker. Readings and presentations were provided in English and/or Chinese, as indicated in Table 11.2. All the specialists prepared PowerPoint

Table 11.2 Specialist lectures: Themes and materials

Week	Guest speakers	Lecture themes	Reading materials
8	A senior research fellow in environmental policy [E]	Challenges and opportunities in international collaborations on environmental issues related to the Belt & Road Initiative	• "Belt and Road insiders: What we think about 'greening' the initiative" [E] • "Belt and Road countries will make or break the Paris Agreement" [E] • "China is quietly reshaping the world" [E]
10	A senior research scientist in hydrology and meteorology [C]	Drinking water crisis in China	• "China is heading towards a water crisis: will government changes help?" [C&E] • "Re-evaluating China's water crisis" [C&E] • "Chinese countryside facing more serious drinking water crisis than cities" [C&E]
11	A professor of environmental sciences [C]	Panda conservation and biodiversity in Southwest China	• "China's endemic vertebrates sheltering under the protective umbrella of the giant panda" [E] • "Panda Nation: The Construction and Conservation of China's Modern Icon" [C&E]

Note. [E]: conducted in English; [C]: conducted in Chinese

slides in English. Each guest lecture lasted 40–45 minutes and was followed by a Q&A and open discussion in Chinese. After each guest lecture, students were required to summarize the main content and their reflections in Chinese in the following class.

Creating opportunities for students to learn from each other

To facilitate students' understanding of the essential roles of language and culture in sustainability issues worldwide, the instructor of ENVIRON 201 and the three tutorial instructors created a course project website for students in the four courses to share their final projects. Students in ENVIRON 201 were required to view and comment on at least three videos (including the PSA videos made by students in CLAC tutorials). In addition, the three tutorial instructors organized a joint session in English at the end of the semester. In this session, students were first assigned to different breakout rooms to present their final projects to each other (see Table 11.3 for the group arrangement and students' final project topics). Students then came back together as a class to discuss the differences and similarities of the sustainability-related issues they identified in different parts of the world and reflect on the connections among language, culture, and sustainability.

Table 11.3 Breakout room arrangement and students' final project topics

Groups	Chinese	French	Spanish
1	e-waste	plastics pollution	air pollution; water pollution
2	e-waste	food waste	petroleum use
3	fast fashion	luxury products	environment system
4	fast fashion	heat pumps and renewable energy	car emission; nature and humans
5	water safety	algae and water pollution	water resources; future of animals
6	water safety	indigenous rights and forestry	tree-cutting; animal and planet

Through discussions and reflections, students discovered many overlaps in their projects. For instance, similar environmental issues (such as water pollution, air pollution, and waste problems) exist in countries worldwide regardless of their development stages. Some students also recognized that all their projects were related to environmental injustice because decisions or actions made by the United States and other major superpower countries would affect those underdeveloped or previously colonized nations. One example is the e-waste problem in China. American people import all sorts of digital gear from countries like China and then send the waste back when they dump the devices. Thus, China has become another trashcan for the United States and has suffered from environmental damages, whereas many Americans never consider the negative consequences of their actions.

One difference that students identified is the roles of government, markets, and individuals in responding to sustainability-related issues across different cultures. As one student summarized based on their group discussion, the government in China has more direct control of everything, so many questions about sustainability are directed at the government. Meanwhile, in Latin America, foreign companies are blamed for making a lot of harmful impacts on the local environment, and the government is expected to protect the local communities over foreign companies. In many Francophone countries, however, individual actions are more emphasized as opposed to cooperative or government actions. Another significant difference that students pinpointed was that the vernacular of each language used to talk about sustainability is different. For example, when talking about environmental justice, there are different terms in different languages that deal with phenomena occurring in different areas.

Student-led class discussions

In the Mandarin CLAC course, students had an opportunity to lead a class discussion with one or two partners on a theme of their choice during the semester. Before the presentation, they first needed to identify at least one article and one video or audio on the theme from a list of library and internet sources recommended by the instructor. They then needed to check with the teacher whether the materials were appropriate in language and content. After getting the teacher's approval, they needed to share the materials and a list of 10–15 keywords with other students at least 72 hours before the class. Finally, they needed to prepare a summary of the materials, several discussion questions for each material, and a game or an activity to review the essential concepts or information related to the theme. Table 11.4 lists the details of these student-led discussions.

Students' learning outcomes and feedback

To better understand students' perceptions of the CLAC tutorial on their learning, in the last class the students were invited to complete an anonymous survey developed based on the AAC&U's (2014) VALUE rubric. This survey asked about students' perceived gains in linguistic knowledge, content knowledge, and global learning skills. All seven students completed the survey. The results are presented in Table 11.5, Table 11.6, and Table 11.7.

The results indicate that students thought that the CLAC tutorial had improved their language learning, content learning, and global learning skills. Moreover, students reported that taking the Mandarin CLAC tutorial made them very likely or somewhat likely to take a content course in the core discipline and enroll in an additional language course. They would also be very likely to recommend this CLAC course to another student. When asked why, one student explained that

Table 11.4 Student-led discussions: Themes, materials, and wrap-up activities

Week	Theme	Materials	Wrap-up activity
4	Environmental activism and activists in China	• One video and one article about mass protest against a polluting project in Shifang (both in Chinese) • One news article and a video clip of Chai Jing's documentary entitled "Under the Dome" (in Chinese, but with English translation or subtitles)	Kahoot game reviewing important facts and concepts
6	Climate change and food security in China	• An article titled "Climate change will make rice less nutritious" (in Chinese) • A YouTube video featuring local farmers' combats against climate change in Guang Xi and Yunnan provinces (in Chinese, but with English subtitles)	Kahoot game reviewing the important facts and concepts
12	Biodiversity conservation and ecological tourism in ethnic minority populated areas in China	• An article titled "Deep history in western China reveals how humans can enhance biodiversity" (in Chinese and English) • Two YouTube videos featuring biodiversity conservation and ecological tourism in villages populated by Li ethnic minorities (in Chinese, but with English subtitles)	Padlet discussion about the pros and cons of the ecological tourism

Table 11.5 Students' perceived gains in the target language (Chinese)

# Question How much growth do you think you've made in the following areas? "I can . . . about the course content"	Substantial % N	Moderate % N	A little % N	Very little to none % N
1 carry on a conversation with a native speaker	28.57% 2	57.14% 4	14.29% 1	0.00% 0
2 deliver an oral presentation in class	57.14% 4	42.86% 3	0.00% 0	0.00% 0
3 listen to a presentation or watch a video without subtitles	42.86% 3	28.57% 2	28.57% 2	0.00% 0
4 read and comprehend a newspaper or short article	28.57% 2	42.86% 3	28.57% 2	0.00% 0
5 write a short report or paper	57.14% 4	28.57% 2	14.29% 1	0.00% 0
6 exchange email or text to discuss ideas and opinions about the related topics	42.86% 3	57.14% 4	0.00% 0	0.00% 0

Table 11.6 Students' perceived gains in the course content

# Question Did working in/through Chinese . . .	A great deal % N	A lot % N	A little % N	Not at all % N
1 improve your understanding of the content in the core discipline?	28.57% 2	71.43% 5	0.00% 0	0.00% 0
2 improve your ability to identify environmental challenges related to the culture of your CLAC course?	71.43% 5	28.57% 2	0.00% 0	0.00% 0
3 help you develop a culturally specific understanding of the effect of environmental problems on local populations?	57.14% 4	42.86% 3	0.00% 0	0.00% 0

"the course reaffirmed my commitment to strengthening my Chinese skills and looking for jobs in the Chinese clean energy space." Another student said, "I think this course is great for people who want to improve their language skills in a low-stress environment while discussing significant issues. I genuinely enjoyed this class and felt more educated about the world because of it." A third student shared that "it was super interesting and great to learn about a specific issue in a different language and from the perspective of a different culture."

Pedagogical reflections

Interdisciplinary collaborations for content and language integration in higher education is less studied (Wallace et al., 2020). Although a handful of pedagogical projects have been reported on the interdisciplinary collaborations in FLAC/

Table 11.7 Students' perceived gains in global learning skills

#	Question How much growth do you think you've made in the following areas? "I can..."	Substantial % N	Moderate % N	A little % N	Very little to none % N
1	understand the interrelationships among myself, local, and global communities	42.86% 3	57.14% 4	0.00% 0	0.00% 0
2	learn from perspectives and experiences different from my own and understand how my place in the world informs and limits my knowledge	14.29% 1	85.71% 6	0.00% 0	0.00% 0
3	stay curious to learn the cultural diversity of other people and recognize the origins and influences of my cultural heritage	71.43% 5	28.57% 2	0.00% 0	0.00% 0
4	recognize my responsibilities to society—locally, nationally, and globally	57.14% 4	42.86% 3	0.00% 0	0.00% 0
5	understand complex and overlapping worldwide natural and human systems	71.43% 5	28.57% 2	0.00% 0	0.00% 0
6	apply knowledge and skills gained to real-life problem-solving, both alone and with others	57.14% 4	42.86% 3	0.00% 0	0.00% 0

CLAC courses (Chikamatsu, 2019, 2022; Kisselev & Comer, 2019; Reisinger, 2018; Reisinger et al., 2022), little is known about how to develop and teach Mandarin FLAC/CLAC courses. Thus, this chapter features a Mandarin CLAC course on environment studies and highlights collaboration among faculty across disciplines and languages. Student feedback clearly indicated that the course design contributed to students' perceived gains in language learning, content learning, and global learning skills.

According to the transdisciplinary framework (DFG, 2016), L2 learning is complex and involves three levels of social activity: micro level, meso level, and macro level. At the micro level, in the Mandarin CLAC course under discussion, the instructor provided students with or led them to explore various multimodal materials in both Mandarin Chinese and English where the fluid usage of the two complements and stimulates learning and thinking (García & Li, 2014). The integration of community speakers across languages also provided additional semiotic resources that can enrich learners' experience in the complex social contexts.

At the meso level, learners participate in social activities in different sociocultural institutions and communities (such as families, schools, neighborhoods, places of work and worship, and social organizations). In the Mandarin CLAC course, students were given opportunities to collaborate in leading class discussions, doing a case study of an environmental challenge in China, and creating a two-part campaign (PSA poster and video) to address the challenge. These collaborations enabled students to engage with their peers in and outside of the classroom, which—according to the transdisciplinary framework (DFG, 2016)—would contribute to students' multilingual repertoires and their learning agency. More importantly, they were able to exchange ideas about environmental issues in China, work together to analyze the complex factors underlying the environmental challenges they identified, and come up with culturally appropriate suggestions or solutions to address the challenges. Therefore, such collaborative learning among students could improve their communication, critical thinking, and problem-solving skills with increased awareness of their own social identities in the L2 context.

At the macro level, learners' L2 repertoires, motivations, investment, and agency for L2 learning are impacted by what teachers teach and how they teach. The collaborations among instructors across languages and disciplines made it possible to align the content of the CLAC courses with that of the parent course. The CLAC instructors also worked together to develop course goals, identify instructional components, design student projects, and create opportunities for students in different languages to learn from each other. This new approach integrating language, culture, and content emphasizes the importance of creating complex social contexts to enable learners' access to and learning of multimodal resources needed for meaningful social interactions in Mandarin Chinese (DFG, 2016; Hall, 2019).

Finally, as previous research has shown, working with faculty across languages and disciplines was mutually beneficial for language teachers and content area teachers (Chikamatsu, 2019, 2022; Davison, 2006; Kisselev & Comer, 2019; Li, 2020; Lo, 2015; Reisinger, 2018; Reisinger et al., 2022). The collaborative teaching encouraged the CLAC instructors and the instructor of ENVIRON 201 to acquire knowledge across disciplines and beyond their specializations. This collaboration also expanded their potentials in developing and teaching interdisciplinary courses. Taking myself as an example, if I had not taught the CLAC courses, I would have had little chance to work with instructors outside of my department or know much about the instructional approaches used in other language programs and disciplines. With the experience gained in developing and teaching the Mandarin CLAC course, I also developed an interdisciplinary course on China-U.S. relations, which has increased the Chinese program's enrollment and promoted the development of Chinese interdisciplinary courses at the university.

Conclusion

This chapter has reported on the design and implementation of a Mandarin CLAC course guided by the transdisciplinary framework in SLA (DFG, 2016). Collaborations among different stakeholders (i.e., teachers, students, and the community of specialists) at different levels of learning have exemplified how to develop and teach Mandarin interdisciplinary courses successfully.

Hopefully, this study will encourage more Chinese language educators to explore the possibilities of codeveloping or coteaching CLAC courses or programs at their institutions. More importantly, it provides a successful model for language faculties and nonlanguage specialists to collaborate in designing and teaching CLAC courses or programs. Student-student collaboration is not new as collaborative learning has been widely used in classrooms since the late 1980s (Brufee, 2000). However, the collaborative tasks/projects designed at the micro and meso levels are noteworthy because they promote students' translingual, transcultural, and critical thinking abilities, which are the fundamental goals of CLAC courses.

Despite its significance, this project has several limitations. First, the current Mandarin CLAC students were not concurrently enrolled in ENVIRON 201. To enforce content and language learning in the FLAC/CLAC model, we hope to promote the registration of the two courses among advanced Chinese learners. Second, this study did not include area studies specialists' reflections or perceptions of the interdisciplinary collaboration, which could otherwise provide additional insights. Finally, although this project demonstrated the potential benefits of the CLAC courses on students' learning outcomes, the number of students is small, and the learning outcomes were measured by perceived gains and not by assessment tools. Therefore, more rigorous studies are needed to validate the benefits of CLAC courses.

Note

1 www.google.com/maps/d/u/0/viewer?msa=0&dg=feature&mid=1R70M9vbPN104K-YqFlUnK1xUDoY&ll=34.781473738473444%2C114.22005875000002&z=5.

References

Association of American Colleges and Universities. (AAC&U). (2014). *VALUE rubrics: Global learning*. www.aacu.org/value/rubrics/global

Beckett, G. H., Slater, T., & Mohan, B. (2019). Philosophical foundation, theoretical approaches, and gaps in the literature. In H. G. Beckett & T. Slater (Eds.), *Global perspectives on project-based language learning, teaching and assessment* (pp. 3–22). Routledge.

Bettencourt, M. (2011). Languages across the curriculum: A response to internationalization in foreign language education. *Multicultural Education, 19*(1), 55–58.

Brufee, K. (2000). *Collaborative learning: Higher education, interdependence, and the authority of knowledge* (2nd ed.). John Hopkins University Press.

Chikamatsu, N. (2019). Collaborative teaching of a Japanese content-based course: 3.11 and nuclear power crisis. In C. Melin (Ed.), *Foreign language teaching and the environment: Theory, curricula, institutional structures* (pp. 215–232). The Modern Language Association of America.

Chikamatsu, N. (2022). Translanguaging in language and area-studies curriculum: A Japanese FLAC course of Minamata and Fukushima in environmental humanities. In M. J. de la Fuente (Ed.), *Education for sustainable development in foreign language learning: Content-based instruction in college-level curricula* (pp. 197–214). Routledge.

CLAC Consortium. (n.d.). *Consortial members*. https://clacconsortium.org/institutional-descriptions

Davies, D. K., & Gonzales, S. (2017). Empowering learners: A win—win solution for students and educators. *New Directions for Student Services, 158*(Summer), 23–35.

Davison, C. (2006). Collaboration between ESL and content teachers: How do we know when we are doing it right? *International Journal of Bilingual Education and Bilingualism, 9*(4), 454–475.

Douglas Fir Group. (2016). A transdisciplinary framework for SLA in a multilingual world. *Modern Language Journal, 100*(S1), 19–47.

García, O., & Li, W. (2014). *Translanguaging: Language, bilingualism, and education*. Palgrave Pivot.

Hall, K. J. (2019). *Essentials of SLA for L2 teachers: A transdisciplinary framework*. Routledge.

Kisselev, O., & Comer, W. (2019). Interdepartmental collaboration and curriculum design: Creating a Russian environmental sustainability course for advanced students. In C. Melin (Ed). *Foreign language teaching and the environment: Theory, curricula, institutional structures* (pp. 110–118). The Modern Language Association of America.

Klee, C. A. (2009). Internationalization and foreign languages: The resurgence of interest in languages across the curriculum. *The Modern Language Journal, 93*(4), 618–621.

Klee, C. A., & Barnes-Karol, G. (2006). A content-based approach to Spanish language study: Foreign languages across the curriculum. In R. Salaberry & B. A. Lafford (Eds.), *The art of teaching Spanish: Second language acquisition from research to praxis* (pp. 23–38). Georgetown University Press.

Kumagai, Y., & Kono, K. (2018). Collaborative curricular initiatives: Linking language and literature courses for critical and cultural literacies. *Japanese Language and Literature, 52*, 247–276.

Li, Y. (2020). Language: Content partnership in higher education: Development and opportunities. *Higher Education Research & Development, 39*(3), 500–514.

Li, Y., Wen, X., & Xie, T. (2014). CLTA 2012 survey of college-level Chinese language programs in North America. *Journal of the Chinese Language Teachers, 49*(1), 1–49.

Lo, Y. Y. (2015). A glimpse into the effectiveness of L2-content cross-curricular collaboration in content-based instruction programmes. *International Journal of Bilingual Education and Bilingualism, 18*(4), 443–462.

Lomicka, K., & Lord, G. (2018). Ten years after the MLA report: What has changed in foreign language departments? *ADFL Bulletin, 44*(2), 116–120.

Modern Language Association (MLA). (2007). *Foreign languages and higher education: New structures for a changed world*. www.mla.org/Resources/Research/Surveys-Reports-and-Other-Documents/Teaching-Enrollments-and-Programs/Foreign-Languages-and-Higher-Education-New-Structures-for-a-Changed-World

Mooney, L. A., & Edwards, B. (2001). Experiential learning in sociology. *Teaching Sociology, 9*(2), 181–194.

Plough, I. C. (2016). Cultures & languages across the curriculum: Strengthening intercultural competence & advancing internationalization. *Multicultural Education, 23*(2), 46–52.

Porter, C. (2009). The MLA recommendations: Can we get there from here? *ADFL Bulletin, 40*(1), 162–177.

Reisinger, D. S. (2018). Measuring the impact of cultures and languages across the curriculum: New research directions. In D. Soneson & C. Zilmer (Eds.), *Developing responsible global citizenship through cultures and languages across the curriculum (CLAC):*

Selected papers from the 2016 CLAC conference (pp. 17–40). University of Minnesota, Center for Advanced Research on Language Acquisition.

Reisinger, D. S., Clifford, J., Deardorf, D., & Whetten, K. (2015). Cultures and languages across the curriculum in global health. In W. Green & C. Whitsed (Eds.), *Critical perspectives on internationalising the curriculum in disciplines: Reflective narrative accounts from business, education and health* (pp. 261–274). Sense Publishers.

Reisinger, D. S., Quammen, S. V., Liu, Y., & Virguez, E. (2022). Sustainability across the curriculum: A multilingual and intercultural approach. In M. J. de la Fuente (Ed.), *Education for sustainable development in foreign language learning: Content-based instruction in college-level curricula* (pp. 197–214). Routledge.

Straight, H. S. (1997). Language-based content instruction. In S. B. Stryker & B. L. Leaver (Eds.), *Content-based instruction in foreign language education: Models and methods* (pp. 239–260). Georgetown University Press.

Wallace, A., Spiliotopoulos, V., & Ilieva, R. (2020). CLIL collaborations in higher education: A critical perspective. *English Teaching & Learning, 44*, 127–148.

Zilmer, C. (2018). A CLAC framework. In D. Soneson & C. Zilmer (Eds.), *Developing responsible global citizenship through cultures and languages across the curriculum (CLAC): Selected papers from the 2016 CLAC conference* (pp. 9–15). University of Minnesota, Center for Advanced Research on Language Acquisition.

Section 5
Across borders
International collaboration

12 The United States-Japan online magazine project

International telecollaborations as translanguaging spaces

Yuri Kumagai and Momoyo Shimazu

Introduction

This chapter introduces an international telecollaboration project, Telecollaborative Online Magazine Project, between a third-year Japanese language course at a U.S. college and seminar courses at two Japanese universities conducted during the fall 2020 semester. International telecollaboration has rapidly gained popularity for language instructional projects (O'Dowd & Lewis, 2016). Increased access to personal computers and other mobile devices, the worldwide development and expansion of the internet, and the diffusion of new communication technologies have facilitated this popularity by providing language educators with new resources and opportunities. Thorne (2016) went so far as to call the trend "the virtual internationalization turn in language study" (p. ix). Many international telecollaboration projects tend to focus on developing learners' language skills and intercultural competencies by having them interact with native speakers of the target language—a language education model shaped by monolingual ideology (Flores, 2013; Ortega, 2019).

Instead of aligning with the monolingual ideology, our project was informed by the translingual practice—specifically, translanguaging (García, 2009; Li, 2018). Unlike many other international telecollaboration projects or collaborative online international learning initiatives, our goal was not language learning or cultural learning *per se*, although such learning was certainly expected to come about. Rather, we aimed to offer a space for students from both countries to learn to relate to each other, negotiate with each other, and collaborate toward a shared goal of producing an online magazine.

In what follows, we first describe the theoretical framework that informs our project and then describe the project in detail along with its learning outcomes. We conclude this chapter with a discussion of future pedagogical implications.

Theoretical framework

International telecollaboration

Telecollaboration—a term originally coined by Warschauer (1996)—can be variously referred to as online intercultural exchange (O'Dowd, 2007; O'Dowd &

Lewis, 2016), virtual exchange (Helm, 2015; O'Dowd, 2018), and collaborative online international learning (COIL) (Rubin, 2016), to name a few. Although the organizational structures and educational objectives of previous telecollaborative projects vary depending on educational contexts and pedagogical focus (Dooly & Vinagre, 2021), they share commonalities in that they involve

> the engagement of groups of learners in extended periods of online intercultural interaction and collaboration with partners from other cultural contexts or geographical locations as an integrated part of their educational programmes and under the guidance of educators and/or expert facilitators.
> (O'Dowd, 2018, p. 5)

Since the early 1990s, educators in the field of foreign language education have seen the potential of connecting language learners with counterparts in other countries in order to provide authentic interactions with native speakers of the target language (Kern et al., 2008; O'Dowd & Waire, 2009). Many telecollaborative studies have reported learning outcomes in areas as diverse as learner autonomy (O'Rourke, 2005), linguistic accuracy and fluency (O'Rourke, 2005; Ware, 2005), online intercultural communication skills (Belz & Müller-Hartmann, 2003; O'Dowd & Ritter, 2006), and electronic and digital literacy (Hauck, 2007). More recently, telecollaboration has become understood as "a form of language-mediated social action that brings the complex reality of communication across cultural and linguistic borders into direct experiences" (Thorne, 2016, p. ix). Importantly, telecollaboration shifts the learners' experiences away from a sole focus on learning languages and toward an approach that develops capacities for creating social relationships by using the language (Lewis & O'Dowd, 2016). O'Dowd and Waire (2009) argued that, unlike regular classroom-based task activities carried out in monolingual and monocultural contexts, telecollaborative tasks carry a strong possibility of producing meaning-centered activity that allows for the negotiation of linguistic and cultural meaning.

Although it is important to acknowledge that many telecollaborations focus on negotiations of meaning through experiential leaning approaches and regard culture as part and parcel of language learning, we find it problematic that cultures have been dichotomized (i.e., my culture versus your culture) in many previous telecollaborative practices. Furthermore, static relationships between native speakers and nonnative speakers (i.e., language learners) have been perpetuated (Train, 2006) with more power given to the former—a practice drawn from monolingual ideologies.

Translanguaging

In foreign language instructional practices, the target-language-only or one-language-at-a-time monolingual ideologies still dominate much practice and policy (Li, 2018; Ortega, 2019). Li Wei (2018) further critiqued the current practices by noting that the actual purpose of learning new languages—to become bilingual and multilingual, rather than to replace the learner's L1 to become another monolingual—often gets forgotten or neglected, and the bilingual, rather than monolingual, speaker is rarely used as the model for teaching and learning.

(p. 16)

To challenge such practices, the current project was designed based on the theory of translingual practices (Canagarajah, 2013)—specifically, translanguaging (García, 2009; Li, 2018). Learning spaces created through the telecollaboration were thought of as translanguaging space, which is

a space that is created by and for translanguaging practices . . . where language users break down the ideologically laden dichotomies between the macro and the micro, the societal and the individual, and the social and the psychological through interactions.

(Li, 2018, p. 23)

From a translanguaging lens, language practices are viewed as "fluid and dynamic practices that transcend the boundaries between named languages, language varieties, and language and other semiotic systems" (Li, 2018, p. 9). In our everyday lives, we use all available linguistic and other semiotic resources as a repertoire rather than adhering to one named language or another. Treating language as a separate system that stands free from other semiotic resources (including other languages) and is detached from its context does not accurately describe how we engage in meaning-making practices.

The idea of translingual practice has changed both scholars' and practitioners' views of language plurality from being a hindrance to being a resource in world language classrooms (Horner et al., 2011; Li, 2018). As such, instructional practices that align with translanguaging encourage students to take advantage of and deploy all available linguistic (and other semiotic) resources and support students in their development of "the ability to work across differences, not just of language but of disciplines and cultures" (Horner et al., 2011, p. 312). In this way, learners gain agency to use language critically and creatively and become empowered to nurture a sense of ownership of their own language use (Creese & Blackledge, 2015; Kato & Kumagai, 2020; Li, 2011).

Translanguaging is aligned with the transdisciplinary framework (Douglas Fir Group, 2016; Hall, 2018), which is the overarching theme of this volume. This framework emphasizes the multifaceted nature of language learning that considers three nested levels of contexts that mutually shape each other: micro contexts of social action and interaction, meso contexts of sociocultural institutions and communities, and the macro level of ideological structures (Douglas Fir Group, 2016, p. 39). This project fits well within the framework as it challenges notions of monolingualism and native-speakerism. Furthermore, it views learning (language and otherwise) as a complex, multidimensional, and socioculturally situated activity. At the micro level, individual students engage in interactions by employing available language resources for accomplishing the communicative goals while surrounded by meso-level social contexts wherein each student assumes various identities (or positionings) for building relationships with others; at the macro level, various ideologies of language learning (e.g., monolingualism and native-speakerism) permeate.

Telecollaborative online magazine project

Project description

During the fall 2020 semester, three instructors involved in the field of Japanese language education collaboratively designed (i.e., general framework, goals, and procedures) and implemented a telecollaborative online magazine project. An educational technology staff member from the U.S. college also played a critical role in identifying technological tools to be used for the project, conducting workshops for students to become familiar with technologies and other important issues related to online-based materials, and offering support to the instructors throughout the project.

Ten students in a third-year Japanese course in the United States and nine students from two Japanese universities—six students from a seminar on Japanese discourse analysis at a university in Osaka and three students in a global study seminar on Japanese communication at a university in Tokyo—participated in the project. Participation in the project was a part of the course requirements and counted toward the course grades for the students in the Japanese course (United States) and in the discourse analysis seminar (Osaka). For the students in the global study seminar (Tokyo), participating in this project was one of several options from which students could choose in order to satisfy the seminar requirements. The students mostly worked in groups of four[1] to create their online magazines, which were to address social issues pertaining to the United Nations's sustainable development goals (SDGs).[2] The audience of online magazines included those studying Japanese as well as those interested in learning about various issues related to SDGs. Throughout the semester, each group engaged in a weekly exchange using Zoom and Slack.[3] Each group also used Google Docs to share documents (e.g., a list of resources, possible images for a magazine) among the group members. The online magazines were created using Google Slides. The following were presented to the students as project goals shared by all three schools.

- Learn about a social issue of your interest (both global and local levels)
- Generate ideas for actions to help solve the issue as a group
- Develop communication skills that go beyond the different languages and cultures
- Learn to collaborate
- Create a multilingual and multimodal online magazine
- Contribute to wider communities by sharing the online magazine

The participating students' language profiles demonstrated their rich linguistic resources. All students were familiar with Japanese and English, and 10 of the 19 students had Chinese as a language resource (with varying levels of proficiency).[4] In accordance with the notion of translanguaging, the students were encouraged to draw upon any language that would facilitate effective communications. However, students used Japanese as the main medium of communication because, as the questionnaire responses revealed, the Japanese language students wanted to try using Japanese as much as possible and the students from Japan were also enrolled in the seminar addressing issues of communication in Japanese. For the students' final product, an online magazine, they were instructed to use both Japanese and English (and other languages, if they chose) along with multimodal elements (images, graphs, etc.). We also asked students to articulate why their language choices were effective for the purpose of achieving their goals.

Procedures

Because of the differences of academic calendars in the United States and Japan, the group activities did not commence until the fourth week of the U.S. fall semester. We held the kickoff meeting, conducted in Japanese, via Zoom to introduce each other and to set the general rules for the interactions; students were sent to separate breakout rooms[5] to meet with their group members and engaged in icebreaker activities. From that point on, each group met weekly on their own via Zoom. Three specific tasks were assigned during the semester to pace and monitor the students' progress: deciding the group theme for the project, creating a magazine outline, and reporting the progress of creating the magazine.

In the eighth week, we posted on Slack a prerecorded interactive workshop video (about 40 minutes) regarding copyright issues pertaining to the use of images and other information found on the internet. The video also discussed design elements that would help the students create an effective magazine. The video was closed captioned in English to help facilitate those students in Japan who were not used to hearing English instruction.

The students finished their Google Slides magazines by the end of the fourteenth week. All magazines were featured on the U.S. college's WordPress site (https://sophia.smith.edu/sdgs-magazines/), which is open to the public. At the end of the semester, we all met synchronously via Zoom for a final presentation where the students shared their online magazines and reflections on the process of collaboratively creating a magazine. We did not specify which language(s) to use for the presentations; however, all students conducted their presentations in Japanese. Figure 12.1 demonstrates the procedures of the project.

Learning outcomes

In the following subsections, we discuss our findings about students' learning on three themes: translanguaging for building rapport, communication with the magazine readers, and sensitive language choices and their impact.

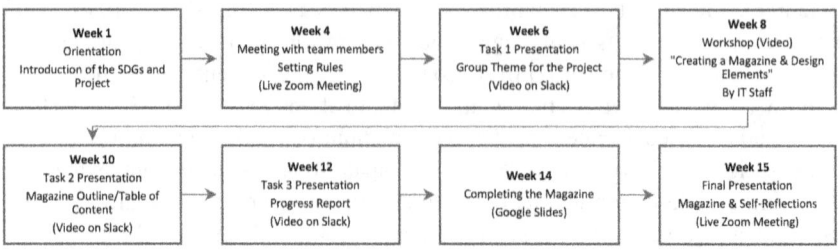

Figure 12.1 Project procedures (based on the U.S. college schedule)

Table 12.1 Language profile of the group members (*all names are pseudonyms)

Name*	College	Home language(s)	Academic language at college	Foreign language(s)
Rou	USA	Chinese	English	Japanese
Emi	USA	English and Japanese	English	Japanese
Xinran	Osaka, Japan	Japanese (Kansai dialect)[7] and Chinese	Japanese	English
Rei	Tokyo, Japan	Japanese	Japanese	English Chinese

Translanguaging to build rapport with group members

To discuss how translanguaging was employed to accomplish the tasks, we first look at one group as a case study. We selected this group because they presented a great diversity in language and cultural backgrounds, as shown in Table 12.1.[6]

Based on our analysis of the various video recordings, we found that students engaged in translanguaging in order to establish and maintain good relationships with others. We observed that students shifted between named languages—in this case, Japanese and English—when the students in the U.S. college wanted to express something that was too difficult or complex to communicate in Japanese.

Example 1 is an excerpt from a group meeting in which the members were discussing whether or not they should change their chosen SDG. Initially, the group selected "Goal 16: Peace, Justice, and Strong Institutions" and intended to address LGBT+ issues as a topic of focus. However, Rou found that LGBT+ issues were specifically addressed under "Goal 5: Gender Equality," which prompted her to bring up the topic during the meeting.

Example 1: group discussion[8]

1. **Rou:** これは [this] ... I don't know if that counts, I think it counts ... but I think, I just thought they had a specific LGBT category in ジェンダー平等 [gender equality], so

2. **Xinran:** うん、うん、うん [Yes, yes, yes]
3. **Emi:** 違うトピックにするってことですか [Are you saying we should change the topic?]
4. **Rou:** 違うゴール [change the goal]
5. **Xinran:** ゴール 5 の「ジェンダー平等を実現しよう」にチェンジしてやる...のが早いのかな [It may be quicker to ... *change* to Goal 5, "Achieve Gender Equality"]
6. **Emi:** ああ、そうかもしんない [Ah, it may be so]

In Line 1, Rou shifted to English and rather hesitantly started to explain that, although LGBT+ topics would probably "count" under the Peace and Justice goal, they may be a better fit with the Gender Equality goal. Emi immediately asked for clarification (in Japanese) as to whether Rou was suggesting that the group change their topic (Line 3). Rou responded that it was the goal, not the topic, that she was suggesting changing and she shifted back to speaking in Japanese. In Line 5, Xinran tried to articulate Rou's idea and proposed a new direction for the group project, which Emi agreed with.

Interestingly, Xinran used the word "change" in her Japanese utterance (italicized) with a rotating hand gesture to mean "change" (see Figure 12.2). Although we do not know if she used the word "change" as an English word or a Japanese loanword, she nonetheless chose to use the word accompanied by a gesture as a strategy to facilitate better understanding.

The second example is from one of the group's Slack interactions (Figure 12.3).

In these written exchanges, Rou sent a rather lengthy message in English with some suggestions for their group presentation slides. She ended her remark by

Figure 12.2 Xinran's hand gesture

Rou 7:28 PM
Hi everyone, after watching other groups' videos I think we might have to be more specific on the slides? For example, for the first slide we can say more about why we chose the topic, and more specifically point out that our topic is legalizing same-sex marriage (in Japan? I don't think we talked about that actually). The outline can definitely be more specific... can do more research and make more slides before the our meeting. Also I think in order to give everyone more chance to speak maybe you all can explain something from the outline part if you want to? No pressure. Sorry about the long message 😅

October 26th, 2020

Rou 11:03 AM
すみません。英語で大丈夫ですか

Xinran 11:18 AM
大丈夫ですよ！分かりやすい英語を書いてもらってありがとうございます！！
😊
私も調べて来週のプレゼンの準備します😊

Rou.

October 28th, 2020

Emi 12:52 AM
Hey, I agree with Rou. Maybe we can focus on same-sex marriage in one country like Japan or America (whichever is fine, but maybe Japan since we have a couple sources on it). So, our outline could be: 1. intro of same-sex marriage/history 2. Japan or America's (whichever country we decide to focus on) view on same-sex marriage 3. Comparing Japan or America's same-sex marriage to other countries 4. Solutions 5. Our own summaries :This could be a general outline and maybe we could all research the 4 parts to put into our presentation on Friday since the fifth point is open ended and doesn't need an explanation
P.S. Sorry about the long message too 😅 日本語で書きましょうか

Xinran 12:57 PM
わかりやすくありがとうございます！
outlineのとこる理解しました👍

Figure 12.3 Slack interaction

saying, "Sorry about the long message" with an emoji of a smiley face with sweat. The next morning, perhaps worried that there had been no reply from her groupmates, Rou followed up in Japanese: "I'm sorry. Was it okay [that I wrote] in English?" Soon afterwards, Xinran responded by saying, "That is fine! Thank you for writing in English that is easy to understand!!" Two days later, Emi responded to Rou's message and provided suggestions for the outline of their slides, again in lengthy English. As if to mimic the technique Rou employed, Emi also noted, "P.S. Sorry about the long message too," with an emoji for a person apologizing, followed by "Shall I write in Japanese?" in Japanese. To Emi's message, Xinran again replied in Japanese: "Thank you for [explaining] clearly/easily! I understand the *outline*," accompanied by a thumbs-up emoji.

These exchanges demonstrated that each student tried to show their concern for others by taking advantage of various language and semiotic resources, including English, Japanese, emojis, and exclamation marks. The use of semiotic systems besides languages was a strategy the students actively employed to convey emotions that were hard to express in the written language. It is often assumed that it is easier and more effective to express emotions in face-to-face interactions due to paralinguistic cues such as facial expressions, gestures, and tone of voice. However, as the written interaction in Figure 12.3 demonstrates, students skillfully communicated emotions by shifting languages and by making use of textual paralinguistic cues. This demonstrates the complex processes in which students engaged when assessing and deciding what to say, which language(s) to use, and—most importantly—which emotions to communicate in each written utterance.

Example 1 and Figure 12.3 illuminate two aspects of dynamic translingual practices that go beyond mere language: Individuals can naturally and fluidly shift between Japanese and English (Rou and Emi), and English utterances can be smoothly followed by Japanese responses without any interruptions. In other words, translanguaging can be seen within one speaker's utterances as well as among multiple participants in communicative events.

Communicating effectively with magazine readers

The final online multilingual magazines showcased each group's unique interests, talents, knowledge, ideas, and collaborative efforts. Table 12.2 shows specific topics chosen by the groups and the corresponding SDGs. Here, we discuss four aspects of the students' learning that were evident in their magazines.

First, the students gained a deeper understanding (and content knowledge) about their chosen issues by researching the topic, exchanging viewpoints, generating ideas for what one can do to alleviate the problems, and calling for actions by the wider audience. For example, Figure 12.4 shows the cover and a page from the magazine コロナと教育/*The Impact of COVID-19 on Higher Education*, in which the students connected and contextualized the abstract notion of the SDG ("quality [and equality] of education") to their own issue (COVID-19 and its impact on higher education) by incorporating their own personal experiences as

Table 12.2 Titles of magazine and corresponding SDGs

Magazine titles (Translation for Japanese titles by the authors)	SDGs
平等の機会/*Equal Chance*	4: Quality Education
コロナと教育/*The Impact of COVID-19 on Higher Education* (Corona and education)	4: Quality Education
ジェンダー平等の形 (Forms of gender equality)	5: Gender Equality
LOVE IS LOVE /日本の同性婚から見るLGBT+ (Seeing LGBT+ issues from same sex marriage in Japan)	5: Gender Equality
気候変動攻略本/*Climate Strategy* (Strategy guide for climate change)	13: Climate Action

well as ideas for coping strategies. Creating a magazine such as this one requires more collaboration among the group members—namely, finding and sharing information, discussing and exchanging opinions, and reconstructing the information and ideas so that they fit the theme of the magazine.

Second, as each group had to decide how multiple languages would be used for various purposes, they needed to carefully think about language choices in writing. They had to ask questions such as: Who is their magazine's audience? What would be the most effective ways to communicate the message and with what language(s)? What roles can different languages play? Some groups wrote the summaries of their articles in English; other groups wrote the most important information in both Japanese and English. One group created a complete bilingual magazine to cater to a wider audience. Their language selections were not random but were rather based on the groups' careful decision-making processes. The cover page of the magazine depicted in Figure 12.4 serves as a good example. The main title of the magazine is "コロナと教育 (Corona and Education)" written in Japanese. The only writing in English on the cover, "The Impact of COVID-19 on Higher Education," is not a literal translation of the title. It can be understood as either the English title or the main theme of the magazine. Below the English writing, question sentences are added only in Japanese, 私達にできることはありますか？("Is there anything we can do?") and, in a smaller font at the bottom, オンライン授業を受講することで疲労しているでしょうか？("Are we tired of taking online classes?") and 私たちはこれからどのように授業を受けるべきでしょうか？("How should we take courses in the future?"). As shown, the students' use of Japanese and English was based on careful thinking in order to create an attractive cover and to communicate messages with their readers.

Third, each magazine demonstrated the students' creativity and multimodal literacy (New London Group, 1996) in creating a visually pleasing magazine that captures readers' attention. The title of the magazine, page layout, color

Figure 12.4 Cover and sample page from *Corona and Education/The Impact of COVID-19 on Higher Education*

schemes, image selections, and language-image relations and organization, among other components, were carefully considered and incorporated into their magazines.

Take, for example, the cover of *Equal Chance* (https://sophia.smith.edu/sdgs-magazines/2020/12/01/equal-chance-magazine/). The black-and-white picture of a young girl with eloquent eyes looking directly at the camera,[9] the Japanese word for "equal chance" handwritten in bright red brushstrokes against the black background, short key phrases in both Japanese and English in white, the selection of fonts, and overall layout all contribute to creating a gripping cover. One student noted that "we chose clear, visually striking images to grab the reader's attention and communicate our message." We later found out that this image is a very well-known photo of a girl from a poverty-stricken area in China. It is themed as "I want to go to school," and the girl in the photo later became the icon for Project Hope, which aims to foster education for children in China. The selection of this image for the cover highlights the students' skillful use of Chinese semiotic resources in communicating the magazine's messages to its viewers. These commands and practices are particularly important for students living in this hypervisual age.

Finally, the magazines are the manifestations of collaborative efforts. Each group completed a magazine that was a culmination of the individual members' skills and knowledge with the students taking advantage of each other's strengths as editors, illustrators, layout designers, and translators. For example, one student, whose Japanese language proficiency was not very strong, wrote on her post project questionnaire:

> I think I became more confident in my ability to contribute to the overall project as we moved into working on formatting, and English translating and writing, which I'm more comfortable with . . . and translation was super fun to me!

Because the magazine offered a space for translingual practices, it gave this student (and others) a sense of confidence as well as membership and agency, as it allowed them to exercise their strengths.

Becoming sensitive to language choices and their impacts

One significant aspect highlighted by the students' post project questionnaires is that the project provided a space for the students to deeply reflect on their own language practices. The careful attention to, and subsequent adjustment of, one's language—shifting of "language varieties" (Li, 2018, p. 14)—could also be considered a type of translanguaging. Xinran, for example, said the following during the interview:

> What I paid attention to was to try not to speak in Kansai dialect, but to speak in what I thought of as the standard Japanese? [Because their Japanese] was what they learned [in a classroom] and was polite Japanese, like naturally adding *desu* at the end [of a sentence] or saying しませんか (shall we …?) and so on.

Xinran usually speaks a Kansai dialect; however, she attempted to use the standard Japanese and the *desu/masu* polite style rather than the casual styles. These shifts away from her everyday language practices were based on her assessment of the specific context and her desire to communicate better with her groupmates.

Likewise, Rou made conscious decisions to shift her style and tone. She came to recognize that her choice of language represented who she was and influenced the way she could relate to others. She wrote on her post project questionnaire:

> I became more mindful of my tone and tried to let everyone else talk and listened to their ideas. . . . In terms of language, I definitely tried to use polite terms like してもいいですか, しましょうか (is it okay to . . .? shall I . . .?) to try not come off as aggressive.

These meta-linguistic behaviors confirm the Douglas Fir Group's (2016) assertion that "multilingual speakers will deploy their semiotic resources by choosing across their languages and/or varieties and registers in response to local demands for social action" (p. 26).

As demonstrated, students in both Japan and the United States adjusted their language practices if they felt that doing so would help convey their ideas to others. These context-specific and partner-specific language practices highlight the students' self-reflections on their own daily language practices as well as their keen sense of others' needs.

In a regular telecollaboration drawing on the monolingual ideology, students' ultimate goal is to improve their own language proficiency and become a better communicator with the language. In this project, however, the focus was not so much on improving one's language proficiency but on learning to become aware of available language resources and to take agentive actions in choosing which varieties of language(s) to use in order to accomplish the communicative goals.

Discussion

The preceding analysis illuminated some phenomena that differ from many of the previous international telecollaboration projects. Oftentimes, telecollaboration implemented in foreign language classrooms focuses on providing opportunities for students to use the target language and learn the target culture by interacting with native speakers (Train, 2006). In this framework, students join the project with the mindset that they are either learners or native speakers of the language. In other words, a dichotomized power structure is established from the start (Liddicoat, 2016), and students feel that they can only play one of two roles: those who teach or those who are taught.

However, in this project, we observed equal relationships among the students. For example, during the interactions, there was no correction of the language by the native speakers,[10] a phenomenon frequently observed in international/intercultural exchange. One student from Japan stated that "the project confirmed my belief that language does not need to be perfect as long as it is understandable." In other words, students experienced and recognized the importance of language as "a resource for doing things" rather than as the leaning goal in and of itself (O'Dowd & Lewis, 2016, p. ix). We believe that this was partially due to the fact that the project was not framed as a space for language learning in a traditional sense, although it was carried out in a Japanese language course. The translanguaging spaces created in this project encouraged students to negotiate and construct relationships necessary for the successful completion of the project.

To establish and maintain good relationships among the group members, students took advantage of different features that the different platforms afforded. Zoom (synchronous) offered students a space with which to engage in real-time, spontaneous, face-to-face oral communication and negotiations, whereas Slack (asynchronous) provided a space for students to take time to consider what to say, how to say it, and in what modes (e.g., choice of words, languages, and emojis). We agree with O'Dowd (2018) that there is a benefit from using multiple tools with various affordances, not so much to develop "intercultural competence" (p. 11) as he argued but rather to enrich the students' communication repertoires, particularly pertaining to the expression of emotion and affect.

This project relied on students' autonomy and agency, with us, the teachers, only offering the space and creating general guidelines. We use the term "autonomy" here to refer to "socially oriented agency" (Toohey & Norton, 2003, p. 59), which is defined as "the ability to operate effectively in collaboration as a cooperating member with the capacity and willingness to act autonomously and in collaboration with others as a social and responsible person" (Blidi, 2017, p. 5) rather than individualized performance(s). Students were responsible for not only selecting the content/theme of their work for the project but also for scheduling the group meetings and planning the concrete steps and procedures for moving forward with the project. Furthermore, they were given the freedom to choose their language(s) of communication. Allowing the students to exercise their own agency provided them with a sense of ownership of the process as well as for the final product. Many students felt proud of their individual accomplishments as well as their group collaborations.

We believe that having a concrete final product as a culmination of group efforts encouraged students to engage in the group processes more agentively, unlike many international collaborations that focus simply on the process of interactions. In addition, the fact that the magazines would be open to the general public further added significance and motivation for students to create high-quality magazines. Their magazines will function as resources for students who participate in the next round of the project and for readers interested in learning about SDGs. In other words, the students' magazines can be considered a type of e-service learning (Hellebrandt & Jorge, 2013) or e-civic engagement (Woodall & Lennon, 2017).

Going forward

World language education today is still predominantly based on the monolingual approach (Ortega, 2019), which emphasizes maximum exposure to the target language while the use of other languages is frowned upon in classrooms. However, as shown in this project, creating a translanguaging space offered the learners important opportunities to deeply reflect on and observe not only their own language practices but also those of others. This allowed the students to relate to each other and more effectively achieve their shared goals.

As the Douglas Fir Group (2016) argued, "emotions are . . . enmeshed with identity, agency, and power, all central in the learning and teaching of languages in today's multilingual world" (p. 36). Restricting classroom language use to only that of the target language may possibly impede the students' potential for learning as well as their growth as individual persons. Positioning all students as translingual practitioners who possess various skills, prior knowledge, and rich communication repertoires will help them grow into confident, conscientious, and critical social agents who can then contribute to the communities around them.

As we live in a multilingual, transnational, "superdiverse" world (Vertovec, 2007, p. 1025), world language education needs to expand its educational goals and shift its focus toward developing learners' diverse semiotic repertoires, cultivating a sense of empathy for others, and gaining the ability to live and work together with people from other cultural backgrounds (Guth & Helm, 2010). We believe that international telecollaborations that allow and encourage flexible, fluid, and multimodal language practices have the potential to do just that.

Acknowledgements

We would like to express our gratitude to Uichi Kamiyoshi, our collaboration partner, from University in Tokyo. We are also grateful to anonymous reviewers and the editors of this volume, Nobuko Chikamatsu and Li Jin, for their constructive feedback on the earlier drafts. The text's deficiencies are wholly our responsibility.

Notes

1 Due to the unbalanced numbers of participants from the United States and Japan (10 and nine, respectively), one group had only three members: two from the United States and one from Japan.
2 The SDGs are 17 global goals set by the United Nations in 2015 with the aim of achieving them by the year 2030. They are a universal call to action to end poverty, protect the planet, and improve the lives and prospects of everyone, everywhere.
3 Zoom, a collaborative, cloud-based videoconferencing service, became one of the dominant platforms used for online synchronous instructions during the COVID-19 pandemic (Guillén et al., 2020; Kim, 2020). Slack is a cloud-based, team collaboration application; it archives all direct messages and group conversations and hosts documents.
4 Six of the 10 students in the U.S. college were native speakers of Chinese; two students from Tokyo had learned Chinese as a part of their degree requirements; and one Osaka student was a native Chinese speaker; another student had studied abroad in Taiwan.
5 Breakout rooms are a Zoom feature that allows an instructor to assign students to different rooms; students can only interact with others in their own room during a designated period of time.
6 One may notice in the data and discussion the invisibility of Rei. We let students negotiate and solve the problems among themselves for the most part because we believe that it is important for students to take charge of their own learning.
7 Kansai dialect is distinct from that of standard Japanese in terms of intonation, vocabulary, grammar, etc.
8 Translations in square brackets hereafter are done by the authors.
9 Image source: https://kuaibao.qq.com.
10 Although we do not have data regarding how each group went about the final editing process, as the magazine was created collaboratively as a group product, we suspect that they helped each other polish the language used in the magazine.

References

Belz, J. A., & Müller-Hartmann, A. (2003). Teachers as intercultural learners: Negotiating German-American telecollaboration along the institutional fault line. *The Modern Language Journal, 87*(1), 71–89.
Blidi, S. (2017). *Collaborative learner autonomy*. Springer.
Canagarajah, S. (2013). *Translingual practice: Global Englishes and cosmopolitan relations*. Routledge.
Creese, A., & Blackledge, A. (2015). Translanguaging and identity in educational settings. *Annual Review of Applied Linguistics, 35*, 20–35.

Dooly, M., & Vinagre, M. (2021). Research into practice: Virtual exchange in language teaching and learning. *Language Teaching*, 1–15.

Douglas Fir Group. (2016). A transdisciplinary framework for SLA in a multilingual world. *The Modern Language Journal*, *100*(Supplement 2016), 19–47.

Flores, N. (2013). The unexamined relationship between neoliberalism and plurilingualism: A cautionary tale. *TESOL Quarterly*, *47*(3), 500–520.

García, O. (2009). *Bilingual education in the 21st century: A global perspective*. Wiley.

Guillén, G., Sawin, T., & Avineri, N. (2020). Zooming out of the crisis: Language and human collaboration. *Foreign Language Annals*, *53*(2), 320–328.

Guth, S., & Helm, F. (Eds.). (2010). *Telecollaboration 2.0: Language, literacies and intercultural learning in the 21st century*. Peter Lang.

Hall, J. K. (2018). *Essentials of SLA for L2 teachers: A transdisciplinary framework*. Routledge.

Hauck, M. (2007). Critical success factors in a TRIDEM exchange. *ReCALL*, *19*(2), 202–223.

Hellebrandt, J., & Jorge, E. (2013). The scholarship of community engagement: Advancing partnerships in Spanish and Portuguese. *Hispania*, *96*(2), 203–214.

Helm, F. (2015). The practices and challenges of telecollaboration in higher education in Europe. *Language Learning & Technology*, *19*(2), 197–217.

Horner, B., Lu, M. Z., Royster, J. J., & Trimbur, J. (2011). Language difference in writing: Toward a translingual approach. *College English*, *73*(3), 303–321.

Kato, R., & Kumagai, Y. (2020). Translingual practices in a "monolingual" society: Discourses, learners, and language choices. *International Journal of Bilingual Education and Bilingualism*, *25*(5), 1681–1696. doi:10.1080/13670050.2020.1799318

Kern, R., Ware, P., & Warschauer, M. (2008). Network-based language teaching. In N. H. Hornberger (Ed.), *Encyclopedia of language and education* (pp. 1374–1385). Springer.

Kim, J. (2020, April 1). Teaching and learning after COVID-19: Three post-pandemic predictions. *Inside Higher Education*. www.insidehighered.com/digital-learning/blogs/learning-innovatation/teaching-and-learning-after-covic-19

Li, W. (2011). Moment analysis and translanguaging space: Discursive construction of identities by multilingual Chinese youth in Britain. *Journal of Pragmatics*, *43*(5), 1222–1235.

Li, W. (2018). Translanguaging as a practical theory of language. *Applied Linguistics*, *39*(1), 9–30.

Liddicoat, A. J. (2016). Native and non-native speaker identities in interaction: Trajectories of power. *Applied Linguistics Review*, *7*(4), 409–429.

Lewis, T., & O'Dowd, R. (2016). Online intercultural exchange and foreign language learning: A systematic review. In R. O'Dowd & T. Lewis (Eds.), *Online intercultural exchange: Policy, pedagogy, practice* (pp. 35–80). Routledge.

New London Group. (1996). A pedagogy of multiliteracies: Designing social futures. *Harvard Educational Review*, *66*(1), 60–92.

O'Dowd, R. (2007). Evaluating the outcomes of online intercultural exchange. *ELT Journal*, *61*(2), 144–152.

O'Dowd, R. (2018). From telecollaboration to virtual exchange: State-of-the-art and the role of UNICollaboration in moving forward. *Research-Publishing.Net*, *1*, 1–23.

O'Dowd, R., & Lewis, T. (Eds.). (2016). *Online intercultural exchange: Policy, pedagogy, practice*. Routledge.

O'Dowd, R., & Ritter, M. (2006). Understanding and working with "failed communication" in telecollaborative exchanges. *CALICO Journal*, *23*(3), 623–642.

O'Dowd, R., & Waire, P. (2009). Critical issues in telecollaborative task design. *Computer Assisted Language Learning, 22*(2), 173–188.

O'Rourke, B. (2005). Form-focused interaction in online tandem learning. *CALICO Journal, 22*(3), 433–466.

Ortega, L. (2019). SLA and the study of equitable multilingualism. *The Modern Language Journal, 103*, 23–38.

Rubin, J. (2016). The collaborative online international learning network. In R. O'Dowd & T. Lewis (Eds.), *Online intercultural exchange: Policy, pedagogy, practice* (pp. 263–272). Routledge.

Thorne, S. L. (2016). Forward: The virtual internationalization turn in language study. In R. O'Dowd & T. Lewis (Eds.), *Online intercultural exchange: Policy, pedagogy, practice* (pp. ix–xi). Routledge.

Toohey, K., & Norton, B. (2003). Learner autonomy as agency in sociocultural settings. In D. Palfreyman & R. C. Smith (Eds.), *Learner autonomy across cultures* (pp. 58–72). Palgrave Macmillan.

Train, R. (2006). A critical look at technologies and ideologies in internet-mediated intercultural foreign language education. In J. A. Belz, & S. L. Thorne (Eds.), *Internet-mediated intercultural foreign language education* (pp. 247–284). Thomson Heinle.

Vertovec, S. (2007). Super-diversity and its implications. *Ethnic and Racial Studies, 30*(6), 1024–1054.

Ware, P. (2005). "Missed" communication in online communication: Tensions in a German-American telecollaboration. *Language Learning & Technology, 9*(2), 64–89.

Warschauer, M. (1996). Motivational aspects of using computers for writing and communication. In M. Warschauer (Ed.), *Telecollaboration in foreign language learning* (pp. 29–46). National Foreign Language Resource Center.

Woodall, J. S., & Lennon, T. M. (2017). Using Twitter to promote classroom and civic engagement. In E. C. Matto, A. R. M. McCartney, E. A. Bennion, & D. Simpson (Eds.), *Teaching civic engagement across the disciplines* (pp. 135–150). American Political Science Association.

13 Transcending borders and limitations with digitally enhanced pedagogy

Language Learning-focused COIL (LLC) for Japanese learners and prospective teachers

Keiko Ikeda and Nobuko Chikamatsu

Introduction

With digital collaboration among multiple institutions beyond various borders and digital teaching modalities becoming increasingly accessible, educators have been rapidly adopting collaborative online international learning (COIL) within higher education in North America and elsewhere, especially as it has gained greater institutional support (DePaul GLE, 2022). COIL is a pedagogy that connects students and professors in different countries for collaborative projects and discussions as part of the coursework (SUNY COIL, n.d.). It is not a superficial online interaction among international speakers, but rather it provides opportunities for students to form a virtual team and work together collaboratively to accomplish a common objective (Ikeda, 2016a). It uses various web-based communication tools such as videoconference applications for synchronous communication as well as written or recorded message exchange applications for asynchronous communication. The speed of COIL adoption has increased since the COVID-19 pandemic when the majority of teaching and learning at the higher education level pivoted to online methods (IAU, 2020; UNESCO, 2021).

This chapter explores an attempt to adapt COIL into a foreign language learning context known as Language Learning-focused COIL (LLC).[1] LLC is a version of COIL in which the medium of communication is the target foreign language (L2) of the participating students. LLC students have dual purposes for enrolling in a COIL program: They wish to enhance their foreign language skills through communicative practice with proficient speakers, and they wish to participate in a project-based learning experience and challenge themselves to complete a mission as a team. The power of this methodology is that it provides a genuinely authentic learning experience by engaging with others from very different backgrounds (Ikeda, 2016b; Rubin & Guth, 2016).

In the COIL examined herein, Japanese language was the lingua franca as well as the theme for the collaborative project, which focused on translation studies for L2 Japanese students in the United States and on language pedagogy for L1 Japanese students in Japan to provide English translations of an original Japanese work through collaboration. Students in an advanced Japanese language class at DePaul University, a North American university, were matched with a group of

DOI: 10.4324/9781003266976-18

prospective teachers of Japanese language in a teacher-training course at Kansai University, a Japanese university. The joint work provided mutual benefits to the two classes; the American students were able to immerse themselves in L2 communication using their target language while the students in Japan were able to practice teaching with learners of Japanese overseas. All resources from the semiotic repertoire in both languages were accessed and utilized in this COIL project; hence, the practice of translanguaging in their collaboration process was considered part of their learning journey (García & Leiva, 2014).

This chapter discusses two performance analyses of participants' output with interactional data from the group work analyzed utilizing conversation analysis and DePaul students' translation products investigated using textual analysis. The strength of this new practice is illustrated in the framework of the translanguaging pedagogy (García & Leiva, 2014; Marrero-Colon, 2021) and followed with suggestions for future international virtual collaborations.

Theoretical and pedagogical framework: cross-language collaboration in COIL

The authors of this chapter adopt plurilingualism as an asset allowing for the active inclusion of all citizens. Although multilingualism is more popularly referred to in the literature on foreign language education, it focuses on situations wherein multiple languages exist side by side in a society and an individual uses these languages separately. Meanwhile, plurilingualism is an individual's interconnected knowledge of multiple languages. (Council of Europe, 2007). Second language acquisition research has further incorporated plurilingualism into the framework of transdisciplinary approach (Douglas Fir Group, 2016; Hawkins & Mori, 2018) and its application to teaching and learning (Hall, 2019). In today's multilingual society, languages are dynamic, open-ended, emergent semiotic repertoires that change shapes and concepts over time and spaces (Douglas Fir Group, 2016). If language learning is a process to shape such languages, we have to optimize learning settings for learners to access diverse multimodal semiotic resources such as verbal and non-verbal, auditory and textual, and personal and collective resources. International collaboration is one of the ideal settings for L2 learners as it maximizes diverse linguistic exposures beyond their limited contact in the classroom. Furthermore, the dynamic use of multiple languages—namely, first language (L1), L2, and target and instructional languages—helps comprehension and communication among learners from different L1 backgrounds (Douglas Fir Group, 2016).

The term translanguaging has been coined to explain this fluid usage of multiple languages, and this process has been applied in language pedagogy (Li, 2018; Mazzaferro, 2018). We view the translanguaging practice as a protestation to the monolingualism and native-speakerism conventionally valued in language education (Ortega, 2019). As the Douglas Fir Group (2016) articulated in their transdisciplinary framework, language learning is shaped through social activity at the three interactive levels: micro, meso, and macro. In this framework, any named languages are potentially equally useful as multilingual resources for one's meaning-making process (i.e., language learning). Therefore, any language users, regardless of their status as a native or nonnative speaker, can be mutually influential and contributing in a translanguaging setting.

Translanguaging practice in international collaboration also potentially prevents one group from being predominant in communication over the other, which is often an issue with English as the lingua franca in the standard design of COIL practice. For instance, to overcome the dominance of English (Wu & Tarc, 2016), in recent years more LLC projects have been implemented in translanguaging settings with Japanese and English (Murata, 2022). UNESCO's (2015) sustainable development goals (SDGs) are often adopted as collaborative project themes to discuss universally important issues such as climate, gender, poverty, and energy (de la Fuente, 2022; Murata, 2022). The SDGs provide optimal learning contexts in which individuals can relate one's own experience and interests to the themes and compare situations or counter-measurements across cultures and languages (de la Fuente, 2022; Kamiyoshi et al., 2022; Melin, 2019). Nonetheless, challenges have been reported as the analysis tends to be superficial, and counter-measurements remain ideal but impractical due to the complexity of SDG themes or an imbalance in respective groups' language proficiency (Murata et al., 2022). Thus, it is ideal to build a setting in which two groups can maximize their use of their L1/stronger language experience to enhance their counterpart's L2/weaker language use. Translation practice makes this possible as both the source language and target language of translation are equally and mutually valued for the meaning-making process.

Translation is indeed a facet of translanguaging where two languages are closely examined as learners go back and forth between the source and target languages. Gramling and Warner (2016) described their L2 German learners as "translanguagers" (p. 82) in their practice translating German prose poems "to access a continuous flow of applied situations in which the broad endeavor of trafficking meaning across language difference presented speakers with ever new affordances, constraints, and opportunities for reflection" (p. 84). They also valued the process for building agentive power in L2 learning as multilingual experiences of translating "must accompany the learners' own socialization into L2 speaking communities of practice" and require "a means of 'engaging actively with a world' that is unpredictable, unanticipatable, and even risky, rather than tidily monolingual and organized by clearly identifiable social tasks" (p. 96). In Japanese pedagogy, Kumagai and Kono (2018) and Chikamatsu (2019, 2022) employed translation as a key learning task for optimal meaning making and agentive power building in content-based instruction or the Foreign Language Across the Curriculum (FLAC) approach.

The benefit of translanguaging practice is enhanced when translating practice is conducted through international collaboration between two L1 groups—namely, one with L1 as the source language and the other with L1 as the target language (Chikamatsu, 2022; Gramling & Warner, 2016). Thus, the DePaul-Kansai COIL project was designed by including translating practice in the translanguaging pedagogy framework.

The COIL project: design and implementation

The COIL project between DePaul and Kansai has been ongoing since spring 2020. Both universities have promoted international virtual exchanges for more than a decade, provided institutional supports from technology to curriculum development, and taken on a leadership role in COIL in their respective countries. Table 13.1 provides information about the two institutions that is relevant for carrying out a COIL module. Spring terms starting in April have more overlaps in the calendar than fall terms. Of the four most recent COIL courses held, this chapter shares an analysis of the spring 2021 collaboration between DePaul's translation course and Kansai's Japanese pedagogy course.

Course descriptions

Kansai course: Japanese teaching method

Kansai's course is for undergraduate students pursuing a teaching certificate for Japanese as a second/foreign language. Among the series of courses required for the program, understanding teaching methods and applying knowledge in a practicum are the two main objectives of this course, which meets 90 minutes each week for 15 weeks of the semester. In 2021, 42 students enrolled in the course. Outside the pandemic context, this course collaborates with the Japanese language program for international students on campus to provide students with practicum experiences. However, due to the pandemic, the class size for the study abroad program was radically reduced and made it difficult for this course to provide teaching practice opportunities to the students.

Table 13.1 DePaul University and Kansai University information

	Kansai University (KU)	*DePaul University (DU)*
Location	Osaka, Japan	Chicago, United States
Institution	Private	Private
Size	30,000	22,000
Academic calendar	Semester (15 weeks) x 2 • 1st: April to August • 2nd: October to February	Quarter (10 weeks) x 3 • 1st: September to November • 2nd: January to March • 3rd: April to June
COIL initiatives	KU-COIL: www.kansai-u.ac.jp/Kokusai/IIGE/resources/KU-COIL.php	DePaul Global Learning Experience (GLE): https://resources.depaul.edu/teaching-commons/programs/global-learning/Pages/default.aspx

DePaul course: Japanese translation practicum

DePaul's translation course is designed for students who have completed at least 3 years of college-level Japanese. The class meets for 90 minutes, twice a week, for 10 weeks. The course's textbook is *The Routledge course in Japanese translation* (Hasegawa, 2012), which discusses translation theories and techniques as well as challenging linguistic features in translation between Japanese and English. Students are assigned one chapter weekly and apply the knowledge gleaned to analyze and/or translate preselected literary pieces [See the course details in Chikamatsu and Matsugu (2022), and Matsugu and Chikamatsu (2023)].

Students complete an individual term project to produce their own translation of an original Japanese text into English. The text can be from any genre: fiction, nonfiction, journalistic writing, novels, picture books, manga, film subtitles, dramatic scripts, games, etc.[2] After submitting a proposal in the second week, the student divides the selected piece into three sections and translates and submits one section biweekly. In class, as time allows, students peer review and comment on one another's drafts. They revise each sectional draft and submit the final version along with a reflection essay (in English) in the eleventh week after an oral presentation in which they share highlights of the translation work. Class instruction is conducted in Japanese unless any English texts are referred to in the discussion. In the spring 2021 term, 11 students enrolled in the course and worked on the term-long translation projects with Kansai students in 11 groups.

Implementation of DePaul-Kansai COIL

Because of the academic term schedules between the two universities, the COIL unit started in DePaul's fourth week, immediately after students submitted the first sectional draft (one third of the complete text). Each DePaul student was grouped with three to four Kansai students. The primary platform for posting self-introduction videos, Zoom links, schedules, and any other shared printed and visual materials was Padlet; students could also use any other tools, such as LINE or email, for communicating or file sharing.

The DePaul-Kansai student groups were expected to collaborate and produce an accurate comprehension and compelling interpretation of an original Japanese literary work for DePaul students' English translation projects. Through this project, the DePaul students were to (a) interpret the original work and translate it into a new language (i.e., English), (b) understand different cultural and new linguistics perspectives, and (c) develop communication skills with any accessible resources (L1, L2, textual, visual, etc.). The last goal was crucial as two languages were involved in the written texts—namely, Japanese for the original and English for the translation, although Japanese was the lingua franca for communication and discussion. For the Kansai students, the goals of this project were to (a) encounter language learners of Japanese outside of Japan for the first time, (b) experience how to teach using Japanese language to those who are L2 speakers, and (c) build their intercultural competence by working as part of an international team.

Four Zoom sessions (the first one for meeting with everyone at once and the other three for individual group meetings) were scheduled with the following themes:

- Zoom 1 (all in class) in Week 4: Introduction
- Zoom 2 (group) in Weeks 5–6: Comprehension and linguistic expressions of the original work
- Zoom 3 (group) in Weeks 7–8: Content, image/symbolism, characters, tone in the original work
- Zoom 4 (group) in Weeks 9–10: Reflections, challenges, and highlights in translation and COIL.

Students were also encouraged to go beyond the given themes for their future communication during each meeting.

The DePaul students were expected to prepare for the discussion questions in advance, including the comprehension of the original work and word choices in translation. The Kansai students were expected to discuss the questions using any accessible resources such as an individual's language and life experience, major or academic knowledge, and information available via the internet. They were not required to give critiques or revise translation drafts, which could be overwhelming and interfere in the efficiency of collaboration due to their lack of familiarity with the original work in Japanese or language proficiency in English (Chikamatsu, 2022). In addition, the Kansai course included a short online language teaching lesson conducted in real time for the L2 learners (i.e., DePaul students).

Conversation and textual analysis of translanguaging collaboration

Translanguaging practice in COIL occurs in different forms such as multimodal communication to build a community of practice among participants (Nakagawa & Kamei, 2022; Wenger, 1998) and translating practice to develop translingual and transcultural competence for meaning making (Gramling & Warner, 2016; Kumagai & Kono, 2018). The following subsections discuss the conversation and textual analyses of data from Group A in the current COIL project. Group A consisted of one DePaul student (DU1) and four Kansai students (KU1–4). The group collaborated to translate a piece from the manga 魔法使いの嫁 (*The Ancient Magnus' Bride*; Yamazaki, 2014), which DU1 selected for the term project. The story depicts the dark life of an orphaned Japanese teenage girl, Chise, who is sold to a mysterious sorcerer at an auction in London. The sorcerer's intention remains unclear; it is either to rescue Chise from a dark life or push her into deeper despair. The group had three Zoom meetings over the 6 weeks, ranging from 30 to 60 minutes each.

Group interactions with multilingual and multimode resources

First, we examined the interactional data from the group works and identified how the participants made use of their multimodal semiotic resources to make the communication process more meaningful. Excerpt 1 includes interactional data from the video recordings of Group A. It captures a very early stage of their first meeting when they were about to start checking DU1's first sectional translation. KU4 offered to share the screen of the Google document. The background to this interaction is that DU1 was using a device with a very small screen, which made it difficult for KU4 to view the font in the shared document. While KU4 was suggesting which page of the document to start discussing, DU1 found it important to stop for a moment and notify the Kansai students about the situation.

Excerpt 1

1. KU4: ichiban saisho? "is it in the first part?"
2. DU1: uh, it's page. peiji (1.0) *1 ((the eye gaze direction moving rapidly left to right))
3. KU4: un. "yeah"
4. DU1: nana? "seven?"
5. (1.0)
6. KU2: nana peeji "page seven."
7. DU1: I see. hh haha! (1.5) mitsukete: mas- etto "I am looking. uh" (1.0) nana "seven"
8. KU 2: nana peeji. "page seven."
9. DU1: hai. uh "yes uh:"
10. (1.5)
11. KU4: koko desu ka. "is this it?"
12. (1.0)
13. DU1: hitosu wa "one of them is,"
14. KU4: un "yeah"
15. DU1: uh: da- hah ahh. chiisai *2 ((put the hand over their mouth with a smile)) "small."
16. KU3: chiisai "small"
17. KU4: ji ga chiisai desu yo,*3 ((enlarge the document)) "the font is small, is it?"
18. DU1: hehe it's okay. .hh daijoobu desu "it is fine."
19. KU4: uh
20. DU1: watashi wa: eto: screen o.*4 ((open the hands)) "My screen is" (1.0)*5 ((moves the hands closer to the center))
21. KU2: a sukureen ga chiisai. "oh screen is small."
22. DU1: hai. hehe "yes. hehe"
23. KU4: unn "yeah"
24. KU2: somo somo ne "the original size is (the problem)"
25. DU1: hehuh [huh*6 ((nods while laughing))
26. KU1: [*7 ((nods with a smile))

" ": English translation
* (( )): non-verbal behaviors (e.g., gestures)
( ): pauses in seconds
[: overlaps

As Excerpt 1 demonstrates, a potential source of miscommunication emerged. Regarding DU1's first mention of *chiisai* ("small") in Line 15, KU3 simply repeated the same term, *chiisai* without clarifying what item was small. However, KU4 initially interpreted it as the fonts were too small; thus, KU4 enlarged the fonts by zooming into that particular part of the document (*3 in Line 17). DU1 responded in English ("It's okay"), followed by the Japanese equivalent (*daijoobu desu*) in line 18, this time with a different embodied display. In Line 20, DU1 first opened both arms widely (*4 in Line 20) while finishing saying *watashi wa eto: screen o* "my screen is," using both Japanese (*watashi wa eto:*) and English (*screen*) in the utterance. Then DU1 moved both hands closer to show that the screen is small (*5). Upon this delivery, KU2 in Line 21 verbalized "oh screen is small," and in Line 22, DU1 confirmed this (*hai* "yes"). Here, DU1 beautifully performs a translanguaging act by adopting various available resources, including DU1's L1 (English), L2 (Japanese), and embodied semiotic resources (e.g., gesture accompanying Line 20). In Line 26, in overlapping KU2, we see the members smiling and giggling, which implies that they achieved mutual understanding. As this was their first real-time online communication, DU1's translanguaging act served as a great icebreaker for team building. García (2009) defined the translanguaging practice as the act of "accessing different linguistic features or various modes of what are described as autonomous languages, in order to maximize communicative potential" (p. 140). That is exactly what happened in Group A's interaction.

Textual analysis of students' group translation

The translation process is a practice of translanguaging—not because of finding equivalents between the two languages but because of identifying meaning and concepts regardless of any specific languages. Hasegawa (2012) defined translation as a work of collaboration among the original writer, readers, translator, and editor in the process of comprehension, interpretation, and (re)creation. The project enhanced a translation process where a translator (DePaul student) was consulted by readers (Kansai students) in their stronger language. For instance, in the final reflection essay, DU1 identified three challenging linguistic features for which the Kansai students' consultation was highly valued: (a) onomatopoeia, (b) tone of voice, and (c) gendered speech. Using data collected from DU1's drafts and revisions along with self-reflections during three Zoom group meetings, the following textual analysis examines how semiotic resources were accessed through translation collaboration and helped DU1 build agentive power in learning.

Onomatopoeia

Onomatopoeia is widely used in Japanese, especially in comics, not only for the sound representation of actions or motions but also to indicate the psychological and emotional states of scenes and characters. The subtlety of meanings is often hard for learners of Japanese to comprehend, but it would be even more challenging to translate into any English equivalents. In the first Zoom group session, DU1 prepared several onomatopoeic questions for the Kansai students, such as

ぐっ ("yank"), すりっ ("nuzzle"), and ビクッ ("flinch"). DU1 thought that the discussion was challenging, yet together they used accessible resources as they:

> all got dictionaries up on our phones to find the word that best fit the meaning and feeling of the onomatopoeias while keeping them short for the sake of still appearing as sound effects or mood markers in the manga panels.

Such interactions helped DU1 make subsequent revision decisions. For instance, the translation for パタン was changed from "slam" to "click" as the Kansai students all agreed it was soft when DU1 asked them if the door was shut with a soft or strong force. にゅっ was changed from "nyonn" to "peek" after a long discussion as the Kansai students "all agreed that it probably meant that this creature was shyly trying to fly up to Chise (the protagonist)." These discussions seemed to help DU1 build confidence, as evident in the second Zoom reflection 2 weeks later: "We went over a few onomatopoeias, though they were mainly a confirmation of what I had already put."

Tone of voice

One of the most challenging items for DU1 was to identify the tone of voice used by the characters. For instance, DU1 was confused about the feeling and tone of the sorcerer in his speech to Chise after purchasing her at the auction and bringing her to his mansion. DU1 first identified the sorcerer's tone as "it sounded like he was being rather forward saying that he was disappointed that she wasn't what he expected even though she was experiencing a traumatic flashback." In the second Zoom meeting, the group discussed the tones and emotions of the two characters in the more unfolded storyline, and the Kansai students identified this tone as "encouraging and gentle." Consequently, DU1 changed the translation as follows:

> 実際そんな無気力でいられると僕が困るんだ
> 人形も悪くないけど
> せっかく高値で買ったものだもの
> 面白みのあるものじゃないと

(p. 12)

Translation in the first draft before Zoom 2

"To tell the truth, I'm in trouble if I can get lethargic like that. A doll isn't bad either, but this thing I went to great pains to buy at a high price, isn't it interesting?"

Translation in the revision after Zoom 2

"To tell the truth, I'm a little disappointed in your apathy. If you're just going to act like a mannequin, I suppose that's fine. But I went to great pains to buy you at a high price. Shouldn't you at least be worth my interest?"

The tone of voice was also discussed for the sentence-ending particle さ, which is often used in the sorcerer's speech, as in 君は魔法使いの弟子になったのさ ("You have become a sorcerer's apprentice"). DU1 asked the Kansai students if it was masculine and what kind of feeling this phrase evoked. Although one Kansai student did not view it as a gendered expression, all the others did. Eventually the Kansai students all agreed that it made the sorcerer sound gentle and nice again. This changed DU1's perception and image of the sorcerer, and reflected in the translation, as DU1 stated, "I'll do my best to keep that in mind as I do my final revisions."

Gendered speech

Gendered phrases were analyzed in the third Zoom session as DU1 asked the Kansai students how the fairy character talked in the scene where the fairies fly around Chise to comfort her. They used a sentence ending with ン, as in あらン！ ("Oh") or アタシ for the first-person pronoun わたし ("I/me"). DU1 identified these as feminine speech based on the student's research, yet she needed to clarify what kind of feminine it was: "a temptress woman or a cute girl." After a few exchanges of distinctive phrases for the two feminine speeches in both English and Japanese, the Kansai students agreed that a cute girl was appropriate. DU1 reflected that, in English, "cutesy" expressions such as "ohhhh my gosh!," "y'know," "like," and "totally" as well as unconventional terms, such as "peoples" for the plural "people," occurred in fairies' utterances.

Through the discussion with the Kansai students about language use in the fictional manga setting with unique characters, DU1 reshaped meanings and developed context-sensitive literacy in the current LLC unit. Learning was enriched in the translanguaging practice among participants from different linguistic, cultural, and personal backgrounds. Consequently, DU1 gained agency to expand her interest and lead her own course of L2 learning in the future, as DU1 concluded the final essay with the following new goals:

> Going forward as I read more manga in Japanese, I can make more educated guesses now that I've picked up on some consistencies. I've already started a new project translating the short stories. . . . They are in prose, not dialogue, but they are also written in particular characters' voices. . . . I'm sure I'll be translating many character-oriented projects in the future.

Student feedback and pedagogical reflections

Kano (2016) pointed out the benefits of using translanguaging during classroom instruction, primarily when the stronger language (L1) is used to develop the weaker language (L2). In the current COIL/LLC setting, DePaul students used their stronger language (i.e., English) to interpret an original text in Japanese and reproduce it as translation while receiving input and support from Kansai students in their stronger language (i.e., Japanese). This translanguaging practice was designed to optimize the L2 learning environment for DePaul students. The comments collected in the post project survey[3] with DePaul students support such benefits, as the students valued authentic and contextualized language input for their meaning-making process as follows.

> While dictionaries can be helpful, they often don't help explain a certain feeling or emotion sometimes being expressed. The Kansai students were able to really help me better understand what the dictionary English meaning didn't always express.

> Having someone who can provide additional context for a word or phrase that one can't find an appropriate meaning of online was very useful.

The benefit was mutual as the Kansai students could nurture their own linguistic and metalinguistic awareness. They expanded their knowledge and experience through collaboration, as indicated in the following comment collected from the post project survey with Kansai students:

> I think that the difficult aspect of Japanese language is that there are many expressions that are not found in English. Onomatopoeia is one of them. It was good to be able to convey (to the U.S. student) that it means something like this and that because of the particular scene where it is used, rather than translating it because it is supposed to reflect a particular fixed sound. I think I was able to explain it by giving as many examples as possible.
>
> (translated by the authors)

The current collaboration also helped learners build a sense of agency and self-identity in their own learning and communication, as the previously discussed textual translation analysis explained. One DePaul student wrote:

> Even if my language was choppy, it was good to know I could get not just my academic points across but my feelings and personality as well, and that was more important to me. I wasn't sure if I really sounded like 'me' in Japanese before, and now I feel that I do.

On the other hand, identity, as a native speaker or a future language instructor of Japanese, was reclaimed rather critically among some Kansai students. As L1 speakers of Japanese, Kansai students initially had the impression that they would be able to handle it well; however, the translating practice made them realize that their depth of knowledge is not sufficient, as the following comment suggests:

> I felt sorry that the Japanese ability of Kansai University students was considerably lower than that of DePaul University students. I thought I had already taken enough classes about Japanese language, but I really thought that I shouldn't think about teaching Japanese language at such a level as I am now.
>
> (translated by the authors)

This eye-opening experience also served as the catalyst for further inquiry and training of language learning and teaching, as the following Kansai student comment demonstrates:

> [The DePaul student's] unpredictable and unexpected questions provided me with opportunities to reexamine the language with new perspectives. I wish to study and learn more about the language as a prospective teacher.
> (translated by the authors)

The use of each group's stronger languages (L1s) in the current international collaborative project facilitated communication, as previously discussed in the conversation analysis. It also formed a sense of community once each participant identified and pursued his or her own role and responsibility. One DePaul student perceived their contribution in the project as an L2 speaker as follows:

> [My contribution] was my use of Japanese at my own level, which gave the Kansai students a good model of an English speaker learning Japanese. They had to use Japanese that I would understand in their explanations, and this took some getting used to, but we eventually found a comfortable zone where they could express ideas and I could understand.

Thus, the authors argue that COIL adaptation is indeed well suited for language learning and the teaching domain, particularly for the purpose of teacher training, when its design is carefully arranged to meet specific purposes (O'Dowd, 2007). The translating and translanguaging practice nurtured the sense of multilingualism where each individual brings in one's experience and knowledge of their L1 and L2 regardless of their status of a native or nonnative speaker so as to undermine the monolingual and native speaker bias still predominant in language education today.

International collaborative learning requires a range of conceptual and pedagogical commitments, and several pragmatic issues such as time differences between participating institutions need to be carefully addressed. However, the merits that COIL adaptation would bring to the learners are certainly worth the efforts; their positive feedback and their performance in the interactional data demonstrate that they had authentic encounters with intercultural others during the COIL experience, and they applied their communication skills (including both their L1 and L2) to co-construct a social activity. The translation and translanguaging practice nurtured the participants' linguistic sensitivity and sensibility and strengthened their visions and roles as a language user not only in L2 but also in L1, despite the monolingual or native speaker bias. Without the bilaterally collaborative nature of this practice, these opportunities would not have been made available.

Conclusion

The pandemic forced us to put (almost all) things online, and many previously shut doors have suddenly opened. Applying a COIL method to the teaching and learning of a foreign language is one such door that was opened. We now observe more enthusiasm about weaving new practices like COIL into language education, which is one way that the pandemic's impact has created a silver lining (Ikeda, 2020). The "new normal" will likely stick, and a blend of online and on-site curriculum design in foreign language education will become widely available in the near future. Adopting COIL requires faculty to know how to collaborate with an overseas classroom and develop a special module together to generate a project-based learning opportunity for small groups, which consist of both international and domestic students. For COIL with language learners, opportunities to use the target language must be embedded so that they have authentic and communicative interactions in the process of conducting the project. In order to promote this particular pedagogical practice among language teachers, additional COIL/LLC-focused teacher training programs need to be provided.

Acknowledgments

This study was partially supported by the Grant-in-Aid for Challenging Research (Exploratory) Grant Number 20K20709, Kansai University Fund for Supporting Outlay Research Centers (2021–2022), and DePaul University GLE (Global Learning Engagement) Grant (2020–2022).

Notes

1 LLC is defined at Kansai University's Institute of Innovative Global Education (IIGE) at www.kansai-u.ac.jp/Kokusai/IIGE/COILPlus/.
2 The following original Japanese pieces were selected by students for their translation projects in spring 2021. Each student had the original copy or downloaded the part for translation available online.

   ライトノベル： 『キノの旅』(時雨沢恵一　2000年);『やはり俺の青春物語は間違っている』(渡航2013年）；　　　『裏世界ピクニック』（宮澤伊織2017年）;『ブリーチ：Bleach letter from the other side』（久保帯人 2000年）

   短編：『ときどき、きらいで』(川上弘美　2006年）；『夢十夜』(夏目漱石 1908年)

   絵本：『さくらがさくと』(とうごう なりさ 2019年)

   漫画：『魔法使いの嫁』（ヤマザキ コレ 2014年）；『いつでもサメーズ』（アリムラ モハ 2016年）

   アルバム歌詞：『0』(青葉市子2013年);『アニメ ギヴン』(アニメ ２０１９年)

3 Post project online surveys were conducted with both DU and KU students to gather their perceptions and attitudes toward the COIL/LLC experiences. DU students completed the post course survey after submitting the final translation and essay when the course ended.

References

Chikamatsu, N. (2019). Collaborative teaching of a Japanese content-based course: 3.11 and nuclear power crisis. In C. A. Melin (Ed.), *Foreign language teaching and the* environment: Theory, curricula, institutional structures (pp. 146–160). The Modern Language Association of America.

Chikamatsu, N. (2021). Translanguaging in language and area-studies curriculum: A Japanese FLAC course of Minamata and Fukushima in environmental humanities. In M. de la Fuente (Ed.), *Education for sustainable development in foreign language learning* (pp. 215–232). Routledge.

Chikamatsu, N. (2022). 国際協働学習(COIL)における翻訳の意義：日米大学のトランスランゲージングの協働から [Translanguaging in translation: COIL in Japanese with college students in Japan and the U.S.A.]. In A. Murata (Ed.), オンライン国際交流と共同学習：多文化共生のために [International virtual exchange and collaborative learning: Fostering cultural diversity and inclusion] (pp. 195–214). Kuroshio Publishing.

Chikamatsu, N., & Matsugu, M. (2022). Translating literature in an advanced Japanese language classroom: *Izu no odoriko*. *Japanese Language and Literature, 56*, 383–410.

Council of Europe. (2007). *Guide for the development of language education policies in Europe: From linguistic diversity to plurilingual education.* www.coe.int/en/web/language-policy/from-linguistic-diversity-to-plurilingual-education-guide-for-the-development-of-language-education-policies-in-europe

de la Fuente, M. J. (Ed.). (2022). *Education for sustainable development in foreign language learning: Content-based instruction in college-level curricula.* Routledge.

DePaul GLE. (2022). *Global learning experience (GLE)*. https://resources.depaul.edu/teaching-commons/programs/global-learning/Pages/default.aspx

Douglas Fir Group. (2016). A transdisciplinary framework for SLA in a multilingual world. *The Modern Language Journal, 100*(Supplement), 19–47.

García, O. (2009). Education, multilingualism, and translanguaging in the 21st century. In A. Mohanty, A. M. Panda, R. Phillipson, & T. Skutnabb-Kangas (Eds.), *Multilingual education for social justice: Globalizing the local* (pp. 128–145). Orient Black Swan.

García, O., & Leiva, C. (2014). Theorizing and enacting translanguaging for social justice. In A. Creese & A. Blackledge (Eds.), *Heteroglossia as practice and pedagogy* (pp. 199–216). Springer.

Gramling, D. J., & Warner, C. (2016). Whose "crisis in language"? Translating and the futurity of foreign language learning. *L2 Journal, 8*, 76–99.

Hall, J. K. (2019). *Essentials of SLA for L2 teachers: A transdisciplinary framework.* Routledge.

Hasegawa, Y. (2012). *The Routledge course in Japanese translation.* Routledge.

Hawkins, M. R., & Mori, J. (2018). Considering "trans-" perspectives in language theories and practices. *Applied Linguistic, 39*, 1–8.

IAU. (2020). *IAU global survey on the impact of COVID-19 on higher education around the world.* www.iau-aiu.net/IAU-Global-Survey-on-the-Impact-of-COVID-19-on-Higher-Education-around-the

Ikeda, K. (2016a). アウトバウンド促進授業実践としてのCOIL（オンライン国際連携学習） [COIL practices for outbound promotion programs]. グローバル人材育成研究 [Global Human Resource Development Study], 2, 65–70.

Ikeda, K. (2016b). バーチャル型国際教育は有効か―日本でCOILを遂行した場合― [Is online international education effective?: A case consideration for Japan]. 留学交流[International Mobility], 67, 1–11.

Ikeda, K. (2020). ICTを活用し海外の学生と行う国際連携型の協働学習「COIL」の教育効果と課題 [Educational effect and challenges for COIL]. *JUCE Journal, 2*, 20–26.

Kamiyoshi, U., Kumagai, Y., Shimazu, M., Fukuchi, M., & Ngoc, N. H. (2022). SDGsを テーマにしたweb雑誌作成プロジェクトとTranslanguaging: 日米COILから [Creating online magazines with SDGs themes: US—Japan COIL]. In A. Murata (Ed.), オンライン国際交流と共同学習：多文化共生のために [International virtual exchange and collaborative learning: Fostering cultural diversity and inclusion] (pp. 121–138). Kuroshio Publishing.

Kano, N. (2016). トランス・ランゲージングを考える：多言語使用の実態に根ざした教授法確立のために [Conceptualizing translanguaging: To consolidate pedagogy rooted in the language use of multilinguals]. *Journal of the Japanese Society for Mother Tongue, Heritage Language, and Bilingual Education, 12*, 1–22.

Kumagai, Y., & Kono, K. (2018). Collaborative curricular initiatives: Linking language and literature courses for critical and cultural literacies. *Japanese Language and Literature, 52*, 247–276.

Li, W. (2018). Translanguaging as a practical theory of language. *Applied Linguistics, 39*(1), 9–30.

Marrero-Colon, M. (2021). *Translanguaging: Theory, concept, practice, stance . . . or all of the above?* Center for Applied Linguistics. www.cal.org/resource-center/publications-products/translanguaging

Matsugu, M., & Chikamatsu, N. (2023). Translation practicum on Kawabata Yasunari's *Izu no odoriko*. In A. Bates (Ed.), *Teaching postwar Japanese fiction* (pp. 336–350). Modern Language Association.

Mazzaferro, G. (2018). *Translanguaging as everyday practice*. Cham Springer.

Melin, A. (2019). *Foreign language teaching and the environment: Theory, curricula, institutional structures*. The Modern Language Association of America.

Murata, A. (Ed.). (2022). オンライン国際交流と共同学習：多文化共生のために [International virtual exchange and collaborative learning: Fostering cultural diversity and inclusion]. Kuroshio Publishing.

Murata, A., Prefume, Y., Mariotti, M., & My, D. T. N. (2022). 協働の深さの模索: 身近なテーマからSDGsのプロジェクトへ [Collaboration development from personal experiences to SDGs projects]. In A. Murata (Ed.), オンライン国際交流と共同学習：多文化共生のために [International virtual exchange and collaborative learning: Fostering cultural diversity and inclusion] (pp. 27–44). Kuroshio Publishing.

Nakagawa, M., & Kamei, M. (2022). オンライン交流学習における「協働」のあり方の模索 [Collaboration in interactive online learning]. In A. Murata (Ed.), オンライン国際交流と共同学習：多文化共生のために [International virtual exchange and collaborative learning: Fostering cultural diversity and inclusion] (pp. 103–120). Kuroshio Publishing.

O'Dowd, R. (Ed.). (2007). *Online intercultural exchange: An introduction for foreign language teachers* (Vol. 15). Multilingual Matters.

Ortega, L. (2019). SLA and the study of equitable multilingualism. *The Modern Language Journal, 103*, 23–38.

Rubin, J., & Guth, S. (2016). Collaborative online international learning: An emerging format for internationalizing curricula. In A. S. Moore & S. Simon (Eds.), *Globally networked teaching in the humanities* (pp. 27–39). Routledge.

SUNY COIL. (n.d.). *Faculty guide for collaborative online international learning course development*. Retrieved on September 1, 2022 from http://www.ufic.ufl.edu/uap/forms/coil_guide.pdf

UNESCO. (2015). *SDGs (sustainable development goals)*. https://en.unesco.org/sustainable developmentgoals

UNESCO. (2021). *One year into COVID: Prioritizing education recovery to avoid a generational catastrophe*. https://en.unesco.org/news/one-year-covid-prioritizing-education-recovery-avoid-generational-catastrophe

Wenger, E. (1998). *Communities of practice: Learning, meaning, and identity*. Cambridge University Press.

Wu, X., & Tarc, P. (2016). Translations and paradoxes of "Western" pedagogy: Perspectives of English language teachers in a Chinese college. *L2 Journal*, *8*, 55–75.

Yamazaki, K. (2014). 魔法使いの嫁 [The ancient Magnus' bride]. Mag-garden Publishing.

14 Coda

Nobuko Chikamatsu and Li Jin

In February 2021, we brought in a group of Chinese and Japanese language and studies educators from higher education to share their experiences and insights in collaborative teaching with colleagues from other disciplines, professions, and geographical locations at the inaugural symposium *Teaching China and Japan: Pedagogical Collaboration across Languages, Disciplines, Communities, and Borders*, held at DePaul University, Chicago. This symposium was the first to focus exclusively on both Chinese and Japanese as a second/foreign language teaching in North America while featuring Chinese-Japanese cross-language pedagogical collaboration. The Chinese and Japanese Studies programs at DePaul University are unique in their interdisciplinary curricula where both advanced language courses and area studies courses are equally required, and a non-hierarchical structure exists between language faculty and content specialists. The Japanese Studies program also stands out for its continuous advocacy for cross-disciplinary collaborative pedagogy (Chikamatsu & Matsugu, 2009). Due to the COVID-19 pandemic, the symposium was hosted completely virtually, which attracted educators from not only North America but also Japan, China, and England. This book features 10 innovative collaborative pedagogical projects discussed at the symposium.

We believe that collaborations in instructional settings make it possible to provide learners with rich diverse contexts as shown in the collaborative practices across disciplines, communities, languages, and borders reported in this volume. As Douglas Fir Group (DFG) stated,

> The greater the number and diversity of contexts of interaction within and across social institutions that L2 learners gain and are given access to and are motivated to participate in, the richer and more linguistically diverse their evolving semiotic resources will be.
>
> (2016, p. 27)

After more than 2 years of remote teaching due to the COVID-19 pandemic, we now live in a different world with new ways of communication and education. Language instruction has taken an unexpected turn. Learners and educators have connected virtually from one room, community, or country to others to form a learning community readily and effectively. Thus, some of the collaborations discussed in this volume are timely even though many projects' design and implementation started before the pandemic.

The challenges we face in second language (L2) Chinese and Japanese pedagogy are similar to those in any other languages, yet there are some unique obstacles we face in today's second language acquisition (SLA) and language pedagogy fields. One is a mindset often shared among L2 Chinese and Japanese educators in North America who feel that they cannot do it in Chinese or Japanese or that Chinese and Japanese are different from other languages, entrenched from outdated labels such as Category IV or less commonly taught languages. As Mori denoted in Chapter 2, language classrooms in U.S. higher education have traditionally been tailored for first language (L1) English speakers, and the discussion of SLA theories and pedagogies has been led by scholars and educators involved in English as a second language (ESL) or more commonly taught Western languages (e.g., Roman or Germanic languages). Such trends may have suppressed our attempts to develop innovative curricula or to share them with a wider audience as if they were impractical or deviant.

We hope the instructional practices shared in this volume can change the mindsets of L2 Chinese and Japanese educators who may have felt challenged to go beyond their comfort zone or the conventional communicative approach that aims to build proficiency around grammar and vocabulary knowledge with native fluency being considered as the norm. We also hope that this volume encourages administrators involved in language education to reevaluate possibilities and potentials in L2 Chinese and Japanese teaching, whether it is situated in Asian studies programs or world languages departments.

Section 1 in this volume challenges L2 Chinese and Japanese language teachers to think beyond traditional classroom teaching. In Chapter 2, Mori raised four critical questions while discussing the current state of East Asian language education in the U.S. higher education institutions: (a) What kind of language should be taught and how? (b) How can we reach out to diverse learners, accommodate their different needs and aspirations, and create a space where they can learn from each other? (c) What would be the role of classroom-based teaching and learning? and (d) What are the essential qualifications and training requirements for future language educators? In Chapter 3, Li Wei rephrased Mori's questions through the lens of translanguaging in the context of an L2 Chinese classroom in the United Kingdom where a young Chinese teacher confronted challenges with a culturally and linguistically diverse student group.

Reporting on detailed collaborative projects, some case studies in this volume have drawn attention to common pedagogical practices and themes in L2 Chinese and Japanese classrooms that take language learning as a holistic meaning-making process. Translanguaging is one practice adopted in multiple projects, especially with English, learners' L1, or the instructional language in a given institution. The use of English eases learners' cognitive demands in understanding contents or comprehension of materials in the target language (i.e., L2) and consequently facilitates analyses or discussions in L2 via cross-disciplinary collaborations, as discussed in Miyamoto's and Chikamatsu's Japanese ethics FLAC (Chapter 4), Sun's and Patterson's Chinese literature FLAC (Chapter 5), Hoshi's and Yoshimizu's Japanese media studies FLAC (Chapter 6), Li et al.'s bilingual meditation (Chapter 7), and Liu's Chinese environmental studies CLAC (Chapter 11) as well as via international collaborations, as examined in Kumagai's and Shimazu's telecollaboration with students in Japan (Chapter 12) and Ikeda's and Chikamatsu's Japanese COIL (Chapter 13). Translanguaging practice is applied to build language proficiency not just in L2 but in any languages accessed for the meaning-making process, as presented in Chapters 4, 6, and 13. Translation, a facet of translanguaging, is also employed to nurture specific linguistic and sociocultural aspects of language learning, such as gendered languages (Chapter 12) and speech styles (Chapter 13).

Collaborative pedagogy, especially through translanguaging, was also innovatively conducted between a L2 Chinese class and a L2 Japanese one for logographic learning, as presented in Sugimori's and Weng's cross-language collaboration with text-based art (Chapter 10). Logographs of each language, *hànzì* and kanji, were examined visually, linguistically, historically, and culturally through an analysis of the arts as well as learners' written correspondence in their respective L2s. DFG (2016) pointed out the significance of literacy and instruction, which mediate language learning. L2 logographic learning has not been extensively discussed in mainstream SLA theories. We hope this cross-language collaborative project from a transdisciplinary perspective can inspire more instructional innovations to support L2 logographic learning.

Identity is another shared theme discussed in several chapters. DFG (2016) defined language learning as identity work, which "shapes language learning and language learning shapes identity work, both being mutually constructive" (p. 32). Zhang worked with a human resource professional for Chinese workplaces (Chapter 8), and Koyama worked with a Japanese orphanage (Chapter 9) to immerse learners in the environment to (re)configure their identities and activate agency for personal, professional, and linguistic growth. In Sun's and Patterson's Chinese literature course (Chapter 5), L2 Chinese students found the motivation to continue learning Chinese after discovering Chinese traditional values resonating with their own identities. Therefore, L2 Chinese and Japanese language educators need to pay more attention to learners' identities. In particular, professional and community-based learning that can prompt learners to face and act on their desired or expected identities need to be further encouraged and promoted in the future.

Successful collaborative pedagogy demands enormous effort. The case studies presented in this volume also highlight several logistical challenges and suggestions for interested educators to consider when adopting these practices, which are summarized in the following subsections.

Institutional agenda

Educators should observe institutional policies (e.g., liberal studies' mission or structures) and practices (COIL, FLAC, community-based learning, etc.) in their units, programs, and schools and reflect them in their choice of collaboration models. Some institutions have started to think of additional main instructional languages (in which to conduct class) other than English, and such trends may help promote FLAC among faculty. COIL is also attracting more attention in many Asian countries for e-certificates or micro-credentials as well as in the United States (e.g., Kansai University and SUNY[1]).

Theme selection

While it is impossible to find a theme equally interesting or appealing to a diverse student group in collaborative courses or projects, it is important to identify a topic that can bring in each student's past experience and background, such as social justice, environmental humanities, sustainable development goals, and traditional and popular cultures. For cross-disciplinary collaborations, it is important to determine colleagues' interests, observe classes, and learn what is shared in interest. The careful selection of authentic, proficiency-appropriate materials is a strenuous task, in part because the issues related to the topics listed herein constantly change at a fast pace. Therefore, educators should keep an eye out for new publications or the release of visual works as a theme that can be narrowed down with available materials in the target language.

Sustainability of collaborative instruction

Educators can also assess how sustainable their innovative instruction or project is by checking enrollment, instructional support, and faculty teaching load. Most collaborative projects in this volume were designed for advanced learners. Is the advanced language course enrollment high enough to offer a course or incorporate a project once a year or once every other year? If two courses are concurrently offered for FLAC, educators determine the best time to schedule both, inform students about the schedule, and start planning (considering faculty members' sabbatical leave, teaching loads, etc.). Should it be a full credit or a half credit course? What is the cap? What are faculty members' commitment and compensation for it? All these issues and logistics are highly relevant and need to be carefully assessed in order to make long-term plans.

Implementation in lower-level classes and for a whole program

Educators should evaluate or decide what language proficiency students need to participate in collaborative programs such as FLAC, COIL, and internships. Although different types of translanguaging practices exist, they all require careful thinking and planning regarding the semiotic resources that need to be provided to learners at different proficiency levels. If faculty members decide to wait until an advanced class to adopt FLAC, COIL, or translation practice, it is imperative to think about how to prepare lower-level students in advance. Envisioning an entire program from beginning to upper levels can include goals and achievements that lead to upper-level collaborative instructions.

Transformation from the language-literature model to an area-studies model

As non-English language enrollments in U.S. higher education institutions have been declining overall in recent years (Looney & Lusin, 2019), we should resume discussions about language across the curriculum initiated in the 1980s. In particular, the conventional language-literature model can be transformed to an area-studies model in which language education is embedded in the integrative curriculum with other humanities, business, and science, technology, engineering, and mathematics (STEM) courses in the university. Eastern Asian language courses have traditionally been offered in the area-studies model along with area-specific literature, history, and religious studies courses. As the separation or hierarchy between language and non-language faculty is largely questioned, the area-studies model would be an opportunity for cross-disciplinary or even cross-language collaboration. Thus, Chinese and Japanese language programs should take advantage of this model to promote the integration of language and area-studies education and, consequently, serve as a successful model for other more commonly taught language programs that have been built around conventional language-literature models.

Cross-language collaboration

Collaborations with faculty members teaching other languages can promote effective collaborative pedagogical models on a common theme. FLAC with multiple languages is a feasible plan where one core content course (in English) is offered concurrently with different language courses sharing similar themes. Such cross-language collaborations may help make the presence of language courses more visible and shift language courses' status from being a technical skill course to one that cultivates students' critical and analytical thinking skills.

Although we discuss both Chinese and Japanese pedagogy in this volume, each faces unique challenges. After a rapid enrollment increase in the 2000s, reaching a peak around 2013, college-level Chinese language enrollment in the United States has been declining at a faster rate than other non-English languages (Looney & Lusin, 2019). Amid continuously deteriorating U.S.-China relations and anti-China sentiment during the COVID-19 pandemic, it may take a while before Chinese language once again becomes appealing to college students in North America. In contrast, Chinese language enrollment at the precollege level enjoyed more good news around the same time thanks to expanding dual language immersion programs and increasing Chinese and non-Chinese heritage learners (American Councils for International Education, 2017). One way to attract more Chinese language students at the college level while accommodating more students coming to college with prior Chinese language learning experience is to offer more language courses integrating content in business, politics, and international relations as bilingual speakers in these areas are increasingly in demand. More engagement with local Chinese-speaking communities as well as direct intercultural communication with students in China can also help motivate students to develop Chinese language skills. Although Japanese enrollment in U.S. higher education hit a plateau in the 2010s, with a slight increase in recent years (Looney & Lusin, 2019; The Japan Foundation Los Angeles, 2016), advanced courses are often in danger of cancellation due to low enrollments and institutional budget cuts. As the demographic of college learners has changed over the years, learners' interests and motivations for learning Japanese have shifted from career oriented to culture focused such as anime, manga, and J-pop (The Japan Foundation, 2020). In our institution, the largest student group enrolled in Japanese courses comes from the College of Digital Media and Computing (CDM), which exceeds the number from even the College of Business and the College of Liberal Arts and Social Sciences. Cross-disciplinary collaborations with CMD should be in demand not only for curriculum or course development but also for degree or certification programs as they help students continue learning the language and culture.

Nonetheless, the current book is a pioneering effort in terms of its focus on college-level pedagogical practices in both Chinese and Japanese language teaching. Both editors—one as a Japanese language pedagogist whose research leans more toward a cognitive-linguistic perspective and the other as a Chinese language pedagogist whose research is influenced more by a sociocultural theoretical perspective—have also learned a great amount of language practices in their respective language fields and from each other. More importantly, this collaboration has expanded our previous understanding of Chinese and Japanese language teaching, respectively, and stimulated us to explore second language teaching and learning from a transdisciplinary perspective. This entire process has been extremely fulfilling and fruitful. We hope this kind of cross-language collaboration as well as the collaborative projects between language educators and their partners across languages, disciplines, countries, and borders shared in this book can inspire more language educators—not only those teaching East Asian languages but all language educators—to purposefully expand their horizons and explore how to enrich our students' language learning experience by engaging other colleagues in collaborative teaching in the "trans-" era.

Note

1 Kansai University posts a microcredentials initiative to develop a coherent microcredentialing infrastructure at https://global.k-state.edu/faculty/microcredentials/ while SUNY has taken leadership in the United States at www.suny.edu/microcredentials/.

References

American Councils for International Education. (2017). *The national K-12 foreign language enrollment survey report*. www.americancouncils.org/sites/default/files/FLE-report-June17.pdf

Chikamatsu, N., & Matsugu, M. (2009). Bridging Japanese language and studies in higher education: Report from the forum on integrative curriculum and program development. *Association of Teachers of Japanese Occasional Papers*, *9*, 1–28.

Douglas Fir Group. (2016). A transdisciplinary framework for SLA in a multilingual world. *Modern Language Journal*, *100*(Supplement), 19–47.

The Japan Foundation. (2020). *Survey report on Japanese-language education abroad 2018*. www.jpf.go.jp/j/project/japanese/survey/result/dl/survey2018/Report_all_e.pdf

The Japan Foundation Los Angeles. (2016). *The Japan Foundation survey on Japanese language education institutions 2015: U.S. data*. www.jflalc.org/ckfinder/userfiles/files/jle/JF_Survey_Report_2015.pdf

Looney, D., & Lusin, N. (2019). *Enrollments in languages other than English in United States institutions of higher education, summer 2016 and fall 2016: Final report*. Modern Language Association. www.mla.org/content/download/110154/2406932/2016-Enrollments-Final-Report.pdf

Index

Note: Locators in *italics* represent figures and **bold** indicate tables in the text.

affordances 191, 198; environmental 43; language learning 9
agency 3, 62–63, 77; activation 11–12; agentive power 128, 191; critical thinking 137; language classroom 62; language growth with identity shifts 136–138; in language learning 149; L2 development 69, 139, 146, 155; learners and 206, 214; self- 62; teacher 22
àiqíng (romantic love) 75
alphabet/alphabetic 4, 148, 151
American Council for Teachers of Foreign Languages (ACTFL) 7, 67
anime 5, 52, 130, 217
anxiety 5, 99–100, 103
area studies 2, 24, 49, 161, 212, 216
Art for the People for the Met 149
artificial intelligence 40
art (text-based artwork) 11, 147–149
Asian Americans and Pacific Islanders (AAPI) 26
Association of American Colleges & Universities (AAC&U) 164
Association of Teachers of Japanese 24
asynchronous communication 196
Atkinson, D. 21
audio-visual translation 10, 83, 93; course design 82; as pedagogy 10, 81; types and roles 87
autonomy 30, 180, 191
awareness: cultural- 44, 103; language 83; metalinguistic- 83, 146, 154, 206; multicultural- 161; multilingual- 20, 146, 206; student- 3, 31, 99, 123; transcultural- 84

Baker, C. 39
Baynman, M. 84

Bicultural Comparison Project (BCP) 11
bilingual cultural comparison (BCC) project 99, 101–103
bilingual education research community 39–40
bilingual guided meditation (BGM) project 99–101; materials 108–109
bilingualism 8, 11, 28, 38–40, 45, 50, 99–103, 214, 217
Bilingual Meditation Program (BMP) 11
Book from the Sky 148
Brantmeier, E. J. 40–41, 43
Bronfenbrenner, U. 20
Bronfenbrenner's model of human development 20
Buddhism 59, 70, 97, 99, 103, 110
Byram, M. 7

Cai, A. 11
calligraphy 148–149, 153, 156
Cantonese expression 38–39
Category IV languages 1, 23, 27, 161, 213
CBI *see* content-based instruction (CBI)
C2 expectation and third-space personae 11, 113; pedagogical manifestation 116–125; theoretical rationale 113–116; workplace scenarios **117**
Chikamatsu, N. 10, 12, 83, 161–162, 200
CHIN102 (first-year course) 150–154
Chinese and Japanese language teaching: collaborative teaching 6–9; transdisciplinary approach 3–6
Chinese human resources professional 116–117
Chinese-Japanese cross-language pedagogical collaboration 212
Chinese Language Teachers Association 24, 159

Index

Chinese resume workshop **121–122**
CLAC *see* Cultures and Languages Across the Curriculum (CLAC)
classroom-based teaching 32
climate change 163–164, **165, 169, 188**
cognitive: development 2, 5; linguistic approach 1–2, 4, 217
COIL *see* Collaborative Online International Learning (COIL)
co-learning 10, 38–45; example 43–44; language learning as cultural translation 42–43
collaborative instruction 215
Collaborative Online International Learning (COIL) 8, 52, 147, 179–180, 196; *see also* Language Learning-focused COIL (LLC)
collaborative pedagogy 2, 6–9, 11, 72, 160, 212, 214
college-level foreign language enrollments 1
college-level non-English language 7
Communication and composition course 71–72, **72**
communicative: approach 213; competence 78; interactions 208; language learning 82; performance in CSL programs 113; potential 50, 203; skills 145; strategies 122
communicative language teaching (CLT) 82
community: engagement 7, 137, 166; learning 164, 166, 214; neglect 136–137; of practice 41, 135, 201
competence: communicative- 78; cultural- 8, 63, 161; intercultural- 7, 128, 191, 200; metalinguistic- 83, 146, 154, 206; multicultural- 5, 11–12, 130, 132, 161; sociocultural- 4, 10, 20, 29, 50, 52, 62, 69, 83, 181, 214, 217; transcultural- 7, 83, 159, 201; translingual- 7, 32–33, 128, 200
computer simulation 40
confidence 63, 77, 100, 125, 164, 190, 204
content: knowledge 50, 81, 169, 187; learning 49–50, 68, 78, 82, 159, 161–162, 169, 171
content-based instruction (CBI) 51, 68, 81, 97, 161; content-based language instruction (CBLI) 82; critical content-based language instruction (CCBI) 96
content-based language instruction (CBLI) 82
Cool Japan 26
COVID-19 pandemic 71, 116, 166, 196, 212, 216
critical content-based instruction (CCBI) 82
critical literacy 29, 83
critical pedagogy 83
critical thinking 50
cross-disciplinary collaboration 7, 10–11, 67–78, 97, 99, 145–156, 159–173; collaborative literature and language teaching 72; Communication and composition course 71–72; designing the FLAC courses 71–74; FLAC model 68; interdisciplinary 93, 98, 156, 161, 170, 173; language learning from transdisciplinary perspective 68–69; language teaching 72; linguistic and cultural references 74; multidisciplinary 68; pedagogical reflections 74–78; planning 69–71; *qíng* 73–74; rationales 146–147; Two Chinese novels course 71; Xu Bing's text-based artworks 147–152
cross-disciplinary projects 67, 99–103
cross-discipline collaboration 99
cross-language 11, 145–156, 159–173, 197, 212, 214, 216–217
cultural gazing 114
cultural translation 10, 39, 42–44, 84
Cultura model 8
Cultures and Languages Across the Curriculum (CLAC) 6, 147, 160, 162–163; faculty members across languages and disciplines 163–168; student-led class discussions 168–169; students' learning outcomes and feedback 169–170

Dai-yu, Lin 70
De Costa, P. I. 22
demographics: learner 1, 5, 26, 217; student 1, 5, 26, 32
DePaul-Kansai COIL 200–201
digital literacy 180
dispensers 40
dominant ideologies 21
Douglas Fir Group's (DFG) transdisciplinary framework 2, 19–22, *21,* 22, 31, 33, 50, 69, 81–82, 104, 130, 146, 160, 197, 212, 214
Dream of the red chamber 70–74, 76
Duff, P. A. 20

East Asian: cultures 26; languages 1, 10, 19–34, 146, 150, 155–156, 213, 217; language teaching 2; studies 44, 150, 154, 156
East Asian languages 22–23, 29, 32; cultural diplomacy 26–27; education 213;

enrollment *25*; languages of national security interest 23–24; rapid enrollment growth and teacher shortage 24–26
ecological: framework 22; layers 20–22; systems 10, 20, 31, 43
ecology 42
emoji 151, 187, 191
emotion 57, 104, 191, 206
emotional bonding 138
empathy 154, 192
emptiness 104
English as a second language (ESL) 213
enrollment 1, 7, 12, 24–26
ENVIRON 201 164, **165,** 167
environment(al): activism 165, 169; ethics 51–62, 162; humanities 209, 215; injustice 165, 168; justice 162, 164, **165,** 168; science 11, 162–163, **167**; studies 166, 214
Essentials of SLA for L2 Teachers: A Transdisciplinary Framework (Hall) 3
e-tandem 8
ethics, environmental 51–52, 162
ethnic minorities in Japan 83
expression, uses of 38
extralinguistic effect 81, 86, 88

film 50–55, 57–58, 86, 88–89, 200; screening and discussion 52–55; *see also* Japanese films
first language (L1) English speakers 213
FLAC *see* Foreign Languages Across the Curriculum; Foreign Languages Across the Curriculum (FLAC)
food and ethics in Japan (JPN) 52
foreign language (FL) 6; education 82; instructional practices 180; requirement 27–29
Foreign Languages Across the Curriculum (FLAC) 6, 49, 68, 82, 147, 159, 198; in environmental ethics 51–52; film screening and discussion 52–55; food and ethics in Japan (JPN) 52; Japanese and ethics courses **53**; L1 course 51–52; L2 course 52; pedagogy 50; religion and ethics in Japanese foodscapes (REL) 51–52; structure 49; translanguaging pedagogy in 52–62; translating poetry 55–57
Foreign Service Institute (FSI) 23
French tutorials 163

Gao, X. 22
García, O. 6, 40

Geisler, M. 30, 67
gendered speech 84, 203, 205
gender equality 184–185, **188**
gesture 5, 86, 88, 90–91, 185, 187, 203
Gramling, D. J. 198
growth: holistic- 128, 131, 139; human- 103; language- 128–140; linguistic- 128; personal 103

Hall, J. K. 3, 98, 160
Hanabusa, A. 52
Hasegawa, Y. 203
hànzì 5, 11, 145–155, 214
He, Y. 7
heritage language education 40
heritage learners 1–2, 34, 163, 216
hierarchy: content 55; faculty 59, 216; hierarchical relationships 1, 50, 52; language 67, 149; non-hierarchical nature 57, 212; social 54
hiragana 55, 57, 61, 145, 153
Hongloumeng (Dream of the red chamber) 70
Hoshi, S. 10
Huang, M. W. 9
human resources (HR) 26, 29, 116, 118
Hush! 88
Hyōjungo (standard language) 4, 32

identity: collective 62; gender 10, 88–89, 93; personal 128, 138; self 5, 61–62; sexual 88–89; shift 136–139; social 116; transgender 90
ideology: dominant 21–22, 81–82, 87, 90, 145; gender 88–89, 93; language 4, 40, 93–94, 146, 149–150, 152; language education 31; language learning 155; monolingual 179–180, 191; pervasive 31
I give you my life (poem) **58,** 63
Ikeda, K. 12
imagined community 11, 77, 130, 132–136
immerse learners 214
immersion 27; classroom 69; learning opportunities 129; program 97, 216
indexicality **85,** 88; indexical relationship, gender and sexuality 86, 88–90
Indo-European languages 1
ingroup mentality 5
Institute of International Education (IIE) 26
institution: agenda 214–215; policy 10, 20–22, 27–31, 214; principles 22, 43, 122; structures 22
institutional policies 21
integral education 98, 103

Index

integrated curriculum 159
intercultural citizenship 7
intercultural competence 7, 128, 191, 200
interdisciplinary collaborations 98, 161, 170
international internship 8, 139–140
international telecollaboration 179–180
Internship preparations **133**
internships at Japanese orphanages 128; buzz words, retorts, and being a foreigner in a Japanese community 135–139; first-year Japanese language student's holistic growth 131–135; interactions and communities 130–131; Japan Children's Home Internship Program (JCHIP) 128–130
interview: job 118, 121–122; mock 118–120, 122–123; questions and corresponding C2 expectations **123**, 124–125; student 122
investment 3, 5, 29, 67, 146, 172; cognitive 78; emotional 78
Ito, H. 59

Japan Children's Home Internship Program (JCHIP) 11, 128–134, 136
Japanese films 81
Japanese media and translation **85**
Japanese studies 51, 212
Japan Foundation, The 26
JAPN302 (third-year course) 150–154
JCHIP *see* Japan Children's Home Internship Program (JCHIP)
Johnson, K. 21, 33
joint sojourners 40
Journey to the West 70–74, 77

kanji 5, 11, 145–155, 214
Kanno, Y. 130
Kano, N. 6, 205
Karera ga honki de amutoki wa 89
karma 75
katakana 91, 145, 153
K–16 foreign language 7
Kono, K. 83
Korean enrollment 26
Korean wave 26
Koyama, N. 11, 214
Kramsch, C. 19, 30, 84
Kumagai, Y. 11, 83

language: acquisition 82; avoidance 128; educators 4, 12, 21; pedagogy 196; proficiency 5; requirements 27–29; specialists 29–30, 67, 70, 74, 81, 173;
teaching 21, 44, 72; transformation 149, 151–152
language education and institutional policies 27; academic unit structures 29–30; classroom-based teaching 32–33; diverse learners, reach out to 32; foreign language requirement 27–29; future 31–33; kinds of language 31–32; qualifications and training requirements 33
language for specific purposes (LSP) 82
language learning 159; content knowledge 81; as cultural translation 42–43; landscape 44; overseas internship 130; and teaching *21*; from transdisciplinary perspective 68–69
language learning-focused COIL (LLC) 12, 196–208; conversation and textual analysis of translanguaging collaboration 201–205; cross-language collaboration 197–199; DePaul-Kansai COIL 200–201; design and implementation 199–200; student feedback and pedagogical reflections 205–207
Languages Across the Curriculum (LAC) 6–7, 68, 160
LaScotte, D. 57
Lave, J. 130
learning environment 3
Leaver, B. L. 97
less commonly taught languages (LCTLs) 23, 25, 51, 213
letter writing 151
LGBTQ (LGBT, LGBTQ+) 184–185, 188
Li, C. 11
Li, W.-y. 40, 73–74
lingua franca 28, 196, 198, 200
linguistic medium 73
linguistic politeness 43
linked model 161
literature: classical 69, 71–72, 74, 78; literary work 73, 200
Little Egg (poem) **60**
Liu, D. 11
Living Word 148, *148*
LLC *see* language learning-focused COIL (LLC)
logograph: character 5, 145; ideograms 148; ideograph 73, 148; orthography 1; pictogram 148
Lomicka, K. 30, 159
Lord, G. 30, 159
L2 (second language) learning 3–5, 69, 128

Index 223

macro: layer 10, 19–20, 31; level 3, 9–10, 20, 31, 33, 68–69, 98, 131, 139, 154, 160, 172, 181–182
Mandarin Chinese 7, 67; tutorial 164
Mandarin CLAC course 159–160, **165**; faculty members across languages and disciplines 163–168; FLAC/CLAC framework 161–162; pedagogical collaborations 162–163; student-led class discussions 168–169; students' learning outcomes and feedback 169–170; transdisciplinary framework of SLA 160–161
manga 52, **53**, 130, 200–201, 204–205, 217
Matsugu, M. 200
meaning making: process 3, 42, 55, 62, 114, 122, 125–126, 146, 181, 198, 201, 206, 213; resources 3, 20, 42–43, 62, 75; sense-making 6, 42
meaning potentials 4, 6, 10, 33, 49, 52–55, 57
media studies 10, 81, 86, 93, 214
meditation 99–101
Menon, K. D. 54
meso: layer 20, 31; level 3, 20, 22, 68–69, 98, 126. 136, 139, 146, 154, 160, 171, 173, 182
micro: layer 98; level 3, 20, 22, 33, 68–69, 98, 131, 137, 139, 146, 154, 160, 171, 180
migrants 34
mìngyùn (fate) 75
minority: minoritization 32; minoritized language 28, 32; minoritized students 6. 69; students 6, 27, 69
Miura, A. 24
Miyamoto, Y. 10
Modern Language Association (MLA) 1, 7, 23, 67, 159
Modern Languages Department (MOL) 51
monolingualism 2, 4, 23, 27, 32, 50, 69, 83, 114, 126, 146, 149, 179–182, 191, 197–198; *see also* translanguaging
Mori, J. 10
motivation 3, 5, 12, 22, 32, 44–45, 76–77, 131, 133, 135, 137–138, 146, 160, 192, 217
multilayered ecological systems 20
multilingualism 114, 197, 207
multimodality 4, 6, 9, 22, 62, 69, 93, 131, 160, 163, 171–172, 182–183, 188, 193, 197, 201
multimodal literacy 188

nationalism 49, 52, 59
nativeness 114–115

native-speakerism 2, 4, 26, 181–182, 197; *see also* monolingualism
neglected languages 23–24
negotiation: C2 expectation 113–126; third-space personae 11, 113–126
Nishio, T. 9
non-government organization (NGO) 164–165
non-tenure-track 30, 159
Norton, B. 22, 130
nuclear: disaster 51; issue 63

onee kotoba ("queen's language") 90
one-language-at-a-time monolingual ideologies 180
online magazines 11, 179–193
onomatopoeia 203–204
orphanages 129, 136
orthography 1; orthographic writing system 5
othering, self 23
overseas internships 128
ownership of language 149, 154–155, 181, 192

paralinguistic: cues 187; repertoires 131
Parker, W. R. 23
Patterson, S. 10
pedagogy of vulnerability 41
personae 116
pictographic language 148
Pines, Y. 73
plurilingualism 45, 50, 197, 209
poetry 50, 52, 55–57, 74, 77; creating 59–62; to express identity 57–62; responding to 57–59; translation 55–57
pop culture 130
pragmatic expressions 38–39
Professional Networking in China 117
proficiency development 29
project-based learning (PBL) 164, 166, 196
public service announcement (PSA) 166
Pǔtōnghuà (common language) 4, 32

Qin, X. 7
qíng 73–74
Qing dynasty 70
Qín Kěqīng 73
queer 85, 90–92

religion and ethics in Japanese foodscapes (REL) 51–52
repertoire: integrated 50; semiotic 3–4, 10, 49, 75, 145, 197

resume: workshop 119–122; writing 119–120, 125
Ruan, J. 26

scene-subtitling projects 86
second/foreign language education 6
second language acquisition (SLA) 1–2, 50, 68, 98, 146, 160, 197, 213
self-expression 50
semiotic resources 2–5, 9–10, 32–33, 42, 49–50, 57, 61–62, 68–69, 75, 77, 82, 93, 98, 104, 114, 116. 122, 125, 131, 136, 160, 171
service learning 7–8, 192
Shanahan, D. 75
shi 74
Shimazu, M. 11
Shirane, H. 24, 26, 29
sinograph 146, 149, 151, 154–155
SLA *see* second language acquisition (SLA)
Slack 182–183, 185, *186,* 191
social constructs 51, 59
socialization 198
sociocultural: diversity 171; factor 29; linguistic approach 88; theory 29, 213; variables 88
sociolinguistics 10, 81–82, 86, 88, 150; theory of indexicality 88
Spanish 1, 11, 23, 67, 163, 168
square word 148–149, **151,** 151–153
standard languages: *Hyōjungo* 4, 32; Putonghua 4, 32
standard variation 32–33
strokes 146, 153–154, 189
Stryker, S. B. 97
subtitle 82–88, 92–94
Sugimori, N. 11
Summer China Dialogue of Civilization Program 97
summer cultural comparison project 110
Sun, J. 10
sustainability 161, 164–165, 167–168, 215
Sustainable Development Goals (SDGs) 182, 198, 215
synchronous communication 196; asynchronous 196

Tale of a Butcher Shop 52
Tangerine 86, 90
target-language-only ideology 180
target-language-speaking 166
Tarone, E. 57
Taylor, E. 129

teacher agency 22
teacher-*versus*-learner dichotomy 40
telecollaboration 8, 11, 179–191, 214
tenure-track content-area faculty 30, 159
text-based arts into Chinese and Japanese L2 courses 145; *see also* Xu Bing's text-based artworks
textual analysis 197, 201–205
Third Space persona 11, 116, 125
tonal system 1
tone of voice 204
transcultural: competence 7, 83, 159, 201; literacy 10, 81–94
transdisciplinary: approach 2–6, 62; framework 4, 6, 19–22; in SLA studies 21
transdisciplinary approach to SLA 98
transdisciplinary framework 98, 146
translanguaging 6, 10, 38–40, 50, 181; approach 39; with food and ethics 49–63; framework 50; in Japanese FLAC course 50; pedagogy 40; practice 39; space 73, 78; United States-Japan online magazine project 180–182
translanguaging practice in international collaboration 198
translation: culture 44; languages 49–62; practice 81, 86, 198, 215; process 81, 90, 93, 203; translator 87, 189, 203; *see also* audiovisual translation
translingual and transcultural literacies 10, 81–82; course assignments 86; course materials 86; course outline 84–86; critical content-based instruction (CCBI) 82–83; critical subtitles studies 87–88; indexical relationship to gender and sexuality 88–90; Japanese subtitles 90–93; pedagogical translanguaging and translation 83–84; student profile 84; two disciplinary approaches 86
transmigration of souls 75
transmodality 19
transspatial utopias 19
Tsu, J. B. 24
Two Chinese novels course 70–71, **72**

United States-Japan online magazine project 179; description 182–183; international telecollaboration 179–180; learning outcomes 183–191; procedures 183; translanguaging 180–182
Ushida, E. 22

VALUE rubric 169
videoconference applications 196

virtual exchange 180
virtual internationalization 179

Wang, W. 26
Warner, C. 198
Warschauer, M. 179
web-based communication tools 196
wellbeing and Chinese language study 11, 97; bilingual cultural comparison (BCC) project 101–103; bilingual guided meditation (BGM) project 99–101; cross-disciplinary projects 99–103; cross-discipline collaboration 99; integral education 98; pedagogical reflections 103–105; transdisciplinary approach to SLA 98
Welsh revitalization 39
Weng, L. 11
Wenger, E. 130
Williams, C. 39
Williams, R. 73
Wukong, S. 78

Xiyouji (Journey to the West) 70
Xu Bing 11, 147–156
Xu Bing's text-based artworks 147–149, *148*; *Art for the People for the Met 149*; in Chinese and Japanese language teaching 150–152; letter correspondence 152–153; *Living Word* 148, *148*; pedagogical reflections 154–155; square words 152–153; student learning outcomes 152–156; students' paths 155–156
Xueqin, C. 70

Yoshimizu, A. 10
Yu, A. 73

Zhang, X. 11, 116
Zheng, B. 69
Zhu, H. 42
Zoom 52, 71, 116, 166, 183, 191, 200–205; meeting 204; workshop 120

For Product Safety Concerns and Information please contact our EU representative GPSR@taylorandfrancis.com
Taylor & Francis Verlag GmbH, Kaufingerstraße 24, 80331 München, Germany

www.ingramcontent.com/pod-product-compliance
Lightning Source LLC
Chambersburg PA
CBHW050302010526
44108CB00040B/2030